D1277289

Pastoral Care in Context

Pastoral Care
in Context

*An Introduction
to Pastoral Care*

John Patton

WESTMINSTER
JOHN KNOX PRESS
LOUISVILLE · KENTUCKY

MARY M. STRIBLING LIBRARY

© 1993 John Patton

All rights reserved. No part of this book may be reproduced or transmitted in any form or by any means, electronic or mechanical, including photocopying, recording, or by any information storage or retrieval system, without permission in writing from the publisher. For information, address Westminster John Knox Press, 100 Witherspoon Street, Louisville, Kentucky 40202-1396.

Scripture quotations from the New Revised Standard Version of the Bible are copyright © 1989 by the Division of Christian Education of the National Council of the Churches of Christ in the U.S.A., and are used by permission.

Book design by Drew Stevens

First edition 1993
Paperback Edition 2005
Published by Westminster John Knox Press
Louisville, Kentucky

This book is printed on acid-free paper that meets the American National Standards Institute Z39.48 standard. ∞

PRINTED IN THE UNITED STATES OF AMERICA

05 06 07 08 09 10 11 12 13 -- 10 9 8 7 6 5 4 3 2 1

Library of Congress Cataloging-in-Publication Data

A catalog record for this book is available from the Library of Congress.
ISBN 0-664-22994-8

To students and colleagues in the
Georgia Association for Pastoral Care,
past and present,
who have helped me learn that
although there is no such thing as pastoral *cure,*
there is pastoral *care.*
And that may be enough.

Contents

Acknowledgments

I have talked with so many people about the issues involved in this book that it is impossible for me to acknowledge all of them by name. I began thinking about this project with Liston Mills of Vanderbilt Divinity School, who contributed significantly to my early thinking about it but declined to become a coauthor. Students in an introductory pastoral care course at the Candler School of Theology, Fall semester, 1990, helped by giving me feedback on a course structured somewhat like this book. Paul Johnson, an Emory graduate student and coleader in the course, was also helpful with his comments.

Brian Childs, Jasper Keith, Ben Kline, Beverly Gaventa, Charles Cousar, Lucy Rose, and Walter Brueggemann, all faculty colleagues at Columbia Seminary, have read or discussed parts of the manuscript with me. Ruthanne Huff gave valuable library assistance. Edward Wimberly of the Interdenominational Theological Center and Melvin Drucker of Georgia State University offered comments and encouragement. My daughter Rebecca Patton Falco of Duke University read and commented on a chapter that fell within her area of work with victims of abuse.

I have been richly influenced and informed by conversation and interviews with many lay pastoral carers introduced to me by their supervisors and consultants. Clinical pastoral educators Sr. Barbara Sheehan, Ron Sunderland, and Peter Thomas have made it possible for me to interview some of the lay carers associated with programs that they have directed. Mac and Anne Turnage of Memorial Drive Presbyterian Church in Houston have helped me to be in a dialogue with several lay ministry programs there. Betty Asbury of Glenn Memorial Church in Atlanta and David Shew, a graduate student in pastoral counseling at Columbia Seminary, discussed lay pastoral care programs in which they

1

have been involved. Sr. Nora Ryan shared the theological journey growing out of her hospital ministry, and Sr. Jude Connelly helped me understand how a Roman Catholic religious might interpret my views of pastoral identity and authority. Several participants at the International Congress on Pastoral Care in Holland in the Summer of 1991, including Breda McGee from Ireland, Fr. Leo Pessini from Brazil, and Sr. Shirley Mills from Zambia, shared stories of the lay pastoral care they were involved in or directed. Also, an invitation to address the Finnish Chaplains Association stimulated my work on some of the material in the book.

Finally, I express my deepest appreciation to Helen, my wife and partner in many things, who knows, better than any writer could possibly hope for, how to offer both criticism and support.

Introduction

Things have changed in pastoral care. One can no longer assume that the audience for a book such as this is the male clergyperson of European ancestry working professionally in a parish or hospital setting. Pastoral care today is being offered competently and creatively by "all sorts and conditions" of God's people, and the dynamic for that care is found not only in professional responsibility of individual clergypersons but also in small communities of persons committed to the work of caring for others as they care, spiritually, for themselves. Thus, this book is addressed to the clergy but also to the other members of those caring communities, including the Hispanic woman who is leader of a Christian care group based in her Catholic parish, and the retired insurance salesman in a small Baptist church that is temporarily without an ordained pastor. It may also be useful to members of a hospice care team in a geriatric center or acute care hospital who want to think seriously about the care they are offering in relation to their religious heritage.

A guiding assumption of this book is that it is the caring community, inclusive of both laity and clergy, that provides pastoral care. The ministry of pastoral care should be understood holistically rather than hierarchically, following the body image of Paul in 1 Corinthians 12 and Ephesians 4. This means that the theory, or theology, of pastoral care for laity and clergy should be the same. James C. Fenhagen has persuasively argued that a new sense of mutuality must exist between the clergy and the laity if the church is to be faithful to its task. The church is not "a community gathered around a minister, but a . . . community of many ministries. . . . We must address the gap which continues to exist in many areas between the clergy and the laity."[1]

3

Much of the material on lay pastoral care unwittingly maintains the assumption that lay care is always adjunct or second best to that offered by clergy. I do not believe this to be the case. While there are significant differences between clergy and lay care in terms of time available for pastoral caring, education, and responsibility for training others, the ministry of the caring community is the same ministry whether performed by laity or clergy.

While things have been changing in pastoral care, a similar phenomenon has taken place in Christian theology. Peter Hodgson, one of the theologians interpreting this change, has said that it is possible "to distinguish three great paradigms of the Christian theological tradition: the *classical* (from the patristic period through the Reformation . . .), the *modern* (from the early eighteenth to the late twentieth century: the 'Enlightenment age'), and the *postmodern*."[2] Although the time frames and the contents of the paradigms are not the same, I believe that one can also distinguish three major paradigms for the ministry of pastoral care: the *classical*, the *clinical pastoral*, and the *communal contextual*.

Briefly stated, the *classical* paradigm for pastoral care extended from the beginning of Christendom beyond the Reformation to the advent of modern dynamic psychology's impact on ministry.[3] Its major emphasis has been upon the *message* of pastoral care, the caring elements in Christian theology and tradition. The *clinical pastoral* paradigm which has extended over approximately the last fifty years has emphasized the *persons* involved in giving and receiving the message of care. Edward Thornton has described the emphasis on the person in clinical pastoral education as beginning with a concern with what a minister must *do*, moving to a concern with what the minister must *know*, then emphasizing what a minister should *say*, and, finally, evolving to the question of what a minister must *be*.[4]

Although there have certainly been expressions of the communal dimensions of the *communal contextual* paradigm for pastoral care at a number of points in history, its emergence in the last thirty years has been associated with the new ecumenicity exemplified by Vatican II and the Consultation on Church Union. In both Roman Catholicism and Protestantism, it has involved the shifting of ecclesiastical authority away from the church's clerical hierarchy toward particular Christian communities. It has been further developed by the liberation movements related to economic circumstance, to race, and to gender. The communal contextual paradigm broadens the clinical pastoral's focus beyond the clergy to include the caring community of clergy *and* laity. It also calls attention to contextual factors affecting both the message of care and those bringing it and receiving it.

I do not believe that either the *classical* or the *clinical pastoral* paradigm is negated by the *communal contextual* but that, in fact, all three are needed to rethink and carry out the pastoral care of the church at this point in history. In attempting to affirm both the new and the old, I have been informed by Hegel's concept of *"Aufhebung"* or "sublation," which, as Peter Hodgson has interpreted it, is "a process of both annulling and preserving, of both passing-over and taking-up."[5] With respect to the ministry of pastoral care, I also hope to annul and preserve—to preserve the most valuable features of the previous paradigms, but also to annul some of them in order to present a view of care that is less hierarchical, less naively provincial, and less uncritically individualistic than the pastoral care I have learned and taught.

The central feature of the *classical* paradigm, which must be preserved and reinterpreted for today, is the message of a God who caringly creates human beings for relationship and who continues to care by hearing and remembering them. Features of the *clinical pastoral* paradigm that must be preserved are its assumptions that: (1) the way one cares for others is inescapably related to the way one cares for oneself; (2) pastoral caring always involves *being* someone as well as *doing* something; and (3) one can best learn about oneself and how to care for others through experiential and reflective participation in caring relationships.

The *communal contextual* paradigm itself offers both an old and a new understanding of pastoral care. It is old in that it is based on the biblical tradition's presentation of a God who cares and who forms those who have been claimed as God's own into a community celebrating that care and extending it to others. It is new in that it emphasizes the caring community and the various contexts for care rather than focusing on pastoral care as the work of the ordained pastor. In the *communal contextual* paradigm, pastoral care is understood to be a ministry of a faith community which reminds members of God's scattered people that they are remembered. Pastoral care today should employ elements of all three paradigms, being attentive to the message, the persons communicating it and receiving it, and the contexts that affect its meaning. Thus the book presents a rethinking of pastoral care in terms of its *message, person,* and *context* and calls for the carers to remember God's action for them, to remember who they are as God's people, and to hear and remember those to whom they minister.

The central theological conviction or thesis of the book is that *God created human beings for relationship with God and with one another. God continues in relationship with creation by hearing us, remembering us, and bringing us into relationship with one another. Human care and community are possible because of our being held in God's memory; therefore, as members of caring communities we express our caring analogically with the caring of God by also hearing and remembering.*

As the thesis suggests, the book argues that the central biblical theme for pastoral care is being remembered and remembering. The use of the term *biblical theme* is indicative of a point of view on the use of the Bible as authority for the ministry of pastoral care.[6] This point of view holds that the Bible does not tell us how to do pastoral care, but it offers empowering themes for expression in the contexts for care today. This thematic view of scripture suggests that although the authority for care as remembering is biblical and expressive of the *classical* paradigm for pastoral care, it can be expressed through the *clinical pastoral* and the *communal contextual* paradigms as well.

Writing a book like this is an intimidating task. There are so many possibilities for organizing the material, so many different pastoral problems to be addressed, that I have felt somewhat like a character in one of Walker Percy's novels who was described as having "to know everything in order to do anything."[7] Fortunately, however, I was able to take comfort in the insight that Percy's character achieved in the novel. He "came to see that he was not destined to do everything but only one or two things." Similarly, I hope to content myself with doing only one or two things: (1) developing the theme of pastoral care as hearing and remembering and (2) relating that theme and the three major paradigms for care that I have identified to some of the more profound human problems to which pastoral care must be addressed. I attempt to do this using the structure described below.

The first section of the book considers communal and contextual elements in pastoral care and attempts to relate them to the theme of hearing and remembering. The specific concern of chapter 1 is to broaden the focus of pastoral care beyond the individual pastor to the larger group of carers within the Christian community. It discusses care as a central dimension of our humanity and relates it to an understanding of community and of remembering as a means by which care is expressed and community is developed. Care and community, however, are not simply momentary experiences. They exist through time, just as God creates but also remembers what has been created. God continues relationship with creation, symbolically forgetting through forgiveness what human beings have done to break relationship with God and with one another. Human beings, in turn, respond to what God has done by keeping covenant, remembering and caring for what God has given into their care.

Community, as discussed in this book, is in most cases a Christian congregation or a group within such a congregation. In some cases, however, it may be a community existing in other situations for ministry, such as a hospital or a social service agency. The church differs from other caring communities because of its responsibility for remembering and celebrating a particular history and experience. It is like other communities in that it expresses the nature of community ambiguously—sometimes with more clarity, sometimes with less. The chapter attempts to demonstrate how pastoral caring grows out of the community's remembering and in turn contributes to the building of a community that cares.

Chapter 2, "The Contextual: Care as Re-membering," addresses some of the important contextual questions related to care. Care, understood as remembering, must also "re-member," or re-vision, the person or persons cared for in the light of the various contexts that may affect the situation of care. "Re-membered" persons are those who can be seen and can see themselves differently from the dominant vision of that person or situation. In many ways the contextual question is a variation of the question of what is common and what is unique in a person or culture and of the human problem of blindness to one's own context and its particularity rather than universality.

The chapter addresses the questions of how class, race, and gender affect the carer and the care rendered. How do theological and ethical assumptions and beliefs impact pastoral care? The chapter also introduces the idea that the problem presented by the person to whom care is addressed is itself a context. If the primary task of pastoral care is hearing and remembering, then the problem presented is a context affecting what kind of care should be offered, the background for understanding the person or persons cared for. Pastoral care may contribute to the solving of problems, but that is not its primary task.

The second section of the book discusses the carer as person, learner, and teacher. Chapter 3, "Characteristics of the Carers," focuses on the person of the carers, or to put it in a question as it has been expressed in both the classical and clinical paradigms, "What are the pastor's personal qualifications, and how do they affect the pastor's ministry?" In recognition of the relational character of human beings, the chapter describes the features of the caring person or minister in terms of how he or she is in relationship rather than drawing a psychological profile or character type. This description applies to "all the saints," not just to the clergy, and involves a dynamic relationship between what one is and what one does. Members of the community of faith maintain their membership and minister to others by remembering that God remembers them. Thus the memory dimension of caring functions as a means of discovering and using their identity as ministers.

Chapter 4, "Care Through Consultation on Caring," examines the way in which members of the caring community learn ministry or, to use the Ephesian letter's term, how they are "equipped" for ministry. The distinctiveness of *pastoral* as a modifier of supervision and consultation is in designating these functions as ministry themselves, not simply practical techniques designed to accomplish a more important task, such as preaching, teaching, or parish visitation. The chapter touches on the New Testament view of leadership and authority, insofar as that can be discerned and interpreted for today, and relates it to the clinical pastoral understanding of supervision, applied in the new paradigm to the members of the community, not just to the professional clergyperson.

Some of the administrative dimensions of the term "pastor" are more often associated with the function of the clergy, but being pastoral is not limited to the clergy. As members of a community of faith, clergy and laity may be thought of as differing primarily in terms of an administrative responsibility and ecclesial accountability. The chapter will develop another, somewhat more unusual way of conceptualizing the clergy-laity difference—viewing the clergy as "generalists" in ministry, representatives of the "whole" ministry of the community of faith, whereas the laity are more often than not "specialists" in a particular type of ministry, such as this book's concern, the ministry of pastoral care.

The *clinical pastoral* paradigm, growing out of the experience of ministry in hierarchical health care institutions, has understood "equipping the saints" as primarily involving the pastor's role as supervisor. It has not sufficiently recognized the peership involved in the image of mutual intercession. The paradigm shift in this chapter, therefore, involves the dynamic relationship between supervision and consultation and what those relationships reveal about the members of the community. Because the norm for community is nonhierarchical, the teaching-learning relationship should be more consultative than supervisory. In fact, however, there is a powerful human resistance to peership, so that much of the teaching-learning relationship involves the tension between supervision and consultation and the way that the community's members both seek and deny peership. The importance of memory appears here in focusing the learning experience on recalling and learning from pastoral events imaginatively reconstructed.

The next section of the book, "Human Problems as Contexts for Care," presents four of the major human problems to which pastoral care is addressed. Pastoral care is certainly faced with many more problems than these, but the problem contexts that I have chosen to address seem to me to point beyond themselves to shed light on the nature of the human condition and on the various modes of care designed to address it. Good pastoral care addresses the details of a particular situation but it is also attuned to how that situation is an expression of the human situation common to all people. The pastoral carers attempt to adapt their caring response to meet specific needs and particular problems, such as addiction or illness, but they also must listen to what each problem has to say about the human condition and the character of the caring response of the community. To use the ancient image, lost sheep have something to say to the shepherd and to those in the sheepfold as well as the other way around.

In the first four chapters of the book I have been particularly concerned to present the care of the Christian community as the work of both laity and clergy involved together in ministry. In considering the human problems in the second four chapters, however, I see some significant differences in the responsibilities of laity and clergy. Both laity and clergy can be fully and effectively involved in addressing the problems of "limit and loss" and "patience and patienthood." The problems of "abuse of self and others" and of "special relationships" involving intimacy and closeness, however, seem to call for a professional dimension of the minister's role. The clergyperson or one whose full-time ministry is pastoral care and counseling is usually in a better position to take the "hard line" needed to address problems of addiction and abuse. She or he also is in a better position to assure the confidentiality necessary in dealing with the personal issues involved in the special relationships of the family. Lay carers are involved in addressing all four problems, but in chapters 7 and 8 and in chapter 9, on pastoral counseling, I will be more concerned in addressing clergy and persons in a full-time ministry of care and counseling.

Chapter 5, "Limit and Loss—The Risks of Care," deals specifically with the acceptance of human limitation and the pain of grief. Obviously, it deals with death and dying as the first, if not the most important, problem that members of the caring community need to respond to. But like Judith Viorst's popular book, *Necessary*

Losses, it broadens our view of grief to include many kinds of losses and the fact of limit and loss itself. It touches on the problem of disability as well as other limits and losses provided by the circumstances of life. What does limit and loss tell us about human being and about care and community? How do hearing and remembering contribute to the care of those who are becoming aware of their limits and losses?

Chapter 6, "Patience and Patienthood—The Need for Care," deals primarily with the problems of disease and illness as major concerns of the caring community and its pastor. It looks for the "pastoral" meaning in the words "being patient" and "being a patient." It argues that patience in ministry to the sick is perhaps the most important dimension of hearing and remembering. It also explores the way in which pastors themselves are patients. How is patienthood accepted or denied, and how is the fact that human beings are "those who wait" related to where they are with others and with God? What, then, is the patient dimension of caring?

Chapter 7, "Abuse of Self and Others—The Failure to Care," attempts to deal with addiction, violence, and victimization under the larger heading of abuse. It understands abuse as the failure to care, usually growing out of deprivation in one's being cared for. Any position taken in this problem area is necessarily controversial because of the mass of popular "ideological" literature on the subject today. Nevertheless, a critical position that can give practical guidance to the caring community and its pastor in identifying what can and cannot be done is particularly important now. Moreover, what can and cannot be done in ministry to the abused and the abuser is related to the larger theological question of what one can do to save oneself and to what degree others can assist in that process. How are addiction and abuse related to care, community, and memory?

Chapter 8, "Special Relationships—The Balances of Care," is a chapter on problems in the family and in other close or "special relationships" in life. It interprets the various problems that appear in this area of life in relation to the balance between one's individuality and relationality and the balance of care among the three generations closest to us. One cannot adequately develop a special relationship to a family member in one generation without dealing also with relationships to the other two proximal generations. It addresses the problem of intimacy in relationships that are given by kinship, such as that between parent and child, and those that are chosen, such as that between husband and wife and those between friends. It argues that "caring for our generations" is the most appropriate image for dealing with special relationships today and that this is the case for persons with children of their own and for those who invest in the future generation in other ways. Finally, it is concerned with the contribution that family relationships and living within them have to make to understanding human relationality and the calling to care.

The final section of the book deals specifically with the pastor's function as counselor and as a theologian of care. Chapter 9, "Pastoral Counseling: A Ministry of Availability and Introduction," is different from the chapters immediately preceding it in that it is not focused on a particular type of pastoral situation, but on more structured methods of care—pastoral counseling and referral. It emphasizes what can and what usually cannot be done in counseling by the pastor who is not specially trained in counseling and how pastoral counseling can be a ministry of introduction to other helping persons.[8]

The most effective learning of pastoral care involves reflection upon one's own experience of caring and being cared for. Optimally, this experience takes place in a clinical setting with a qualified pastoral supervisor. Courses in pastoral care often have such a clinical component as well as a classroom component. When that is not possible, individual reflection or, better yet, dialogue or small-group discussion on issues of care may be substituted. With that in mind, at the end of the first nine chapters of the book there are questions for reflection and discussion. At the end of the book there is an Appendix with assignments that may facilitate learning from one's own experience. The assignments involve the description of an event or the telling of a story in order to encourage a group of students and their leader to focus on the experiential rather than the more abstract and conceptual.

Chapter 10, "Theological Reflection on Pastoral Caring," is a brief concluding chapter which examines several methods of theological reflection on the theory and practice of pastoral care. It touches on questions such as, How does pastoral experience contribute to theological understanding? and, How do one's theological convictions affect the work of care? It concludes with a reflection on the theological method of this book.

My writing of this book grows out of my experience as a pastor for over thirty-five years, the majority of that time in a specialized ministry of chaplaincy or pastoral counseling. This experience has been enriched by extensive dialogue with a variety of persons associated with the international pastoral care and counseling movement and—during the last two years—through interviews I have conducted with lay pastoral carers and those involved in educating and facilitating their ministry.

The book is intended to be a background resource and guide-book for courses in pastoral care for theological students moving toward ordination and for members of caring communities who are involved in learning to care more effectively. The book is a "rethinking" of pastoral care—more theoretically than clinically. It makes use of case material, but it assumes that the best learning cases are not those of this author but those of persons involved in pastoral caring themselves. It further assumes that the best courses in pastoral care are those which have strong clinical compo-nents—caring persons involved in situations of care where they can reflect upon and learn from their own experience.

I have tried, insofar as possible, to correct for the limitations of my perspective as a white male clergyperson, pastoral counselor, and professor by incorporating the results of extensive dialogue with women ministers, persons from other countries and cultures, laity and clergy, on their understanding and experience of the task of pastoral care. I have no illusion that I can speak for those whose perspective is radically different from mine. What I do be-lieve, however, is that there are significant commonalities of care that cut across differences in race, culture, and gender and that if one is aware of one's own particular perspective and at least some of its biases, important things can be said that are relevant for car-ing communities quite different from one's own.

Pastoral Care in Context

Part One

The Communal
and the Contextual

1

The Communal:
Care as Remembering

What are human beings that you are mindful of them,
mortals, that you care for them?

—Psalm 8:4

Patient (after a visit from the hospital chaplain): "Remember me,
Reverend. Remember me."

The understanding of pastoral care in this book is based on the
theological conviction that human care and community are possible because we are held in God's memory; therefore, as members
of caring communities, we express our caring analogically with
the caring of God by hearing and remembering one another. God
created human beings for relationship and continues in relationship with creation by hearing us, remembering us, and meeting us
in our relationships with one another. The *communal contextual*
paradigm views pastoral care as a ministry of the Christian community that takes place through remembering God's action for us,
remembering who we are as God's own people, and hearing and
remembering those to whom we minister. This chapter argues
that thesis by examining the meanings of care, community, and
memory and their relationship to one another.

The Meaning of Care

In an address to the Association for Clinical Pastoral Education,
Parker Palmer used a quotation from Annie Dillard to affirm care

15

as a fundamental part of the human spirit. "In the depths of the human being," he said, "underneath the violence and terror of which psychology warned us, you find what our sciences cannot locate or name . . . the unified field, our complex and inexplicable caring for one another and for our life together here. This is given. This is not learned."[1]

Whether this "inexplicable caring for one another and for our life together here" is given or learned—I believe that it is learned in the first relationships of life—is less important than the affirmation of its fundamental nature. One can express the same affirmation biblically:

> Then God said, "Let us make humankind in our image, according to our likeness; and let them have dominion over the fish of the sea, and over the birds of the air, and over the cattle, and over all the wild animals of the earth, and over every creeping thing that creeps upon the earth."

> So God created humankind in his image,
>   in the image of God he created them;
>   male and female he created them.

> God blessed them, and God said to them, "Be fruitful and multiply . . . and have dominion over . . . every living thing that moves upon the earth."

> (Gen. 1:26–28)

A major conviction on which this book is based is that scripture reveals a God who cares and who creates a community with authority to interpret scripture in a way that empowers its life in the world. The material above from Genesis 1:26–28 has been the church's classic text for the doctrine of the *imago Dei*, the image of God in human being, but it also provides an important biblical basis for pastoral care. It is the Bible's earliest attempt to say what the human being is and does. The theological understanding of the human being created in the image of God has been conceptualized in a number of ways, but traditionally it has been seen as a capacity given by God to humankind, a capacity associated with power. More recent interpretations, however, have argued that humankind's responsibility is not dominion or power over the earth but care for it.[2] According to one of my former professors of theology, Joseph Sittler, "The word *dominion* is a direct English effort to translate the Latin. In English *dominion* suggests *domination*, but that is an incorrect translation. The Hebrew statement is, 'And God said you are to exercise care over the earth and hold it in its proper place.'"[3] I think that this newer interpretation is not so much a more nearly correct translation as it is translation informed by a newer theological interpretation.

In another place Sittler insists that the "fundamental term *imago Dei* is not a term that points to a substance, an attribute, or a specifiable quality, but one which specifies a relation."[4] Humankind, according to this reinterpretation of the Genesis text (from dominion to care) has been given the vocation of caring for the earth.[5]

Considering the concept of care more broadly, the *Oxford English Dictionary* traces two basic views of care in the development of the English language. The first understanding involves the concept of anxiety; the second, of solicitude. To care is to be anxious, troubled, and even to grieve, but it also means to be concerned with, to regard, and even to love, in the sense of care for the other rather than for oneself. Both meanings are important in understanding pastoral care.

In one of its meanings, care expresses the basic human concern with control and predictability. It is concerned with preserving the present and/or controlling the future. To be "care-full" is to be anxious. It involves the restless waiting for the future to unfold. But care also has the meaning of solicitude and concern for the needs of the other, based not on the subjective needs of the caregiver but on the objective perception of the other's needs. The classic image of the shepherd still usefully illustrates the meaning of care. The shepherd tends the whole flock but is ever vigilant about the needs of the individual member of the flock while being concerned for the needs of the whole.

One of the names strongly associated with the meaning of care is that of Martin Heidegger. As in the definitional views noted above, Heidegger affirmed the importance of understanding care both as the anxiety that we feel about our own lives and also as the solicitude we direct toward others. He views care as "the basic constitutive phenomenon of human existence, and the clue to its interpretation."[6] Care is what makes the human being human. If we do not care, we lose our humanity.[7] Yet, our finitude and our temporality are what make care possible. We are limited by time and, therefore, challenged to care both for ourselves and for others in order to deal creatively with the limits that time imposes. Heidegger is helpful in reminding the pastoral carer that care is more than what we feel or think or do. As "constitutive of our being," it is what we in fact are—caring.

A useful recent interpretation of care comes from ethicist Nel Noddings, who identified caring as the moral virtue necessary for reducing alienation and guiding moral action. She argues that the "highest" stage of moral judgment is "not so much concerned with the rearrangement of priorities among principles," but "with maintaining and enhancing caring." Finding an ethical norm in what women do rather than in what men do, she argues that women "do not abstract away from the concrete situation those elements that allow a formulation or deductive argument; rather, they remain in the situation as sensitive, receptive, and responsible agents."[8]

To care "is to act not by fixed rule but by affection and regard." Thus, the actions of caring will be varied rather than rule-bound, and, while predictable in a global sense, will be unpredictable in detail. What is important for Noddings is that "the rational-objective," which is so much a part of ethical thinking today, be reestablished and redirected from a fresh base of care and commitment. If this does not happen, the caring person can become "inextricably enmeshed in procedures that somehow serve only themselves" and her thoughts "separated, completely detached, from the original objects of caring."[9]

Noddings reminds us that the caring attitude has as its prototype the mother-child relationship. That attitude "which expresses our earliest memories of being cared for and our growing store of memories of both caring and being cared for, is universally accessible."[10] Ethical caring is based developmentally in that original relationship, but it differs in being intentional. It may be accompanied by love, but it always involves responsibility for the other—the cared-for. "As we care, we hear the 'I ought'—direct and primitive—and the potential for suffering guilt is ever present." Guilt is most likely, however, in caring that is sustained over time. Although the one caring affirms responsibility for the other, she also insists on "a deep and steady caring for self."[11]

Commenting on Noddings's work, a recent interpreter has offered a useful addendum, namely, that the successful use of an ethics of care requires a moral agent who is clear "about the boundaries of the self so that she can practice the demanding task of engrossment without the loss of self being a problem for her." Furthermore, a care ethic also presupposes "an agent who has a realistic sense of her own competencies and a sense of that which she can reasonably take responsibility for so that she can separate from situations in which caring is not effective."[12]

Many of the things that Noddings has presented in her view of care resonate strongly with pastoral care as it has developed within the clinical pastoral paradigm. The development of those sensitivities to relationships that have been identified as feminine is, in fact, a quality essential to becoming a good pastor of either gender. Noddings's emphasis on being aware of one's own involvement in what one does and the impossibility of evaluating thoughts and acts apart from the one who has them and does them is a central feature of what is best in the *clinical pastoral* paradigm. Learning to deal with one's responsibilities for caring and the necessary guilt that accompanies the impossibility of fully carrying out those responsibilities is one of the most important things that supervised clinical experience has offered.

It is hard to overemphasize the importance of care in human life. It may be a painful or a satisfying part of the most important human relationships. One of the earliest feelings and some of the earliest words in our experience have to do with whether the person most important to us cares or does not seem to care. Negatively expressed, the words "You don't care" are, perhaps, the most painful ones that we hear or say. To care is central to being human, from the perspective of theology, philosophy, or ethics.

What care means and some of the implications of that meaning may be summarized as follows:

1. The image of God may be seen in relationality and responsibility—one's response to God expressed through care for self and others. Care's two meanings, anxiety and solicitude, express the self and other foci and exist in relationship to each other in a way similar to the individuality and relationality discussed in the section on community that follows.

2. Care as anxiety, or Heidegger's "care for being," expresses finitude, one's own and the finitude of others. Those for whom we care most may die and leave us without relationship to them.

3. Care of the other—which cannot be separated from care of self—is based not only on our relation to God and our God-given vocation to care, but also on the fundamental relationship between parent and child, usually between mother and child. All other relationships emerge out of that basic relationship, and disappointment and denial of that relationship results in distortion of all our relationships.

4. Because of our relationality and our call to care, guilt is inescapable as a result of our failure to care fully and adequately. Thus, to be human is also to be guilty and to find ways of dealing with that guilt.

5. Care is fundamental for humanity and, as Tillich has suggested, an unconscious expression of who we are. However, ways of caring and caring more effectively can and should be learned by those called to a ministry of pastoral caring.

The Meaning of Community

In reflecting upon the meaning of community as I had experienced it and discussed it with caring communities involved in ministry, I recalled a lecture by theologian Daniel Day Williams in which he spoke personally of his experience of Christian community.

> What was most important was the experience itself . . . this sense of being in an unfriendly world, a world full of all kinds of threats—the struggle to adjust to the group, of being alone—and then discovering that there is a group in which there is real love. In the church there is a community which truly cares about you. There is the sense of sin, of being involved in evil that you cannot overcome and being estranged from what is essentially right in life. And then the discovery of grace—that the sinner is still within the circle of the care of God—that there is a possible restoration of life. There is the experience of a new kind of life itself, a life beginning to be restored to what it ought to be. . . . Whatever philosophy or world view or general knowledge about the world comes along, it must help interpret this most important thing of all.[13]

I also remembered talking about the meaning of community with one of the elderly church members in a small church on the South Side of Chicago, where I was pastor during my days as a graduate student. Dr. Matthies had grown up in a German community in South Dakota. When I asked her how she happened to be a Methodist instead of a Lutheran, her simple answer was: "The Methodists called me 'little sister Mabel.'" That community had named her as belonging to them.

Much more recently, when I was interviewing a group of lay ministers in a large Presbyterian church in the Southwest about how they understood themselves as ministers, one of the women, whom I will call Natalie, said:

> I grew up in this church. A lot of these people were here when I lost my father, and they gave me something I didn't even know I needed. I guess you could call it a sense of being part of a group that cared. When I visit people I want to give them the same kind of thing, a feeling that there is something important that they are a part of.

Natalie wanted people to feel "that there is something important that they are a part of." She remembers being cared for herself, and wants others to experience care as she has. Her loss will help her be sensitive to the losses of others, but what she has to offer is not only what her life experience has been, but what she has experienced as a member of a caring community. Professor Williams, Dr. Matthies, and Natalie all remember being cared for and experiencing community. In sharing these reflections I am underscoring the importance of community as a basis for ministry, not attempting to develop a singular way of describing it.

One way of describing community has been suggested by William Willimon, who has identified five characteristics that are applicable to most of the caring communities that I have studied and experienced. Those characteristics are: common identity, common authority, common memory, common vision, common shared life together, and common shared life in the world.[14] All caring communities may not exhibit all five of these characteristics with equal strength, but I believe they have some elements of all of them.

Common identity in caring communities is most seen in the way the community functions. The lay pastoral carers with whom I met all seemed to have an identity as a ministering community and a sense of being an important part of a larger Christian community. "We are the ones involved in this particular ministry, and we're proud of it." As I have experienced these groups and interviewed their leaders, the common authority they express is the authority of experience. They tell stories of what has happened to them in their ministry and express confidence in the value of that experience to aid them in their future work. They also speak very positively of the training and supervision in ministry they have received and how that has helped them learn from their experience.

Another aspect of community is shared memory. I was particularly aware of shared memory as I visited ministry groups to listen and learn about their experiences in pastoral caring. Their shared memory was expressed in stories about the particular congregation or groups and significant individuals within it, or simply, "This is how we started, and here are some of the things that have happened to us." Lay pastoral carers speak of the importance of the Christian message and tradition and seem aware that their ministry of care grows out of that message, but the message may not be expressed with much theological sophistication. It is more likely to be pointed to, identified with the sermons the minister has preached or with memory expressed in the eucharistic liturgy.

Not all caring communities are related to congregations. Some offer care in secular settings, such as a hospice team in a general hospital or the staff of a community service agency. These groups also speak of their particular history and the difficulties they have overcome in performing their ministry together. The common memory is virtually inseparable from their shared life together. Among the groups I have interviewed, the shared life in their particular type of ministry has most commonly been the visitation of the sick. The common vision is most often the acceptance of their particular ministry as central in the life of the larger congregation or community of which they are a part. The members of Natalie's lay ministry group, for example, seemed unanimous in their conviction that what they were doing was much more than making visits as individuals. They felt "a part of something" and found a variety of ways to say that what they were doing as pastoral carers was representing a community in which they felt cared for.

Parker Palmer has commented that community is an inward fact long before it can be an outward reality. "Our common life, our true community, or what Thomas Merton once called our hidden wholeness is found originally not in outward reality but in our inner life." Community, "which we normally think of as a sociological phenomenon, is in fact a contemplative act. It is a reaching for deep, inner insight about our connectedness with one another, with the world, with God's reality. It is a given. It is a knowledge that's in our backbone. There is no external ethic which can teach community."[15]

Palmer is concerned, however, that when clergy and laity say they want "Christian community" they often mean they want the opposite of what they see in society at large. Instead of conflict, the church should offer comfort; instead of distance between persons, intimacy; instead of criticism, affirmation. He questions this "ideal family" image of community and suggests that it inappropriately constricts our understanding and experience of community and forces people to hide their conflicts. "Such a church does everything in its power to eliminate the strange and cultivate the familiar. Such a church can neither welcome the stranger nor allow the stranger in each of us to emerge."[16]

Palmer argues convincingly that the identity of community with idealized family intimacy must be abandoned. Similarly, one of my students, preaching on community in the seminary chapel, recently commented that those who think of community as a congenial and happy family are forgetting about the fights in the back seat of the car when the family was trying to go someplace together. Palmer's image of community is that of a "company of strangers"—a place where people confront the stranger in each other and in themselves, and "still know that they are members one of another."[17]

Thus, as important as the experience of community is, Palmer's image of a company of strangers suggests convincingly that *experiencing* community is not an end in itself. Although it appropriately expresses the human need for relationship, community can also be an elusive ideal which sometimes is compulsively sought to avoid the action of ministry. The church and other caring communities are a community of ministers who are together not primarily to be together, but because as human beings their members need one another in order to do the work of ministry. Relationships with the members of the community are important, but seemingly more important is the awareness of participating in a common task and of not being alone in the difficulties and responsibilities of life. To use an image from the Synoptic Gospels, Peter appears to be tempted to stay on the Mount of Transfiguration with Jesus, Moses, and Elijah rather than going down the mountain to minister to the needs of the people below. The symbolic inner connection of persons involved together in ministry appears to me to be more important than experiencing the pleasure of particular communal relationships. Being with another in ministry is more important than the satisfaction of simply being with.

Theoretical Views of Community

The theoretical and theological basis for these more experiential views of community may be found in a number of places, first of all in Canadian theologian Douglas John Hall's argument that the basic ontological category is not "being" but *being with*. "To claim that the rudimentary ontology of the biblical tradition is being-with is to say that all being, from the Being who is the source and ground of being to the smallest of created things, is being-in-relationship."[18]

Focusing in a similar way on the importance of relationality, Frank G. Kirkpatrick has affirmed a "mutual/personal" model of community which attempts to express dialectically the needs and concerns of both individual and community.[19] Following religious philosophers Martin Buber and John Macmurray, he argues that the "notion of a biblical community needs to be grounded in an adequate metaphysical view of persons, God, and interpersonal relations."[20] With Buber he believes that the concept of the isolated individual is a fiction. Relationship is primary. "There is no I taken in itself, but only the 'I' of the primary word *I-Thou* and the 'I' of the primary word *I-It*."[21] Human beings have been given the task of becoming a community. Buber defines "community" as a connection of persons "who are so joined in their life with something apportioned to them in common or something which they have apportioned to themselves in common that they are just thereby, joined with one another in their life." But community cannot be achieved without God, who is the creator of its conditions, as the center of community.[22]

Complementing Buber's point of view is the work of philosopher John Macmurray[23] who was concerned with the egocentricity of modern philosophy in taking the self as its starting point and in viewing the self as purely individual in isolation. Macmurray argued that thinking must be done from the standpoint of relationality, a relationality that is possible only if the self is first a doer and secondarily a thinker. He believed that action, in contrast to thinking, was "a full concrete activity of the self in which all our capacities are employed." It is in the practical encounter of action that the other is discovered both as the resistance to, and the support of, action. For Macmurray, the unity of persons in community is a unity in which each remains a distinct individual and in which each realizes him- or herself in and through the other.

Hall, Buber, and Macmurray present different but complementary interpretations of community. Hall emphasizes the ontological nature of relationality, of "being with" as what being means. Buber emphasizes human relationality in partnership with God. Macmurray brings together action and relationship, and is concerned that the distinctiveness of the individual self in action not be lost in the affirmation of the fundamental nature of relationship. Thus, the unity of persons in community is one in which each remains a distinct individual, but also one in which each realizes him- or herself in and through the other. Relationality does not negate individuality; it requires it. Genuine and mutual relationships, which are the community's life, are possible because individuality exists, because there are differences between persons, and because those differences are needed to fulfill and enrich the relationships. There is, however, always a tension or dialectical relationship between the claims of relationality and of individuality, and the life of the community is most often expressed in terms of that fundamental tension.

God is the author of community, creating it as an expression of human relationality. This relationality, however, is not a passive condition. It is brought into being through human action, empowered through relationship to God. Through their vocation of caring for the earth, human beings learn to care for one another. Thus, although human beings are created as relational and find their individuality through relationship with one another and with God, the purpose of Christian community is not only to experience relationship, but also to experience relationship in order to empower ministry.

The church and other caring communities may be character-ized as communities of action, of relationship, and of meaning. No one of these three is more important than any other. Each serves to challenge and correct the other two.[24] The church exists to facilitate care of the earth and the human beings that inhabit it, through offering genuine relationship and enabling persons to discover meaning in life and the world.

Natalie and other lay pastoral carers have not been explicitly theological in most of their references to the church and the church's meaning for them. Part of the reason may be lack of comfort with the language. They have learned to do the work of ministry before learning to talk about it in a theological way. They use the language fairly comfortably in worship and in study groups, but in groups that involve a focus on what they have done or are doing ecclesial language is less comfortable and fa-miliar.

I believe there is another reason as well. Laity involved in the ministry of the church are very much aware of the ambiguity of the church that they serve. This comes out in their talk of the church's failures or the failures of its leaders. They know from ex-perience the separation between the church as it should be and as it is. They know and speak of in everyday language what theolo-gian Peter Hodgson has spoken of dialectically. How can the church, he says, "be both a divine gift and a human activity, both a spirit-filled community and a historical institution, without there being an identity of these dimensions of its being but with-out there being a separation of them either?"[25] Although the per-sons in the ministry groups I have interviewed did not have either the theological training or the familiarity with the language to ar-ticulate the problem like this, they recognized that the church as they had experienced was both ideal and actual, and they could speak of it both critically and lovingly.

Hodgson deals with the ambiguity of the church by relating the concepts of *basileia*, usually translated kingdom or kingdom of God, and *ecclesia*, the church, traditionally characterized by its unity, catholicity, apostolicity.[26] *Basileia* is an image of a new way of being human in the world in relation to God and neighbor— new community, communion of love, liberation, a new and radi-cal family based not on blood relationships but on human and ethical ones. The church inevitably becomes an institution that seeks to maintain itself through time, but this *ecclesia* is also "an image, sign, sacrament, and foretaste of the *basileia*, embodied in the diversity of historical churches. As such, it discloses the *basileia* vision unambiguously but actualizes it only fragmentarily."[27]

Although I am speaking theoretically here about the nature of the caring community, this kind of dialectical "yes" and "no" or "yes" and "but also" is experientially understandable to pastoral carers who have experienced the "yes" and "no" of the church as caring community in a variety of ways. Care for the church and ambivalence about it have consistently appeared in a variety of ways in my interviewing of lay pastoral carers. This dialectical view of the church is important not only in dealing with the intellectual issues identified by Hodgson, but also in accepting the practical ambivalence about the church expressed by its members. They have experienced community there, but know only too well the church's human limitations and have difficulty in claiming too much for it. It is important that the church exists, but its power and authority remain problematic. Stating this ambivalence toward the church theologically, it is important to affirm the reality of *ecclesia* as a necessary structure and enduring sociological reality in the world, and also *basileia* as the dynamic function of God's action in the world, criticizing and correcting all its structural expressions, particularly the church.

Summarizing this understanding of community and what it means for ministry:

1. God is the author of community, creating it as a dimension of human relationality and being involved in it by enabling the mutual personal relationships that take place within it.

2. This relationality, however, is not a passive condition. Action is the means of encountering the other. Human beings risk themselves in acting on behalf of themselves and of others and in that process engage persons who are different from themselves. The process of working with those differences to achieve genuine relationship is the substance of the community's life.

3. Human relationality does not negate individuality—in fact, it requires it. Genuine and mutual relationships which are the community's life are possible because individuality exists, because there are differences between persons, and because those differences are needed to fulfill and enrich the relationships. There is, however, always a tension or dialectical relationship between the claims of relationality and those of individuality, and the life of the community is most often expressed in terms of that fundamental tension.

4. Further expressions of the community's life may be seen in its common identity, the shared memory of its life, the vision of

its possibility as a community and in relation to those outside it.

5. Even though God is the author and sustainer of any genuine community of human beings, the community *is* and *is not* expressive of that relationship to the divine. That persistent problem has been expressed theologically in a variety of ways. One way has been in terms of the tension between *basileia* and *ecclesia,* or dynamic and form, each judging and challenging the other. The ongoing task of the church is to witness to the possibility of community, but also to recognize that often it is not expressive of it and that genuine community may exist elsewhere.

6. Pastoral care is the person-to-person response that grows out of participation in a caring community and which seeks to enable persons to give and receive care and to experience community.

7. The communal dimension of the communal contextual paradigm is corrective of the classical paradigm in emphasizing that the Christian message is heard, experienced, and remembered in community. The classical Christian affirmation that there is no salvation outside the church can now be understood not in terms of the church as mediating between the individual and God but as emphasizing that the church is a community in which a person may know God in the context of communal relationships.

8. The clinical pastoral paradigm emphasized the person of the pastor and the inseparability of the person and the message. The communal dimension of the communal contextual paradigm enlarges the clinical pastoral by emphasizing the Christian community and its members as the messengers of care. In emphasizing human relationality, the communal dimension does not look at the ordained pastor apart from the community but in relation to it and as a leader and facilitator of the relationships that take place as a part of it. Pastoral care is an action of the community which may be nurtured and led by the ordained pastor, but which is first a responsibility of the community.

The Community Remembers and Cares

Caring . . . implies remembering, that is to say, keeping the other person . . . in mind. Thus, it comes as a confirming fact to learn that "memory" is also cognate with the Greek *merimna,* "care," "solicitude," "anxiety," "sorrow." Remembering *is* caring for what we remember—intensified, once more, in commemorating.[28]

Care and community are obviously related to each other, but it is memory that brings them fully into relationship. Community "is lost knowledge that must be remembered and recovered.

Remembered means to re-member. It means to put the body back together. The opposite of remember is not to forget, but to dis-member. And when we forget where we came from . . . we have in fact dis-membered something."[29] Because I remember I can care. Because I remember I can experience community in celebrating a God who remembers. Moreover, in the strength of knowing that I am remembered I can express care for others through hearing and remembering them.[30]

"Jesus, remember me when you come into your kingdom" (Luke 23:42). Without really knowing what we were singing, many of those in my generation echoed those words as we sang the rhythmic spiritual, "Do Lord, O Do Lord, O Do Remember Me!" in youth groups many years ago. Only recently have I begun to realize how profound those simple words are. They represent the human need for care and, perhaps, the primary authorization for the ministry of pastoral care. They are not isolated words. The petition appears in many ways in scripture, but it also appears in the corridors of the hospital and nursing home: "Remember me, Reverend," even from those who are hesitant to use the word prayer in their request. Similarly, resonating with many other places in the Old Testament is the psalmist's petition about God's remembering Israel: "Remember your congregation, which you acquired long ago,/which you redeemed to be the tribe of your heritage" (Ps. 74:2).

We Remember Because God Remembers

"The extraordinary feature of the biblical picture of God," says theologian Don Saliers, "is . . . that God will remember God's people." The God revealed in Hosea speaks poignantly, "How can I give you up, Ephraim?" Central to biblical faith is a God who has covenanted not to forsake us:

> In remembering us and all those in any adversity, God acts out of the compassion and covenant with which the whole creation was loved into being. . . . Like all generations before and after us, we need to learn the remembrance of God and to call upon God to re-member us.[31]

Old Testament scholar Brevard Childs argues that in the Old Testament there can be no dichotomy between God's thought and action, that God's remembering always implies God's movement toward the object of God's memory. "The essence of God's remembering lies in his acting toward someone because of a previous commitment."[32] "The object of God's remembering is either the recipient of the covenant (Noah, Gen. 8:1; Abraham, Gen. 19:29) or the covenant . . . itself."[33] A more recent interpreter, Ralph W. Klein, has claimed that the memory of God is "virtually equivalent to his acts of deliverance"[34] and is the most usable theme for organizing the theological message of the "P" document in Genesis.

In his commentary on Genesis, Gerhard von Rad speaks eloquently of God's remembering Noah on the ark as

> a bold anthropomorphism which makes the freedom of the divine resolve for salvation especially impressive. A turn toward salvation has occurred, and it can be founded only on the fact that God remembered Noah. God checked the chaotic powers by which the entire earth was already engulfed, before they also brought Noah and those with him to destruction.[35]

Commenting on the same passage, Walter Brueggemann speaks of God as "not immune to the flow of human events." It is

> the gospel of this God that he remembers. . . . His remembering is an act of gracious engagement with his covenant partner, an act of committed compassion. It asserts that God is not preoccupied with himself but with his covenant partner, creation. It is the remembering of God, and only that, which gives hope and makes new life possible (cf. I Sam. 1:11, 19; Judg. 16:28; Ps. 8:4; 10:12; 74:1–3; Jer. 15:15). Above all, Job 14:13 articulates the conviction that God's memory is the last ground of hope in the realm of death.[36]

Most important for us here, Brueggemann affirms that the "issue of being forgotten is not just a concern of Israel. It is a genuine pastoral issue."[37] I agree and further believe that there is no more fundamental biblical basis for pastoral care than the Old Testament faith in the memory of God and the New Testament conviction that Jesus as the Christ is evidence of God's remembering. The God who remembers Israel is the God of Jesus' Sermon on the Mount, whose "eye is on the sparrow" (Matt. 6:26), and whose human creatures are affirmed as being remembered as of even more value.

In response to God's memory of them, Christians find faith and renew it by remembering the story of Jesus as it is told in words and retold in sacrament. They remember what Jesus did and what he said. Perhaps the most important example of this is from 1 Corinthians: "For I received from the Lord what I also handed on to you" (1 Cor. 11:23). And then Paul remembers:

> The Lord Jesus on the night when he was betrayed took a loaf of bread, and when he had given thanks, he broke it and said, "This is

my body that is for you. Do this in remembrance of me." In the same way he took the cup also, after supper, saying, "This cup is the new covenant in my blood. Do this, as often as you drink it, in remembrance of me." (1 Cor. 11:23b–25)

As a community of anamnesis, of remembering, the church is challenged to remember as an act of caring. Although in the history of the church there have been many theological debates about the "remembering" involved in the eucharistic celebration, the central meaning of anamnesis is not simply memory of a past event. It is the re-presenting of something that is not absent but alive and active in the present. The kind of remembering involved in the eucharistic liturgy binds past, present, and future together.

The pastoral dimension of this can be seen in some of Paul's letters. Paul remembers, but not just as reminiscing. He has in mind at the present time the power of those past relationships. The letter that seems most personal and most exemplary for pastoral care, Philippians, begins with the affirmation of his readers, "I thank my God every time I remember you" (Phil. 1:3) and later, "It is right for me to think this way about all of you, because you hold me in your heart, for all of you share in God's grace with me"(v. 7).[38]

Even the letter of Paul that seems most impersonal, the letter to Romans, ends with a striking recital of memories and greetings. If I have counted correctly, no less than twenty-three persons are named and greeted, some with particular memories associated with their names; for example: Prisca and Aquila, "who work with me in Christ Jesus, and who risked their necks for my life" (Rom. 16:3–4), and Rufus and his mother, "a mother to me also" (v. 13). The letter to the Ephesians, which may not be an actual writing of Paul, is certainly written in the spirit of Paul's relationship to those to whom he ministered. The author presents a picture of pastoral remembering as he requests prayer "for all the saints . . . [and] for me" (Eph. 6:18–19).

The Human Condition: Amnesia vs. Memory
A great deal of the literature on memory is both fascinating and relevant for a pastoral care understood as hearing and remembering. Memory seems particularly important for today because forgetting is so characteristic of our time. The work of Sigmund Freud and much of the literature of psychoanalysis have emphasized the importance of memory in life and health. Philosopher Edward Casey, in his study of remembering, points to Freud's comment that "the weak spot in the security of our mental life [is] the untrustworthiness of our memory," and he speaks of psycho-

analysis as consisting of "a continuous struggle against the forces of forgetfulness."[39] Freud's work underscored the painfulness of many memories and how they are repressed or denied. His classic paper on "Recollection, Repetition, and Working Through" discusses how psychoanalytic working through overcomes the compulsion to repeat and allows persons to remember and change.[40]

German pastor-psychoanalyst Joachim Scharfenberg characterizes Freud's method of treatment as taking "ahistorical" persons who cannot be open to the future because of their compulsions to repeat the past and helping them return to history.[41] The analyst helps them rediscover their memory. The patient reconnects with his life story and makes a new one freer from denial. Thus, psychoanalytic remembering tries to discover a more integrating form for the past by disclosing and reinterpreting painful memories which have been unnoticed or repressed.

Czech novelist Milan Kundera has posed the question of the relationship between remembering and forgetting. What Kundera has called "splendid lightness" is fostered by actively forgetting that which becomes intolerably heavy when remembered. But, Kundera wonders, "Is heaviness truly deplorable and lightness splendid?" The answer of his novel is "No." In fact he affirms that the heaviest of burdens "can be an image of life's most intense fulfillment. The heavier the burden, the closer our lives come to the earth, the more real and truthful they become."[42]

Memory means something other than the psychologically demonstrable ability to retain an idea of something in the past. Memory, according to Martin Heidegger, "is the gathering of recollection, thinking back."[43] Memory, Heidegger said, did not initially mean the power to recall. Originally memory's meaning was similar to that of "devotion: a constant concentrated abiding with something—not just with something that has passed, but in the same way with what is present and with what may come."[44]

Augustine believed that remembering creates and maintains continuity of the self, and that it is concerned not only "with the past and the present but also with the future."[45] Memory, as Augustine understood it, contributes to one of the central concerns of the *clinical pastoral* paradigm for pastoral care, a sense of identity, of "persistence over time as continuously the same person."[46] Don Saliers has also spoken of remembering in that way. "Our deepest emotions are intimately linked with how we remember and what we recall. . . . Without the capacity to remember, we lack a sense of narrative about our lives and our world."[47]

Memory, according to Augustine, not only contributes to a sense of personal identity, but it is where one should search for

God. Believing that the events of his life could reveal God's will and purpose, he systematically engaged in bringing his lifetime to mind and sought to discover the call God addressed to him. Like creative imagination, Augustine believed that remembering could be a spiritual activity. Because of the power of memory he could speak of things that he could not see; therefore it was fitting that God should reside in memory."[48]

Pastoral Care as Hearing and Remembering

It was sometime around midnight, and I was in the Dallas airport. I had been scheduled to fly home from Houston to Atlanta some four hours earlier, but after getting on and off and on and off the plane, due to the plane's mechanical difficulties, we were told that our flight had been canceled. My only chance to get home that night was to fly to Dallas and there to catch the last plane out for Atlanta. So there I was in Dallas, farther away from home than when I had first gotten on the plane. I was tired and, at best, frustrated by the experience.

I was waiting impatiently for my flight to be called when a bright-faced young woman in a flight attendant's uniform came up to me and said, "You're Dr. Patton, aren't you?" Surprised and curious, I nodded, "Yes," and the young woman identified herself as the daughter of someone who had cleaned our office for many years. "I remember you from when I used to work with my mother," the young woman said. And then I remembered her mother, Jean, and the family she brought with her to help her do their work. I remembered their surprising pleasantness on other nights I was tired and for some reason late at the office. The young woman and I chatted for a few minutes about her family and her new career, and then she hurried off to her flight. With some surprise I found that I was no longer tired and that the hours of delay seemed unimportant—all, apparently, because I had been remembered.

The work of Carl Rogers was a powerful influence on pastoral care, and it became a part of the clinical pastoral paradigm's emphasis on the person of the pastor. Rogers and his disciples democratized psychotherapeutic techniques and made them available to a broad audience, offering practical training in helping skills to many people who would not otherwise have acquired them.[49] Unfortunately, many of those who have learned these skills have learned them superficially and stereotypically.

One of Rogers's most influential disciples, Eugene Gendlin, has insisted that the technique is not at fault. It is simply that the capacity to listen has not been learned well enough. What he has to say about listening is extremely important to pastoral carers with varying degrees of experience. What he says is that traditional client-centered response, as taught by Rogers, attempts to convey to the person whose life situation is being attended to that the carer has indeed heard what has been said to him or her. Accuracy in hearing and in conveying what has been heard is the essence of the technique. What most often happens in response, however, is only a vague approximation of what has been said—a response that is, as Gendlin puts it, "deprived of its specific edges." The person who is trying to convey his concerns to a carer is left trying to *hold on to* what he originally felt, despite the interference of the carer's inaccurate response.[50]

In trying to hold on to what they have shared, persons seeking help may try to deal with the listener's inaccurate response by trying to clarify what they have said: "It's not so much that, because after all, the way things were was such and such." The carer, most often not realizing that all of that is a comeback to an inaccurate response, restates what has been said to her. By this time what the seeker had sought from the alleged listener has been lost in generalizations and "lowest common denominators."

> Without being able to listen, to hear, to respond exactly, to help the person share what is felt, the therapist is actually leaving the client basically alone. However useful the other things a therapist does may be, if the therapist can't hear, the person is left alone inside. What the person is really up against is not dealt with, is not even brought in, is not even touched. Without listening, the inward sense of the person is not expanded, it remains not only alone, but compressed, sometimes nearly silent, dumb. That way there can be no relationship. . . . Responding in a listening way is a baseline prerequisite for any other modes of responding. It is not just one of many ways, but a precondition for the other ways.[51]

It is hard to imagine a stronger appeal for the importance of careful listening, clarifying, and responding to the feelings and facts of what a person shares with you about her or his life. All pastoral carers need some kind of regular supervision and consultation on the way they hear and remember. Those who have ears, let them listen!

Finally, although memory generally is associated with time, place is equally important for our remembering. One of the most important aids in remembering is what Edward Casey has called "a given sense of place." Place "acts as a grid onto which images of items to be remembered are placed in a certain order. The subsequent remembering of these items occurs by revisiting the place-grid and traversing it silently step by step in one's mind."[52] Memories "seek out particular places as their natural habitats. . . . Places are *congealed scenes* for remembered contents; and as such they serve to situate what we remember." What is remembered "is well grounded if it is remembered as being in a particular place—a place that may well take precedence over the time of its occurrence."[53]

Place has too often been overlooked as compared with time because it has too simply been identified with site or location, as on a graph or a map. But place is far more important than that. The pastoral carer is well advised to give great attention to the places that have been important to the people she cares for. Sometimes pictures are available. More often, good pastoral care involves assisting persons to paint pictures with words, pictures that stir images in the mind of the pastoral carer that she can remember and celebrate.

Susan Allen Toth is the author of two memoirs, one of her childhood, another of her college days. In an essay in the *New York Times Book Review,* she shared some of the responses of persons from her past at being remembered or not remembered. "What struck me most," she says, "was the hunger of 'ordinary' people to have their lives recorded and valued. In long letters filled with bits of their own biographies, readers said again and again with wistful and belated recognition, 'you've told my story.'"[54]

She recalls meeting her former high school drama coach at a book signing. In one of her books she had written about the death of his small daughter and its effect on him some twenty-three years before. "I had changed names and a few identifying facts," says Toth,

> as I did with anyone easily recognizable. Although her real name was Susie—like mine, so I had never forgotten it—I had called her Mary. After grasping my hand and congratulating me on my book, he paused. Looking intently into my eyes, his face strained and shadowed by that old and terrible loss, he said, 'I have to know one thing. You called her Mary in the book. Did you remember her real name?' I assured him I had, and his face eased.[55]

One can hardly overemphasize the importance of the pastoral carer's remembering the "real names" and all that those names symbolize for those for whom he cares. It is a way of conveying the affirmation, "I can't possibly know what it's been like to live your life; but I remember some of it, and I respect and value it."

Remembering and being remembered are key elements in care

and in the development of community. I recall the recent memorial service for my mother which took place in the church where I had grown up. Clearly the focus was on my mother and what people remembered and were thankful for about her life. But I was keenly aware that I was being remembered as well. "You're still one of my boys," said my old Sunday School teacher. "I still remember what you wrote to me when Herman died," said a woman who was a friend and contemporary of my parents. "You sure look like your dad," said another. And somewhere in the midst of those words and feelings it became clear to me that I was cared for and accepted as a member of that community.

Some Final Reflections

Caring is remembering. Remembering is caring. This is affirmed in both Old and New Testaments by the picture of God's remembering God's people, by the early Christians remembering God's action in Jesus Christ, and by Paul's remembering particular members of the Christian community. Moreover, the notion that remembering is caring is affirmed repeatedly in pastoral experience by those who ask pastoral carers to remember them in prayer or just to remember. It is affirmed in a variety of ways by elderly and dying patients or parishioners who find ways to let their carers know that they do not want to be alone at the time of their death. It is, perhaps, the most powerful dynamic in the prayer so long ignored or unknown by Protestant Christians, the Hail Mary. Mary, the powerful maternal symbol of care, is asked to remember, to "pray for us sinners now and in the hour of our death."

One of the major assumptions of the *communal contextual* paradigm is that the power of pastoral care rests in the fact that it is the care given by the community, not by the individual pastoral carer alone. The pastoral carer goes out with the strength and blessing of the caring community and with a conviction that because she, the carer, is cared about, she can offer the community's care to others. Care of self and care of others go together, and perhaps most important, care and community are somehow together in the memory of God.

Augustine saw the importance of memory in maintaining our identity as a place to search for God. One can hardly think of a more powerful way to present the work of pastoral care than as assisting persons in remembering—searching for God in their memory and remembering who they are. Conceptualized in another way, this may be what Henri Nouwen and others have characterized as connecting our human stories with God's story. "To heal," he says, "does not primarily mean to take pains away but to reveal that our pains are part of a greater pain, that our sorrows are part of a greater sorrow, that our experience is part of the great experience of him who said, 'But was it not ordained that the Christ should suffer and so enter into the glory of God?' (cf. Luke 24:26)." In connecting our story to the Christian story which we remember and celebrate, "we rescue our history from its fatalistic chain and allow our time to be converted . . . from a series of randomly organized incidents and accidents into a constant opportunity to explore God's work in our lives."[56]

We care as we remember and enable others to remember and, as Nouwen suggests, "connect" their story to a larger one. The most useful, though it is not necessarily the most efficient, memory device is learning to hear hurts that need healing as part of a story. Just as the fact of Jesus' suffering has no meaning for us apart from the story of who he was and is, ordinary human hurts have meaning and can be remembered when heard as a part of a particular life in a particular context. I examine issues related to context in some detail in the next chapter. Here I am simply saying that a good pastoral carer listens for the times, places, and particularities that give a person's story meaning and allow it to be held respectfully in memory.

Questions for Consideration

The points of view expressed in this chapter are intended to be questioned. The value of this book will come not in the reader's agreement, but in your engaging the issues and taking a position of your own. Some of these issues are reflected in the questions below, but you are encouraged to add your own questions to them.

1. What is the primary authority for pastoral care? Is it scripture, tradition, experience in ministry, or the nature of the community's life together? What is the authority of the ordinary members of the community as compared to the authority of its "teaching elders" or priests?

2. The mutual/personal view of community appears to be the most relevant for the work of pastoral care, but are there not political/structural models that are also relevant? If so, in what way is the mutual/personal view limited?

3. In what way is the church the "true" caring community or the only caring community of relevance to the pastoral carer? How is the Tillich-Hodgson resolution of the church visible and invisible question satisfying or unsatisfying to you?

4. Discuss the positive and negative features of the lay or clergy minister's ambivalence toward being identified with the church. The church is often embraced as the most important factor in ministry, but it is equally often seen as a handicap to ministry because of its imperfections. What does this mean?

5. In what ways are care of self and care of others complementary, and in what ways are they conflictual? Do you agree with Noddings and others that care that takes place over a period of time always involves guilt?

2

The Contextual: Care as Re-membering

I think it's important to be with people who have similar hurts, but the point is that we care, not that we've been through it. The common predicament helps, but you can't limit it to that.
—Lay pastoral carer

What can be learned from context and only there is something of the spirit of the times (*Zeitgeist*).
—Theologian Douglas John Hall[1]

Context may be defined as the whole background or environment relevant to a particular circumstance or event. Contextuality means that the social situation in all its uniqueness informs the thought and action of the reflection of the Christian community. In the first chapter I focused primarily on the *communal* dimension of the *communal contextual* paradigm. In this chapter I explore some of the *contextual* issues most relevant for pastoral care today. In doing this, I do not deny the value or negate the contributions of previous paradigms but attempt to add to them serious attention to some of the important contextual factors in pastoral caring today.

Neither the *classical* nor the *clinical pastoral* paradigms for pastoral care have given much recognition to context. The classical paradigm tended to universalize its understanding of human problems and express them in exclusively religious terms. The clinical pastoral paradigm most often interpreted human problems psychologically or insisted that the psychological context—

most often the personality structure and dynamics of males of the dominant culture—be recognized as normative.

An early exception to this lack of attention to context during the dominance of the clinical pastoral paradigm was Hiltner and Colston's research, published in the early '60s, which attempted to compare the effectiveness of pastoral counseling in a secular setting and in a church setting. They argued that the context in which the counseling took place was a significant factor in determining its effectiveness and concluded that the way one is perceived is a powerful factor in the effectiveness of what one does.[2] Because the research attempted to study only one contextual element in pastoral care, it offered a far narrower view of the components of context than is necessary today. In contrast to this narrow view, the emerging *communal contextual* paradigm insists that there are multiple contexts to be taken into account. In fact, a central part of the ministry of pastoral care today is discerning the contexts most relevant for understanding a pastoral situation.

Douglas John Hall and Peter Hodgson identify some of the contexts that theology must take into account today: (1) the end of the political establishment of Christianity; (2) recognition that there are many religions, not just one; (3) the impact of Auschwitz, symbolizing the radical nature of human evil; (4) the revolution recognizing that the oppressed people of the world have a place in history and society; (5) the ecological crisis or rebellion of nature; (6) the fear of nuclear accident; (7) the rise of religious simplism and apocalyptic consciousness; (8) awareness of the African American church; (9) the Latin American sacramental and communal church-based communities; and (10) the feminist vision.[3]

Because these contexts involve the practice of the faith as well as its theoretical formulation, the above list is suggestive for pastoral care as well as for theology. And a number of those contexts will be addressed directly or indirectly in this chapter. Although any judgment of this type is a matter of personal perspective, the contexts that I have chosen to discuss in this chapter are: *race, gender, power, problem, and morality.* "Problem," viewed as a context, is perhaps the most unexpected member in the list. However, if the people of God are called to care for one another through their hearing and remembering, as I argued in the first chapter, then the central act of pastoral caring is not problem solving. It is hearing and remembering in relationship, and the human problems are the contextual background for the more important task of care.

The Universal and the Particular

Before dealing with the contexts for care I have identified, it is important to address what seems to me to be the more inclusive issue of the universal and the particular. The issue of context is part of the more general human question of what features of being human are universal and what features are particular to a specific context.

> There is no one definition of what it means to be human. Each sub-culture, each ideology, each religion explains the reality of human nature in its own way. Yet it is clear that to be human involves: first, the ability to participate in understanding and shaping the world in which a person lives; second, being accepted as a subject and not as a thing or object of someone else's manipulation.[4]

Recognition of specific contexts for care involves hearing and remembering that (1) tries to discern what is specific and perhaps unique to a particular person or situation, and (2) remains open to the discovery of what appears to be common to many persons and situations. Moreover, this dual perspective assumes that knowledge of what is specific and particular contributes to what is more general and that what appears to be common contributes to the understanding of what is specific and particular.

Social worker and professor Elaine Pinderhughes has approached the issue of human difference and likeness from her perspective as a social worker and clinician. She notes that "while a stance of nondifference and 'all people are alike' may seem to diminish anxiety related to differentness, it also creates problems in that real differences cannot be acknowledged, sameness may be overemphasized, and distortion and misunderstanding may be reinforced rather than avoided." On the other hand, "to focus on difference without attention to similarities," she believes, "can also be anxiety-provoking and defeat the goal of understanding."[5]

Pinderhughes is helpful in reminding us that the uncritically held view that "all people are alike—protects those holding it from awareness of their ignorance of others and the necessity of exerting the energy and effort to understand and bridge the differences."[6] She also emphasizes the importance of the clinician's obtaining clarity about his or her own values. Such clarity "helps guard against use of that well-known defense, expectation of sameness," which makes people comfortable but reinforces a helper's need to see others as like themselves and thus to ignore differences that may mean ignoring the other's uniqueness and strengths. It is important to recognize how one's own values constitute a lens through which one sees others and to recognize the handicap that can be.[7]

Pastoral theologian David Augsburger uses Kluckhohn and Murray's classic text, *Personality in Nature, Society, and Culture*,[8] to identify three fundamental dimensions of being human: (1) the universal, in which every person is in certain respects like all others; (2) the cultural, in which every human being is like some others; and (3) the individual, in which every human being is like no other.

"Anyone who knows only one culture," says Augsburger, "knows no culture." In coming to know a second or a third culture a person "discovers how much that was taken to be reality is actually an interpretation of realities that are seen in part and known in part." One "begins to understand that many things assumed to be universal are local, thought to be absolute are relative, seen as simple are complex."[9]

Virtually everything that Augsburger says about culture can be said about the more inclusive term, "context." Persons who are familiar with only one context for pastoral care are not sufficiently aware of that context to know what is contextual. Many things assumed to be universal are local, thought to be absolute are relative, seen as simple are complex. Moreover, the persons to whom we offer pastoral care and the situations they share with us are in various respects like no others, like some others, and like all others. And, as with culture, the pastoral carer needs an awareness of a number of contexts in addition to his or her own and, in attempting to understand each of them, must work on the boundary line between the more familiar context and the less familiar one.

Augsburger believes that cultural awareness can be learned. Contextual awareness can also be learned. What one needs to develop as a part of this awareness is: (1) a clear understanding of one's own values and basic assumptions and an awareness that others may hold different assumptions; (2) a capacity for welcoming, entering into, and prizing other worldviews while holding onto one's own uniqueness; (3) sensitivity to sources of influence in both the person and the context and appreciation of the impact of the historical, social, religious, political, and economic forces on persons and families; (4) flexibility in responding to the life situation of a particular person without forcing it to conform to a particular psychological theory; and (5) awareness of one's own relatedness to and differentness from other persons, valuing both the differences and similarities, uniqueness and commonality.[10] In attempting to offer care to a person or persons significantly different from oneself, it is important to: (1) discover and dispel misinformation and faulty assumptions; (2) look for values in the other's tradition, wishing to appropriate them for one's own; (3) expect to find new areas of reality and meaning of which one was not aware before.[11]

The Pastoral Carer as "Mini-Ethnographer"

Another guide for the pastoral carer who takes context and culture seriously can be found in psychiatrist and medical educator Arthur Kleinman's picture of what a clinician should be. It is an equally valuable image for the pastoral carer. Kleinman describes the good clinician as a "mini-ethnographer." The task of ethnography is to discover the story of a particular group of people. The ethnographer attempts to understand their myths, rituals, daily activities. The key ethnographic task is observation, and the ethnographer is one who establishes relationships of trust and collaboration in which further observation can be conducted. The ethnographer is particularly skilled in drawing upon knowledge of the context to make sense of behavior. The interpretation made will benefit from the ethnographer's having one foot in the culture being studied and one foot outside it. Master ethnographers and clinicians share a sensibility. They both believe in the primacy of experience and are more like observational scientists than experimentalists. Like the poet and the painter, they are strongly drawn to the details of perception.[12] The good clinician or pastor is a "mini-ethnographer" because he or she takes on these tasks for an individual, family, or small group rather than for a whole tribe or culture.

The pastoral carer, lay or clergyperson, who accepts the image and task of the mini-ethnographer must be deeply involved in observation and description. Another guide for that is anthropologist Clifford Geertz, who enriches our understanding of an ethnographer's work by his concept of "thick description." Most important for us here, however, is his statement, "Understanding a people's culture exposes their normalness without reducing their particularity."[13] This seems to me to be a marvelous description of what pastoral care should be.

"Ethnographic findings," Geertz continues, "are not privileged, just particular."

> The methodological problem which the microscopic nature of ethnography presents is both real and critical. . . . It is to be resolved—or anyway, decently kept at bay—by realizing that social

actions are comments on more than themselves; that where an interpretation comes from does not determine where it can be impelled to go.[14]

He notes that with respect to the study of human beings, "explanation often consists of substituting complex pictures for simple ones while striving somehow to retain the persuasive clarity that went with the simple ones."[15] This, it seems to me, is another beautiful picture of what a pastoral carer should be about. Geertz reminds us forcefully that human beings "unmodified by the customs of particular places do not in fact exist." Thus "drawing of a line between what is natural, universal, and constant in man and what is conventional, local, and variable" is extraordinarily difficult. In fact, "to draw such a line is to falsify the human situation, or at least to misrender it seriously."[16] There "is no such thing as human nature independent of culture." "We are, in sum, incomplete or unfinished animals who complete or finish ourselves through culture—and not through culture in general but through highly particular forms of it."[17]

Finally, the following lengthy quotation from Geertz is extremely important for understanding contextually sensitive pastoral care.

> The human being can be defined neither by his innate capacities alone, as the Enlightenment sought to do, nor by his actual behaviors alone, as much of contemporary social science seeks to do, but rather by the link between them, by the way in which the first is transformed into the second, his generic potentialities focused into his specific performances. It is in man's *career*, in its characteristic course, that we can discern, however dimly, his nature. . . .
>
> To be human . . . is . . . not to be Everyman; it is to be a particular kind of man, and of course men differ. We must, in short, descend into detail, past the misleading tags, past the metaphysical types, past the empty similarities to grasp firmly the essential character of not only the various cultures but the various sorts of individuals within each culture, if we wish to encounter humanity face to face. In this area, the road to the general, to the revelatory simplicities of science, lies through a concern with the particular.[18]

This is rich material for informing us about the importance of attending to the particular in pastoral caring. It deepens our understanding of the classical and clinical pastoral as well as helping us in our sensitivity to context. Geertz's statement that "the road to the general, to the revelatory simplicities of science, lies through a concern with the particular" could, in my judgment, be equally said of the classical theological message in which pastoral caring is grounded. Moreover, the concern of both Kleinman and Geertz with the person of the clinician and ethnographer informs the focus of the clinical pastoral on the person of the pastor.

If the pastoral carer is one who remembers, he must be, as Kleinman says, a keen observer who becomes able to tell a story of the persons cared for that includes their myths, rituals, daily activities, and problems. The pastoral carer "believes in the primacy of experience" and, "like the poet and the painter," is strongly drawn to the details of a person's life, perhaps respecting and seeing in them far more than the person herself sees and values. Particularly relevant for our concern here with context is Geertz's assertion that "the drawing of a line between what is natural, universal, and constant . . . and what is conventional, local, and variable" is "to falsify the human situation, or at least to misrender it seriously." I move now to discuss some of the specific contexts for care.

Race and Gender as Contextual Issues: A Clinical Example

A useful example of working with two of the contextual issues addressed in this chapter comes from two former students, now colleagues in the Georgia Association for Pastoral Care. Eugene Robinson and Miriam Needham have described some of the gender and racial issues in their work together as C.P.E. supervisor and supervisor-in-training.[19] I have chosen this way to explore these issues because I have worked with both Robinson and Needham and am familiar with the specific institutional context out of which the article grows.

Robinson and Needham are both in their forties. Robinson, the supervisor, is an African American male; Needham, the supervisor-in-training, a white female. They examine some of the cultural myths about black-white, male-female relationships in relation to their experience in working together. These cultural myths express untruths about persons and relationships. Although Robinson and Needham use the term "myth" almost exclusively to mean "untruth," the fact that there is a myth about something points to the importance of the issue and the anxiety that surrounds it. Myth is associated with the reconciling of opposites and with organizing a disorganized world. The untrue myths that Robinson and Needham seek to expose are unsatisfactory means of reconciliation and dealing with anxiety that must be replaced with myths that more nearly reveal truth about black-white and male-female relationships.

With respect to some of the family background that helped to actualize the cultural myths, Miriam (I use first names in describing the clinical situation, and last names in presenting the authors' reflections on it) had grown up as the daughter of a successful Salvation Army officer. She had been designated as "Daddy's girl," had acquired many of his social and public skills, but with the modifying gender and cultural messages, "Take care of others," "Daddy will take care of you," "Females can be strong, but not too independent." Gene had grown up in an economically poor but emotionally nurturing environment with strong support from his parents and grandmother. His schooling was in predominantly black institutions from grade school through his seminary training, and he was aware of stereotypical cultural messages, such as, "Black men are studs," and "White women are only second to white males." The messages he received from his father to counter these and other stereotypes were: "Passivity is a sin," "Education is essential for a black man's salvation," and "Depend on yourself."

Robinson and Needham describe a critical incident in relationship in which Needham was invited to accept a position at another institution. The other center offered an upper-middle-class setting, less stressful working conditions, and exposure as a staff member in a well-known academic center. Although he felt angry and competitive with the "white establishment" institution that had made the offer and betrayal from Miriam for considering it, Gene was committed to the principle that Miriam must make the decision and accept the consequences. Within the situation there were the gender and racial messages from the past—"White women cannot be trusted by black men," "Be careful with seductive behavior," and "You're not as smart as . . ." In addition to following his supervisory principle that students should have to struggle with their decision, Gene was also operating from the cultural injunction about being careful with white women.

At the same time, Miriam felt anger and abandonment. Strong males were expected to step forward and fight for her, but Robinson seemed to sit back and do nothing. This must mean he did not care. Both were angry, but the anger, early on, was not expressed directly. "Miriam operated under the assumption that because Gene was black, he needed to be protected from 'white' anger. . . . She felt like she needed to make up for the sins and injustices of past generations."

In this relationship, as is the case with so many, the way out of an impasse or the clue to understanding it came from another relationship, this time between Miriam and an older African American

student. This phenomenon, referred to in the psychological literature on the supervision as "the parallel process," suggests that
many or most relationships have parallels in other relationships,
and if one is "stuck" in working with one relationship, one may
achieve insight and a way out of the impasse by learning from the
parallel relationship. Miriam found that the more she moved toward her student with her typical nurturing and perhaps seductive stance, the farther he moved away from her. She had been
working with the student in a way that assumed that he couldn't
take care of himself and thus had softened her responses to him
so that he would like her. When he continued to resist her and
become angry, she became confused.

In supervision Gene pointed out the difficulty a black male
might have in relating to a warm and potentially seductive white
female. The cultural myth informing his suggestion was that of
the black male slave seduced by the mistress of the big house,
who later stood back and allowed him to be beaten or killed when
the master caught them together. The learning opportunity in the
situation was actualized by testing the theory of parallel process.
"If a white supervisor in training relates to her black students in a
particular way, it is quite possible that the same dynamics are op-
erant in her relationship with her black supervisor." Miriam's insight was that her avoidance of her student's anger by trying to be
gentle and nice was related to her fear of Gene's anger. With this
student and, later, with others she discovered or rediscovered the
importance of offering an honest relationship rather than trying
to manipulate her feelings in order to achieve a particular result.

Robinson's and Needham's careful examination of these interpersonal events caused them to look more deeply at the power of
myth to deal with issues of race and gender. Robinson reflected
on the myth of the innocent and defenseless white female, suggested by the story of Sleeping Beauty, and how that myth had
had the ordering effect of maintaining distances between the
sexes and races, but had been functioning counterproductively in
this relationship by calling for stereotypical rather than direct and
honest relationship.

Miriam, a single woman who had in many ways claimed her
independence in her personal and vocational life, was surprised to
discover that the myth of Sleeping Beauty still held power. The
myth, understood in the context of a traditional, patriarchical
family system, said that the female is to be a desirable object and
should live for another rather than for herself. As interpreted by
Madonna Kolbenschlag, the myth further insists that a woman
should, like Sleeping Beauty, sleep or "wait forever, if necessary,

for the expected other who will make her life meaningful and fulfilled."[20] Miriam's reflections on the myth pointed to her long
history of relinquishing her own personal authority to another,
while at the same time becoming skillful at seduction and manip-
ulation in order to be sure that she would be taken care of. In supervision, this assumption and style of life was brought into
question as Gene challenged her to stand up and take care of
herself.

In the course of their relationship, Robinson and Needham
looked at other myths that had, at first unconsciously, informed
and influenced the way they worked together. One was the myth
that one race is obviously inferior to another and that the superior race has the obligation to take care of the other race as well as
the right to keep it in its inferior place. In rebelling against the
content of the myth, Miriam realized that she had been governed
by it in another way. She had withheld her honest feelings toward
African Americans—in this case Gene and her students—in order
to atone for the guilt she felt for the sins of her white brothers
and sisters toward black people.

Another prominent myth that has ordered relationships between blacks and whites is that of the sexual prowess and promis-
cuousness of black males. This myth has functioned not only to
maintain distance between the races and sexes, but also to give an
identity to black males whose oppression made it difficult to find
other positive identities. As Robinson puts it, he was aware that
he had felt a need to overcompensate to prove the myth erro-
neous for himself and yet has had to live with the pain of the negative black male image which he alone could not change.

In the supervisory relationship with Miriam he became aware
of how the black male myth was impacting his supervision. As he
puts it, "he experienced it mostly in terms of his reluctance to explore the playful/sexual dynamic in the relationship—a dynamic
which is always to some degree a part of any intense and personal
relationship." He became aware of how difficult it was for him to
allow himself to enjoy feelings of attraction and playfulness for
fear of being seen as promiscuous. When the influence of the
myth and his efforts to deny it were acknowledged, there was an
increased openness to playfulness and awareness of sexuality
in the relationship with Miriam and, in parallel, also between
Miriam and her students.

The implications of this presentation of a supervisory relationship go considerably beyond supervision per se and can assist the
pastoral carer in attending to racial, gender, and other contexts
for care. Some of these implications are:

1. Gender issues are always present in any significant relationship, and often there are also inherited myths that affect the way they are perceived and dealt with.

2. It is important to look at conflictual issues in the larger society that may be present in a particular interpersonal relationship.

3. In relationships between persons who have both been oppressed by the way society has been ordered, the similarities and differences in their experience of oppression should be carefully examined.

4. Understanding the power of a myth and some of the issues that it was intended to order and interpret is important, even when the myth is rejected as literal truth.

One can conclude from Robinson and Needham's work that anyone attempting to care or offer training in care for someone different from herself should

> maintain a healthy amount of disbelief if the initial response is, "Oh, that's not a problem for me—the fact that you're a woman (or that you're white, or that you're black, or that I am the only female in a peer group, etc.) doesn't bother me—I really don't see differences but I tend to look at people for who they are, not black or white." A healthy amount of disbelief will tell the supervisor that the student has not reflected upon the impact such differences can have, in personal interactions, or may hold a theology which implies that it is not Christian to be aware of the differences, or finds talking about inwardly held cultural or gender myths too threatening, or feels that the pain of "confessing" her or his racism or sexism is too difficult.[21]

More on Gender as a Context for Care

In spite of an increasing awareness of gender as a contextual issue in many areas of society, most male pastoral carers need help in understanding what is meant when a particular social structure is identified as patriarchal. The features noted below, although presented some years ago by Iglitzin and Ross, may still provide a good beginning point for identifying a patriarchally ordered social system.

1. Sexual division of labor reflects clear differences between the roles of men and women. A useful example is the role of serving or helping. Fulfilling that role at home or in the workplace in jobs such as that of teacher, secretary, or nurse is assumed to be more "natural for women."

2. A woman's identity comes primarily through her relationship with men, and women without an important relationship to

a male deviate from the norm.

3. Women can achieve their highest fulfillment only as wives and mothers. Men are always assumed to be the primary income producers.

4. Women are assumed to be childlike, needing protection from the rigors of the world.

5. Women are assumed to prefer the private sphere of the home to business and political life.[22]

In response to these kinds of assumptions and the social structures supporting them, feminists in pastoral care and psychotherapy have effectively argued that:

1. The inferior status of women is due primarily to their having less economic and political power than men.

2. Gender is more influential than are economic and social class in determining a woman's power.

3. Change should be focused on both the social and external and also the personal and internal world of the women.

4. Friendship, love, and marriage should be based on equality of personal power.

Those involved in the work of pastoral care seldom think of themselves as change agents. Their guiding image is "care, not cure." Nevertheless, care does not mean support for the status quo. It does mean offering a relationship that can allow a person to see possibilities for his or her life. It does mean being sensitive to gender issues in order to understand the context for living of the person or persons cared for. An ongoing question, then, is whether a male pastoral carer can be sensitive in this way with a woman parishioner or counselee.

Family therapist William J. Doherty has answered this question in the affirmative for family therapists. What he says can also apply to those who do pastoral care. He argues that therapists of both sexes can work effectively with "a wide range of clients and client systems and that personal qualities and professional skills are more important factors for therapists than their sex." The fundamental issue "is *consciousness of the issues of power that women and men face in therapy and in society*." Consciousness is gendered and requires therapists to work within their own gendered experience to help a female client to find her own power. "Feminist therapists," says Doherty, "have been working on this problem for over two decades. Male therapists have just begun to face it.[23]

"Work[ing] within their own gendered experience" means that a man must be aware of his gender as a contextual issue in his relationship to a female. In past years and under the influence of the classical and clinical pastoral paradigms, men have not had to do this. The *communal contextual* paradigm presents a new occasion teaching new duties: seeking gender awareness and also the awareness that one's early efforts in achieving it are likely to be ineffective and possibly embarrassing. From my own experience and from what I have observed in other males, embarrassment usually leads to denial and future avoidance of the embarrassing situation. This is just what should not be done. The development of gender awareness will require a great deal of male embarrassment in the years immediately ahead of us, but in order to move to equality of power between the sexes it is worth it.

One of the more useful guides for the "embarrassing years" is feminist family therapist Deborah Luepnitz, who argues that the insights of feminist therapy provide more complex choices than we were formerly aware of about how to live as women and men.[24] As one who is more practitioner than theorist, she also reminds us that feminist theory, or any theory for that matter, is of little value "until the theory turns into who we are—into phrase and glance and gesture—until our intellectual powers and our humor settle into it." Our theory must become "a *sensibility*, or it is nothing useful at all."[25] Again, I believe that what she says about doing therapy is fully applicable to more informal, less sophisticated caring processes.

The focus of Luepnitz's work is on the whole person in relationship, meaning "a person embodied with both capacities and incapacities, living within the idioms of gender, culture, race, and class, enhanced and inhibited by unconscious process, making choices in historical time."[26] Her concern as a therapist is "to help both women and men appropriate their powers to preserve themselves, to prize interdependence, to be freely for-others, to live fearless and principled lives, to have the capacities for critical thought, political resistance, and sexual ecstasy." The goal of the pastoral relationship is more limited in terms of therapeutic change, but the values the pastoral carer supports for persons are quite similar.

A pivotal concept in Luepnitz's work, *"re-membering"* is essential in considering gender as a contextual issue and in bringing this concern into relationship with the discussion of remembering in this book. What she says is different from, but related to, Parker Palmer's view of "re-membering" touched on in the preceding chapter. For Luepnitz hyphenating the word can guide us "in the important activity of not forgetting that we are all capable of both action and reflection, and that we separate the two at our social and personal peril."[27] She wants to bring together the "remembering" associated with psychoanalysis, to which I referred in the preceding chapter, with the "restructuring" associated with family therapy.

Psychoanalysis is generally more reflective, whereas family therapy is a more active enterprise. Re-membering the family leads to a change in the roles and functions of the family members and a new insight and understanding of them.

"Classical psychoanalytic therapists," she says, "have insisted on *remembering* the past, but have turned their backs on the issue of actively fostering other kinds of change." At the other extreme are family therapists who have focused on "restructuring" or "fixing" the family without attention to insight about the past. My concern here is, of course, not with either type of psychotherapy but with the implication for pastoral caring growing out of each therapy's emphasis. Not only in family therapy but also in a one-to-one relationship of pastoral care, remembering the family contributes to "re-membering" it. This is because remembering one's family emphasizes the family's historicity, the fact that it exists in a particular historical form, which cannot be appropriately measured against an ideal type. The family is contextually specific, but historical, and, therefore, changeable.

Following Luepnitz, the contextually sensitive pastor should think "at the level of both social and personal history."[28] He or she can encourage the reflective process of a person's remembering her family of origin and encourage the "re-membering" of it, that is, each member being seen in roles that, as Luepnitz puts it, are *less patriarchal*, *less father-absent*, and *less isolated from their context* than before. Remembering their early experiences and the emotional lives of their own families leads to a change in the present, to a "re-membering."[29]

Luepnitz's concept of re-membering helps to tie together the emphasis on care and remembering in the first chapter with the contextual issues that concern us here. To remember contributes to the important task of "re-membering" family, church, or a larger social structure. Members of the family, the community, one's self can be "re-membered" or given new roles, functions, or opportunities. Restricted stereotypes and abstractions can be changed into more active, choosing persons and groups. To remember concretely and specifically in the context of a caring and understanding relationship opens the possibility of "re-membering" one's life, an important step toward changing it.

Power as a Context for Care

Power can best be defined functionally, as "the capacity to produce desired effects on others,"[30] as when one person affects another in a manner that may be contrary to the second person's interests. Power may be operative in various forms. Coercive power is the form of power generated by the organization of a particular social system "which, at both the covert and overt levels, serves to maintain the status quo." Expert power, the kind that can be observed in professional relationships, is based on a certain level of expertise in a particular field. Legitimate power is power of an office, belonging to the person holding that office. Referent power is power accrued through association with one who has power.[31]

All four types of power are operative in pastoral caring. We are most aware of expert, legitimate, and referent power as associated with the office of minister, but it is coercive power, particularly when this is covertly exercised, that the pastoral carer needs to be most aware of as a contextual factor. In her book *Writing a Woman's Life*, Carolyn Heilbrun describes power as "the ability to take one's place in whatever discourse is essential to action and the right to have one's power matter. This is true in the Pentagon, in marriage, in friendship, and in politics."[32] Covert coercive power is what is most likely to prevent a person not favored by the organization of a particular social structure from taking her place in that structure. The importance of recognizing and dealing with power issues in pastoral care is underscored by one of the major contemporary writers on psychotherapy, Michael Basch, who has said, "The feeling of controlling one's destiny to some reasonable extent is the essential psychological component of all aspects of life."[33]

In considering personal power as a context for pastoral care, it is also important to consider the meaning of powerlessness. Social critic and therapist Michael Lerner, who was involved in the antiwar and social justice movements of the '60s, speaks of how powerlessness "corrupts in a very direct way: It changes, transforms, and distorts us." What happens is that we "look at our world and our own behavior, and we tell ourselves that although we really aren't living the lives we want to live, there is nothing we can do about it." We conclude that we are powerless. The sad part of growing up, says Lerner, "is not the process of learning about reality. It is the process of accommodating to deformities in the world, and then allowing oneself to be shaped by a desire to fit in and be part of the world as it is currently constituted."

Although he continues to believe in and work for social and personal change, Lerner believes that one of the major reasons things tend to stay as they are is because of our "deep belief and conviction that nothing can or will change." This belief is what he calls "surplus powerlessness." "It is inside our own heads, and it is recreated by us in every thought that assumes that how things are is the equivalent of 'reality.'"[34]

Writing from an explicitly pastoral perspective, Judith Lynn Orr discusses the way that working-class women "are silenced by sex and by class in both church and society." She believes that the pastoral needs of the working class have largely been ignored.[35] Orr focuses her research and her concern on the industrial laborers, service workers, beauticians, waitresses, keypunch operators, and others who do routine labor or provide basic human services and usually receive low compensation. Because women are paid lesser wages for their work—even for the same work that men do—marriage becomes a major economic factor for them. Many working-class women "are only a divorce away from poverty."

She notes a difference in the shaping of a working-class woman's personality as compared with that of the middle-class woman. The cycle of adult life begins and runs its course several years earlier than in the middle class. Working-class women finish school earlier, leave home, get their first job, marry, have their first child, their last child, enter menopause, retire, and die earlier than middle-class women. Having given over control of their lives to others, working-class women placate, "show deference to perceived superiors and struggle merely to survive."[36] They are, says Orr, "living examples of learned helplessness."

Pastoral care with these women does not involve helping them to interpret or discover identity, autonomy, and meaning in life in spite of periodic crises. Rather, it involves confronting the ongoing crisis of their inequality and lack of power. It involves enhancing skills for conflict resolution and attempting to effect change in institutions so that those institutions can more nearly meet the needs of these women and their families. In order to do this, Orr turns to Adlerian psychology as a resource. She believes that it views those in need, "not as sick, but as discouraged and in need of reeducation for social living." She sees the Adlerian perspective as addressing the need of working-class women for disengaging from "learned helplessness" and discovering the importance of directing their own lives.

Judith Orr's interpretation of the way their class and gender affect the lives of working-class women is valuable for the pastor in recognizing the importance of power relations as a context for care.

Christine Wiley also recognizes the importance of power as a contextual factor in care, but differs from Orr in emphasizing that a variety of approaches to care can be relevant for poor and working-class persons. Wiley discusses her experience with the black church as "a community of caring . . . in which faith is combined with action, the individual is cared for in the context of community, the sacred is coexistent with the secular, and one's inner experience must be in dynamic relationship with one's outer reality." She believes that a variety of caring ministries can be useful to persons with minimal power, influence, and economic resources. Individually focused pastoral care can be quite appropriate for the African American community as long as other needs for care are also addressed. Training in pastoral care and counseling, although it continues "to reflect Eurocentric systems dominated by white males," can be broadened to make cross-cultural counseling and the examination of gender issues and sexism a part of its curriculum.[37]

Elaine Pinderhughes, whose work I touched on earlier in the chapter, emphasizes the importance of dealing with power issues clinically by engaging clients in ways that enable them "to experience themselves as competent, valuable, and worthwhile both as individuals and as members of their cultural group." When this occurs, she says,

> they no longer feel powerless nor do they collude in their own victimization or the denigration of their cultural group. . . . Successful intervention means that clients can now see themselves as persons of power who belong to a group that has value and can behave in ways that aim to change their powerless status, including acquiring the resources necessary to cope with this reality.[38]

Speaking more explicitly about engaging persons on power issues in the context of therapy, family therapist Monica Mc-Goldrick offers some suggestions that are directly relevant for pastors working with individuals and families. It is important, she says, to pay attention to the relative income and work potential of husband and wife and how that may affect the balance of power. One should also be aware of their comparative physical strength because "40% of women experience violence by their husbands at some point in the marriage."

It is important to help the couple clarify the rules by which male and female roles are determined, such as who makes decisions, who handles finances, and who handles emotional matters. Try to place the couple's views on male and female roles in the context of broader economic and social issues and encourage them to look outside their own relationship to learn about these matters. Affirm the wife in her concerns about relationships, but also affirm her capacity to deal with work, money, and other outside-the-home matters. Be aware of the price husbands may have to pay if they give up their success orientation and become more sensitive to personal matters.[39] (I recall one man saying to me in couple's therapy, "You're helping my home life, but ruining me at work.")

Those involved in pastoral caring cannot afford to ignore power as a contextual issue. They need to consider questions like the following: What does the person receiving care have the power to change or not change? How is he or she affected by feelings of powerlessness? What can the pastoral carer do to empower the patient or parishioner through the pastoral relationship? What can be accomplished by involving patient or parishioner with a group of persons with similar power concerns? How does the pastoral carer's own sense of power or lack of it affect the way she responds to the person needing care? (One of the ways that theological students have learned about their own power is in trying to accomplish some kind of change in an institution, such as a large hospital where clinical pastoral education takes place.) Helping a person overcome a sense of powerlessness is an important dimension of pastoral care, but it can happen only when the carer's contextual awareness is attuned to power issues.

The Problem as a Context for Care

How can a person's problem be a context of care rather than the focus of care? The answer to that question lies in a basic assumption of this book that pastoral care is the care of the whole person in relationship, not the treatment of a specific dysfunction. It is in line with the view of the classical paradigm that pastoral care is more concerned with the state of one's soul than with the health of one's body or relationships. It is not unconcerned with the latter, but not concerned apart from the former. Although the carer is constantly tempted to seek appreciation as a problem solver, the aphorism "Life is not a problem to be solved, but a mystery to be lived" is a valuable reminder of some of the limitations of problem solving.[40]

Another way of presenting the issue is to describe pastoral care as bifocal—concerned, certainly, with the problem a person presents, but also concerned with the larger issues of life. Those issues are what my colleague Shirley C. Guthrie identified as "truth about God, about ourselves and about the world we live in. What else is there to talk about?"[41] If those larger issues are recognized as implicit in any pastoral relationship, then the problem a person presents can and should be viewed as a context, the details of which inform the type of care that can be offered. Certainly, it is a very important context that informs the whole approach of one person to another. The "problem" is what a person chooses to share about himself—what life is like for him now. Just like the good physician who believes that a good history can tell her more about a patient's diagnosis than most of the tests she orders, the pastoral carer learns to listen carefully to the problem and attempts to hear and remember. Usually the way a person describes the problem is a doorway into how that person understands life. He or she may not be able yet to talk about "life," so what can be talked about is the problem, which usually reveals important contextual features of that person's life.

I am often reminded of a young woman I had seen in counseling for about three months when she angrily questioned me, "Why didn't you tell me when I first came to see you that I was morally and spiritually bankrupt?" I replied, "When you first came to see me, we didn't know each other well enough to talk about things like that."[42] In that particular session we were talking about "things like that," but it had taken a while to get there. It took getting to know in great detail the pain and struggles of her life. It is quite possible that we might not have gotten there, and persons who offer their pastoral care in more informal, less structured settings may not "get there" in the same way or get there at all. This, however, does not negate the value of the care and the attention to the problem as a way of understanding the context of a person's life. A person who has genuinely been heard on the problem he is facing will have a sense of having been cared for and of not being alone. Care and relationship are important even when the issues of life that appear to be deeper are not explicitly addressed.

Most persons today simply do not know how to address their need for relationship and care without the excuse of having a particular problem. Their problem is the only avenue they have for developing a relationship to a helping person that can allow them to talk with another person about the deeper concerns of their lives. Pastoral care certainly involves assisting persons in reducing their anxiety about a variety of specific concerns, but these specific helps toward solving problems take place in a relational context of care and are carried out with the assumption by the pastoral carer that the fundamental issues of life are not solvable, only livable—in the context of significant human relationship.

In articles written on the same topic for the *Dictionary of Pastoral Care and Counseling*, Shirley C. Guthrie and Rodney J. Hunter have considered the human condition or predicament from different perspectives.[43]

Guthrie, writing from a theological perspective, has identified several polarities within the human being and our tendency to separate or confuse them in our understanding of ourselves and others. The polarities are: body and soul; feeling and thinking; individuality and community; being and becoming; life and death; human nature and human sin; responsibility and grace. Whether or not these are the particular polarities with which human beings must struggle, certainly there are such conflicting issues in human life that must be recognized and a recognition of these "larger issues" contributes significantly to the pastoral care of persons to whom we minister. The patient in the hospital has physical illness, hepatitis or emphysema, but he or she is also implicitly or explicitly involved in questions of the relation of body and soul, of freedom and limitation, responsibility for his or her own life in relation to the grace that might come as a gift. It is important that these larger issues be discerned as the problem context is addressed.

Hunter writes about the clinical pastoral perspective or, we might say here, the clinical pastoral paradigm. That perspective or paradigm does not allow the study of how to help patients or parishioners apart from studying the pastor as well. From that perspective both pastor and patient are understood to be caught in the human condition in such a way that they are challenged to look at their own depths.

Members of caring communities will differ in their abilities and their responsibilities to hear not only the most obvious problem, such as sickness, financial stress, or abuse, but also the more generic human need to be heard and remembered. Persons with more training and responsibility in pastoral care will be more nearly able to perceive the problem as a contextual issue and to discern some of the implications of the specific problem for the care and relational needs of the patient or parishioner. Even for the relatively untrained pastoral carer, it is both possible and important to have a twofold perspective, one that includes "the problem" as presented but that also includes a sensitivity to the caught-ness and the polarities in life which Hunter and Guthrie address.

Morality as Context

Morality as a context for care will be addressed in greater detail in chapter 9, on pastoral counseling, than here. The reason is that it is primarily the ordained pastor who is authorized by the caring community and her faith group to engage in pastoral counseling, whereas both laity and clergy are regularly involved in pastoral caring. Moreover, it is the ordained pastor who is more clearly designated by most faith groups to discuss, interpret, and advise persons on issues of faith and morality; therefore, dealing with moral context in the chapter on pastoral counseling seems to be a reasonable approach.

In a book published in 1976, *The Moral Context of Pastoral Care*, which has contributed significantly to the concern for the context for care, Don Browning argued that every act of pastoral care has a normative horizon, a vision of how things ought to be as well as how they are. He saw the modern secular psychologies as having a morality of their own, although they do not acknowledge it, and he insisted that they were providing too much of the guidance for pastoral care. In order to avoid this "sellout to psychology," Browning advocated a return to a normative—the way persons ought to be—vision of the human life cycle, and said that a significant part of pastoral care's work is to communicate that vision to persons in distress. [44]

My own view as it has emerged thus far in this book is obviously similar. Pastoral care, still affirming much of the classical paradigm, grows out of a vision of what human beings are and need. Pastoral care should attempt to communicate that vision in ways appropriate to the particular person and situation. But that vision of humanity is not only ethical, it is theological. Questions of, Who am I? Where am I going? and, Who is God?—not just, What must I do? are also involved in every pastoral relationship. Bringing together ethics and pastoral care involves not only guidance in moral decision making, bringing the parishioner in relation to the law, but bringing him or her in touch with both. law and gospel. The chapter on pastoral counseling explores contextual issues of morality in more depth.

Some Final Reflections

Although the value of listening as a part of pastoral caring is hard to overestimate, the lay pastoral carer's optimistic "as long as I remember not to talk too much and really listen to someone, it works out" shows too little awareness of the importance of context in caring. As another said, "The common predicament helps, but you can't limit it to that." All pastoral carers, whatever their level of training and sophistication, need to be sensitized to the effect of context on the caring relationship.

I have touched on several of the contexts that are most demanding of our awareness today: race, gender, power, problem. I have deferred extensive dealing with the moral context of care until a later chapter on pastoral counseling. Perhaps most important, I have attempted to confront the issue of the universal and the particular, which is a part of all contextual questions. I have also suggested some ways of dealing with that issue that have implications beyond the specific contexts I have discussed.

In this connection, Elaine Pinderhughes's statement seems profoundly important for all those who care for themselves and others:

> Self-understanding as well as understanding of cultural dynamics requires the ability to consider both the commonalities and the differences between oneself and others. By respecting people's connectedness without lumping them together carelessly, we recognize our own uniqueness and how it emerges from our connection to others.[45]

More specific, but equally important, is Clifford Geertz's reminder that "we must descend into the detail." The road to the general lies through a concern with the particular.[46]

Questions for Consideration

1. What relationship is there between the contextual issues affecting theology and those which affect pastoral care, or to what extent do the issues that affect theory also affect practice?

2. Reflect on what Augsburger means by his statement that "anyone who knows only one culture knows no culture." How is this relevant for the pastoral carer?

3. In what ways are the roles of the pastor and the ethnographer similar, and in what ways are they different? What would be some of the theoretical and practical elements in an "ethnographic" pastoral care?

4. What is the function of myth in general and of cultural myth in particular? Illustrate the function of myth in at least one context other than those of race and gender.

5. Of what value is the perception of power or powerlessness to the pastoral carer? Illustrate how the pastoral carer might assist in the empowerment of an individual or family.

6. What are the two meanings of "remembering" in Luepnitz's concept of re-membering? What theological meanings might this concept have?

7. Discuss the thesis that in pastoral caring a problem can be a context. What are some of the relationships between a person's particular problem and the human problem as that is conceptualized theologically? How is this concerned with the relationship between salvation and health?

Part Two

The Carer
as Person, Learner, and Teacher

3

Characteristics of the Carers

"Don't bother with the beds, Breda. Go talk with the patient in 301."

—Lay carer remembering how she got into ministry

In the first chapter, I discussed care and community and their relationship in God's memory and ours. In chapter 2 the focus was on some of the contexts that affect how care is given and received. In this chapter I consider how the character or person of the carer affects the care that is offered.

Perhaps the major contribution of the clinical pastoral paradigm to the ministry of pastoral care has been its insistence that the person of the carer is deeply involved in the quality of the care. The experience of clinical pastoral education (C.P.E.), on which much of the modern pastoral care movement has been based, has most often worked with the assumption that if the person of the minister or student were impacted by the experience of doing ministry under supervision, the quality of pastoral care would be positively affected. In C.P.E., students have learned skills of listening and communicating, but the focus of their training has been elsewhere—on their person. Whether or not it is appropriate to say that C.P.E. has been overly influenced by psychotherapy in so emphasizing "being" over "doing," concern with the person of the pastor has been a central value.

Although the major emphasis of the classical paradigm has been on the message of care rather than the person of the carer, none of the ecclesial families of Christendom have been unconcerned about the persons of their ministers. The church has struggled with this issue throughout the Christian era and has

65

"ambivalently demanded some kind of ideal type of life and alternately raged or sighed with relief when someone discovered that the minister had failed to live up to it." Expectations about the minister's personal life have been "expressed in a variety of forms, sometimes as virginity and celibacy and other times as the minister's spouse and four perfectly behaved children sitting quietly at worship in the second pew."[1]

Sexuality and family life have been particular areas of concern, but the issue of the "character of the carers" is considerably broader than that. In his now classic volume, *The Christian Pastor*, Wayne Oates wrote about the character of the carers as they appeared in the later epistles in the New Testament. The early Christians, Oates commented, "were not vague in their statement of the personal qualifications of those into whose hands was committed the care of the flock of God."[2]

As an illustration of the classical paradigm, the bishop of my United Methodist annual conference still asks the question, "Are all ministers blameless in life and character?" The question is uncomfortable when asked of clergy, and even though I know that the bishop is simply following John Wesley's precedent, I sometimes feel like saying, "Oh come on, Bishop, you don't really mean that!" Or, "I don't think you really want to know the answer to that question." I'm sure that neither the bishop nor I think that the clergy of the conference are literally blameless.

But what is the meaning of this concern if we are not just talking about expectations and standards for the clergy? What does it mean when there has been a paradigm shift that requires that speaking of ministry is speaking not just of the clergy but of the ministry of all Christians? This certainly seems to be the impact of the ministry documents of the Consultation on Church Union, the World Council of Churches, and Vatican II which insist that "ordained and lay ministries of the Church are differing forms of the one ministry of Christ that is shared by the whole People of God."[3] When I imagine the bishop's "blameless in life and character" question being asked of the pastoral care committee in the church where I am a member, I further imagine all the members of the committee resigning.

In order to keep that from happening, the churches have often ignored questions of the character of their ministry and membership in order to involve persons in the work of ministry. Another strategy has been to deal with the question of character only ritualistically and thus to avoid the issue in practice. The churches have also made sharp distinctions between the character of the "ordinary" Christian and the character and expectations of the clergy, as a way of involving the laity in volunteer work without making serious demands on their life and personhood. At a time when the communal contextual paradigm requires us to see the work of pastoral care being carried out by both clergy and laity, is there a way to take seriously the question of the character of the carer? If laity and clergy are involved in the ministry of pastoral care, what standards for ministry apply to both? Although these questions are not easy to answer, some of the meanings of the word "character" point in the direction of an answer.

"Character" has sometimes been used in psychological theory to speak of a more or less unchangeable aspect of the person, as in the term "disorder of character." The more general meanings of the word, however, seem quite relevant for the church's concerns about ministry. Character is defined as "a distinctive mark, a distinctive trait, quality, or attribute, an essential quality." Secondarily, character has meant "moral strength, self-discipline, fortitude." It has also meant "a definable role," such as a "character" in a play. All these meanings associated with the character of a person grow out of the term's meaning in printing, "a distinctive mark," such as a letter or a symbol. The church has generally agreed that its ministers should have "a distinctive mark," but what this has meant has varied among the various church traditions and in different historical times. Although questions about the character of the carers will always be uncomfortable to both laity and clergy, the image of the "distinctive mark" may be one that can be affirmed as relevant for both.

The Distinctive Mark of Breda McGee

I recently met a woman who seemed to me to have this mark, although she would be surprised at my perceiving her in that way. She is an Irishwoman named Breda McGee. I have met many others, but Breda is representative of the kind of lay pastoral carer who, thank God, is emerging in many places. When I met her at an international conference on pastoral care and counseling, she lived in Dublin. She was a member of my reflection group of eight pastoral carers, all from different countries. As I heard her tell some of her story in our group and observed her sensitivity to other group members, I found myself wanting to hear more of her story and asked if I could interview her about her ministry. This is some of what she told me:

> When my youngest child was five I decided that I needed more than the house, so I thought I would go back to nursing. Even before the

last child was born I began searching for something else in my life and had started to find my faith again. I was doing volunteer work and had trouble getting a job for pay, so I started on a volunteer basis in nursing.

After working as a nurse for a while I noticed that the sister in charge was saying to me, "Don't bother with the beds, Breda. Go talk with the patient in 301." She had discovered and then I discovered that I was good with people. I decided to take a counseling course, and it helped me to use myself and discover my pattern of relating to people. Unfortunately, there was no money in it, and my husband couldn't understand why I wanted to give up nursing when there was beginning to be some money in doing that.

But I went on. I took a year of pastoral care. The supervisor was excellent, and the fact that he was a man helped me a lot. He was a very gentle guy, and I started to recognize that I had similar qualities to his. It helped me give up some of the prejudices I had had toward men in the past. (There are things I don't like about the Roman Catholic Church, but I understand things there.) As a result of the pastoral care course and my search to rediscover my faith, I found that the church's approach to caring for people seemed more right to me than what I had learned in counseling. In the counseling course there was not the recognition of evil and good the way I recognized it and had felt it in my own life. The counseling theory said we were all born good. Things got in the way, but the thing that was important was to get free—to get free of your marriage or whatever was bothering you. When I questioned that point of view I was told that I was just hung up with my Catholic upbringing. The pastoral care course seemed to take more seriously my struggle and other people's struggle just to deal with life.

After that course I was invited to co-lead a group of priests in training. There were seven of them at all levels. They had a compulsory half day of being out in the community, but were getting no supervision. They understood that I was there to help them reflect on the work they were doing. My job was to help them see themselves, where they were too cold or too afraid. The priest co-leader was the academic. I was the one who brought in the female that they had to deal with. Because I was also doing some of the same pastoral work that they were doing, the men knew I knew what was real and what wasn't.

I asked Breda to tell me about some particular experiences in her pastoral caring.

There was a lovely man there who was older than most of the group. He was an introvert and somewhat cut off from the others.

The group members confronted him about the way he kept his distance. I found myself touching him on the shoulder and saying to him, "You don't have to hold back unless you really need to." That seemed to allow him to let his defenses down. It seemed to help that I was a woman.

Outside the group, in my own neighborhood, there was a woman whose father died. I went to the funeral, and a couple of days later she arrived at my door. I just opened the door and took her in. She said she was upset about her father's death. Her mother had died a short time before, and she was left with the burden of experiencing for the first time the feeling that her parents did not love each other. Theirs had been a silent and undemonstrative marriage over many years. I sat and listened for a while and then said, "There are many kinds of love." And somehow that was the right thing to say. She knew it, and I did. On another level we have an ordinary neighborly relationship with each other. She's jealous of my kids, and I'm jealous of hers. We're not really friends in spite of what happened, but she was able to use me as her minister.

Another time a priest came to see me who just needed to cry. You could see that four and a half miles away. He somehow knew he could cry with me. Afterward he just thanked me.

I am sure that neither Breda McGee nor those who know her well characterize her as "blameless in life and character," but as I became acquainted with something of her life and work I perceived her as having the distinctive mark of a Christian minister. In what follows I want to suggest what contributed to that mark and some of the ways that the marking of a minister has been expressed.

Ways of Recognizing the "Identifying Mark"

For many years I have been appreciative of David Duncombe's attempts, begun in his doctoral dissertation, to describe the Christian life. I believe that his 1969 book, *The Shape of the Christian Life*,[4] continues to have value today. In more recent writing, Duncombe has pointed to four major forces underlying and affecting Christian life: (1) the unique set of personality traits of the individual Christian; (2) the life events and circumstances that interface with his or her personality; (3) the particular will, desire, or call of Christ for this person; and (4) the expectations of his or her particular denominational tradition with regard to how a Christian should live.[5]

All these forces can be seen, for example, in the life of Breda McGee. She was, obviously, a particular type of personality. There were circumstances strongly affecting her call to ministry, such as the last child leaving home. Her nursing background made it natural to return to a ministry of care, and her own interpretation of Catholicism seemed more true to life than what she had learned in counseling training.

These are some of the forces in a person's life that affect "marking for ministry." In the remainder of the chapter, I will be discussing three ways in which pastoral carers have been "marked" or identified as ministers: description, discernment, and fostering. And again, I am indebted to David Duncombe. The process of clarifying the meaning of the Christian life moves from a conceptual mode (description) to a much more empirical or experiential one (fostering) through a mode that combines them both (discernment).

Identifying the Character of the Carer by Description

Within the descriptive mode there are six dimensions of spiritual or religious life in the Christian tradition that may be used to describe the marking of the pastoral carer. All six dimensions are dialectical in the sense that they have contrasting meanings which enrich each other when in dialogue with each other.

First is the *mystical/moral*, in which one side of the dialectic suggests a mystical union with God whereas the other reminds us of obedience and social obligation.

Second, there is the *sacred/secular*, representing the encounter with God at special times and places, such as in worship, and at the same time affirming the possibility of divine presence at all times.

Third, the Christian life has emphasized the lonely journey of the pilgrim moving through the trials of life, but has also affirmed the importance of the gathered community. That dimension is the *individual/corporate*.

Fourth is the *belief/faith* dimension. One side considers unwavering convictions as central to the Christian life, while the other side emphasizes the work of the Spirit as relatively unrelated to a particular set of beliefs.

The fifth dimension is *virtue/ability*, one side emphasizing Christian specific virtues as necessary for Christian life and ministry, such as the Galatians 5:22 list which includes love, joy, peace; the other side insisting that any ability can express the Christian life and ministry if it is rooted in God.

Sixth is *perfection/wholeness*. One side is striving for perfection, as commended by Christ in Matthew 5:48 and reflected historically in the holiness tradition. The other side is a wholeness that emphasizes a recognition, balance, or integration of the good and bad which is present in all human beings.[6]

These six dimensions will be echoed by other descriptive formulations of Christian life and ministry which follow.

I continue to find value in the characterization of the Christian life, and by implication, the distinctive mark of ministry, in the work of Karl Barth and Paul Tillich. Barth's radical skepticism of any virtue based in humankind itself prevents him from using the traditional *analogia entis,* or analogy of being, to speak of the relationship between God and humankind. Instead he speaks of an *analogia relationis,* or analogy of relationship. We are like God only in our relatedness. Humanity is "fellow-humanity." The humanity of man, Barth says, "consists in the determination of his being as a being with the other." Jesus could be *for* others. We can only be *with* others. And we must infer that our ministry lies in that "withness."[7]

Barth characterizes that "being with" in four ways, all of which are extremely relevant for the ministry of pastoral care. The human being is with another first of all by *being seen* or being visible to the other, not hiding herself from the other person. Second, there must be *mutual speech and hearing.* (Paul Tillich echoed this point in speaking of the mutuality of pastoral care.) Third, for Barth, being human with another involves *rendering mutual assistance* in a variety of forms. And fourth, our relational humanity depends on our doing all the above with *gladness,* which I would interpret as a kind of childlike openness. "Man is essentially determined to be with his fellowman gladly . . . to choose not to do so expresses not his nature, but his sin."[8]

In his characterization of the Christian life, which can be extended to describe the mark of the minister or pastoral carer, Paul Tillich uses the term *Spiritual Personality* to refer to the "dynamic essence"—what has been referred to here as character—of every active member in the spiritual community. These persons are under the impact of the Spirit and, consequently, transparent to the divine. They are like the Christ, but to a lesser degree. These members of the community exercise all the functions of a priest. (In fact, there is nothing except *degree* of transparency to the divine that prevents them from exercising all the functions of the Christ.) They are functional saints who minister to others both within and outside the church, performing miracles as an expression of their spiritual power. For Tillich, the difference between Jesus and the saints is that in Jesus there are no moments of separation from the "Spiritual Presence" or from transparency to the divine, whereas with others there are many moments of separation.

In order to emphasize his concept of transparency, Tillich went so far as to say that even "Jesus is not good in himself, as the saints are not good in themselves."[9] "The real meaning of saint-hood is radiation, transparency to the holy—or translucency to the holy. . . . 'Radiation' is perhaps the best, since a saint radiates the presence of the divine in a special way."[10] Tillich believed that this understanding of sainthood was lost by the church when it attributed special saintliness to the ascetics and martyrs. Thus, the ordinary members of the church lost awareness of the possibility of their own saintliness. But even in the focus on the special-ness of saintliness, Tillich insisted, the concern was not with moral superiority but with transparency to the divine expressed in words, personal excellence, and power over nature and human beings.

"Saintliness is transmoral in essence."[11] Saints are justified sin-ners and thus equal, rather than superior, to others. They are no different from other members of the spiritual community. As jus-tified sinners they demonstrate in a fragmentary way how one can be both estranged and reunited. With respect to their per-sonal characteristics, they exhibit both *maturity* and *blessedness*. Maturity "means full consciousness and the actualizing of one's freedom"; blessedness refers to a state "in which the conflicts con-nected with freedom are solved, at least fragmentarily."[12]

Continuing for a moment with Paul Tillich's view of life under the impact of the Spirit, it is important to recognize that although Tillich is writing about this in the section of his book on sanctifi-cation, his picture of Christian life is radically qualified by the principle of justification. It is not something that human beings seek to achieve and obtain. He avoids setting perfectionistic goals for the Christian but rather presents life under the impact of the Spiritual Presence as something that cannot be described before it happens. It can be recognized, however, when it does happen in the person's *increasing awareness*—a sensitivity to the ambiguities in oneself and others and the power to affirm life in spite of ambi-guity. It "includes sensitivity toward the demands of one's own growth," toward the hopes and disappointments of others, an ability to discern the feeling and meaning of a concrete situation, and to respond to the authentic elements in the lives of others.[13]

It is further recognized in the person's *increasing freedom*—freedom from law reflected in the power to evaluate a given situa-tion in the light of the Spiritual Presence and decide on an appro-priate action even when this is an apparent contradiction to the law. It also involves the power to resist forces from both within and without that try to destroy freedom.[14] Under the impact of the Spiritual Presence a person is also *increasingly related*. This is a balance to the principle of increasing freedom which may isolate a person. A fourth evidence of the Spiritual Presence's impact is *self-transcendence*. Awareness, freedom, and relatedness each involve self-transcendence, which "is identical with the attitude of devotion toward that which is ultimate. . . . It is like the breathing-in of another air, an elevation above average existence."[15]

In a different vein, a specific effort to describe the personal qualifications of pastoral carers may be found in Wayne Oates's book *The Christian Pastor*. Although it is over forty years old and was originally written to describe only ordained male clergy, I believe it should still be examined seriously. In viewing New Testament writings, particularly the later epistles, Oates finds and comments on the following qualifications for pastors. He understands the New Testament to be saying that pastoral carers need to be: (1) above reproach; (2) not new converts; (3) not divorced and remarried; (4) good managers of their own households; (5) sane, sensible, of a sound mind; having a firm hold on the word of God; (6) healthy and apt teachers; and (7) willing workers.[16]

In presenting this 1950s interpretation of the later epistles' view of the Christian pastor I am reaffirming my belief that it is essential that the church have expectations of its ministry and continually reexamine those expectations in relation to the context in which Christian ministry takes place. However, the specific qualifications for ministry given in the New Testament may not be those most relevant for pastoral care ministry today. In the thinking about the ministry of the people of God today, particularly the ministry of pastoral care, what qualifications are most important? To answer that question I want to reinterpret Oates's listing of the personal qualifications of Christian carers in a way that can be extended to all members of the caring community. The reader's agreement with my reinterpretation is not important, but taking seriously the question of qualifications for ministry *is* important.

All members of the community of faith who do the work of pastoral care:

1. must take seriously how they are viewed by church and community. This does not mean uniformity of behavior, but it does mean that what they do in ministry cannot be separated from the persons they are;

2. must not be naive about or indifferent to the facts and affirmations of the faith. Uniformity of religious education is not required, but serious involvement in such education is;

3. and 4. must be aware of how their relationship to their own family may affect the way they approach and respond to the pain in the families of others. The minister's own marital status is not so important as his or her awareness of the importance of issues of intimacy and closeness in the lives of everyone. Such issues cannot be separated from more explicitly "religious" issues;

5. must be able to handle personal issues with objectivity and wisdom, not using the situations of others to work on their own personal concerns;

6. and 7. must be committed to the importance of Christian faith for their lives. The convictions of ministers, lay or ordained, cannot be casual. They must be firmly, but not defensively, held—held in a way that they are available for dialogue, not indoctrination;

8. must be able to work willingly. Ministers cannot be happy about all the tasks of ministry, but must have a way of doing them that is not resentful and hostile about having to do the work. The attitude toward the task is important.

Although these descriptions of Christian life and ministry can be useful in identifying the distinctive mark of pastoral carers, it is important to recognize the limits of all such descriptions. David Duncombe does this very effectively by reminding us of Søren Kierkegaard's ironic picture of the "knight of faith" in *Fear and Trembling*.[17] Kierkegaard comments that people travel around the world to see rivers and mountains, new stars, and the like. "This does not occupy me," he says. "But if I knew where a knight of faith lived I would travel on foot to him, for this marvel occupies me absolutely." When he finds this marvelous man, "I jump back, clap my hands and say half aloud, 'Good Lord, is this the man, is this really the one—he looks just like a tax collector.'" He certainly cannot be distinguished from his neighbors by the way he looks. "What distinguishes the knight from others," says Duncombe, is something so deep and personal that it cannot be seen, known, or communicated directly—and that is the Christian life, discerned and fostered by its substance and not its form."[18]

Identifying the Character of the Carer by Discernment

Discernment is mostly an intuitive process that is similar to the recognition of a long-lost friend. It can, however, apply both to the recognition of another and to the recognition of something in oneself. Much about the friend has changed. His outer appearance is almost completely different from the way he was, but there is some inner something about him that is recognizable as the person I knew and still know. In the Gospel picture of Jesus, he is one who discerns the mark of a particular kind of character in persons that may not be obvious to others. He sees Nathanael as "an Israelite in whom there is no deceit"(John 1:47). He calls disciples to follow him who appear to be quite ordinary. Discernment is also like Paul's description in 2 Corinthians 2:14–16 of the Christian's having a distinctive aroma. The identifying mark is discerned in a more primitive way that the higher senses of seeing and hearing cannot perceive.

Within the pastoral carer, discernment is the process that allows us to focus deeply on the life and concerns of another person. Because we are discerned and known, we can discern and know others in our care for them. Because God remembers and has discerned us, we can remember other persons in our care of them. Because we have been valued, we can value others as we hear and remember them.

Pastoral Identity

I believe that discernment is very close in meaning to what the clinical pastoral paradigm has called pastoral identity. Although the term "pastoral" has been strongly associated with the clergy, I believe that there are important ways in which the modifier "pastoral" can accurately designate the ministry of both laity and the clergy. Pastoral identity has been a central element in the clinical pastoral paradigm, particularly as this has been a part of clinical pastoral education. Pastoral identity is something that can be discerned as an inner awareness of being a duly authorized representative of a Christian community of faith.

In an article written some years ago, Edward Thornton contrasted this view with a discovery he made during a sabbatical at the Westminster Pastoral Foundation in London. "I realized," says Thornton, "how uncritically I had bought into the assumption that pastoral means ordained for church vocation, or at least functioning under some form of ecclesiastical endorsement." At Westminster, Thornton found that for staff and students alike,

> the word pastoral has no necessary connection with a leadership role in a church vocation. It has to do rather with a religiously serious attitude toward life, with an effort to reflect upon experience in religious categories, and, especially among the European specialists whom I met, a concern to penetrate the theological meanings of psychotherapeutic experience, and to construct a comprehensive pastoral theology.[19]

Thornton, one of the major historians of clinical pastoral education, was not content with either the British or the American view but longed for a day when American specialists in pastoral care and counseling "will risk more involvement in the ambiguities of theological reflection in a secular context" and "British pastoral psychologists invest more energy in the therapeutic potential of religious institutions and in the clinical pastoral education of seminarians and clergy."

Thornton then reflected on his own spiritual pilgrimage as a clue for finding a synthesis between the British and American views of pastoral identity and found it in what he calls "an insatiable appetite for the Presence of God." Paraphrasing Evagrius, one of the desert fathers, he described a pastor as "a theologian who prays aright." The *pastoral*, Thornton says,

> denotes an awaking soul, alive to the Holy Spirit of God, awakened to the delights of prayer, to the excitement of internal dialogue between one's self and the Spirit, and to the enjoyment in awe and wonder of the Presence who makes the internal dialogue something other than introspection.[20]

Thornton's article is worthy of rediscovery as is his book, which offers more guidance on this theme of a spiritually defined pastoral identity.[21]

The importance of Thornton's view is in its broadening the concept of pastoral identity beyond ordination and in relating it explicitly to the awakening of the spiritual or religious life. The difficulties with his view in relating to the pastoral ministry of the caring community, however, is that it unnecessarily narrows as well as broadens the understanding of the pastoral. It suggests that to be pastoral one must be comfortable in expressing one's spiritual quest in religious terms. The majority of lay ministry groups with which I am familiar can only hesitantly use Christian religious language to express what they are doing in ministry and the way they are developing in their own faith or spirituality.

It seems more effective, therefore, to describe emerging pastoral identity in terms of a "quest" rather than something as explicitly religious as an "insatiable appetite for the presence of God." Persons can be well into the process of offering pastoral care and learning from their ministry before they have any sense that they are as spiritually hungry as Thornton's image suggests. To express this another way, pastoral identity begins to develop long before one's ability to identify with and comfortably use the language of one's religious tradition. The "quest," therefore, or Walker Percy's ambiguous and modest terminology in his novel *The Moviegoer*, "being onto something," fits better with the caring communities with which I am familiar. I deal with the meaning of "quest" later, in the section on *fostering*. I am concerned now to say more about the principal elements in a pastoral identity. The most important elements are, in my judgment: *attitude, ability, authority,* and *accountability*.

1. The pastoral *attitude*, perspective, or way of looking at things has most often been interpreted through the use of the biblical image of the shepherd. The shepherd is one who cares for all, but who is particularly concerned for those who are lost or separated from the whole community to which care is extended. In his influential book *Preface to Pastoral Theology*, Seward Hiltner spoke of the "shepherding perspective" as "an attitude or point of view or type of feeling that is basic" to the carer, "not just something tacked on." The shepherding perspective is relational in that it is directed toward a particular person or persons, and its basic content is a "tender, solicitous concern" for those to whom it is directed.[22]

Much of what has been said about care in chapter 1 is applicable in this consideration of "pastoral" as an attitude. Care, however, as we are discussing it in this book clearly involves ability as well as attitude. Paul Tillich has insisted that because care is a universally human function, it cannot be monopolized or controlled by any profession, including the clergy. The difference between those who offer care as clergy and all other human beings is not that the clergy exercise this function and others do not; the difference is that the clergy along with other professionals consciously exercise care, reflect upon it and learn from it, whereas others express their care "indirectly, casually, and mostly unconsciously."[23]

Tillich's distinction between clergy and lay pastoral carers has been valuable for the clinical pastoral paradigm. However, the communal contextual paradigm, which views pastoral care primarily as a ministry of the community and not just the pastor, requires that we go beyond Tillich and affirm intentional care for both laity and clergy. The difference between laity and clergy is not that the clergy are intentional in their attitude of care and the laity are not. The difference lies in the other dimensions of being pastoral: ability, authority, and accountability.

2. To speak of pastoral *ability* is to deal with the capacity to carry out one's attitude of care. It involves action as well as attitude, doing something as well as being and thinking something. It involves the relationship of theory and practice and all those things that the clinical pastoral paradigm has represented. The term "pastoral" is associated with the ability to do something: to listen, to remember a person's story, and to respond empathically. Again, memory is a key element in the process. Learning and change are possible when one can remember what happened,

write and share the events of one's life with others, and objectify the events enough to interpret what the events say about oneself and one's relationship to others.

This ability is not just a skill, something that can be taught technically and behaviorally. It involves what Edward Farley appears to mean by *theologia* (wisdom), and is similar to what Michael Polanyi calls *tacit knowledge*, the knowledge of how to do something gained through observation, performance, and judgment. It includes a sense of context, wholeness that exceeds what can be known, done, and said, and a sense of oneself as a participant in the larger whole. The employer of such knowledge, the person with this kind of pastoral ability, trusts herself and can develop her own way of conceptualizing and doing things. Elements of this kind of knowledge can be given in principles and illustrations, but these fall short of "teaching" a person this kind of pastoral ability. It involves understanding ability as discernment.

An interesting and useful way of underscoring the necessity of the risk of self in practice may be seen in Kierkegaard's concept of repetition,[24] which, in effect, is the power of the individual to forge his personality out of the chaos of events, in the midst of the flux. It is the power to discern who one is and create an identity in the face of the incessant dispersal of the self. The self, like pastoral identity, is not a substance or permanent presence, but a task to be achieved. The self is defined as choice. It is something to be won. Kierkegaard's concern is to move away from abstraction and restore the sphere of actuality and the involvement of the person in the action. However skilled the clergy or lay minister becomes, the risk of foolishness and failure is an ever-present part of what ministry means. A ministry of pastoral care requires some of the radicalness of Kierkegaard's existential point of view to underscore this. This is a part of what pastoral *ability* means.

3. The dimensions discussed above, attitude and ability, have more often been associated with the ministry of the laity than have authority and accountability. The meanings of authority and accountability in ministry are intertwined, but I will attempt to discuss them separately.

Authority as it is discerned in oneself or another involves (1) being under authority; (2) being an authority; and (3) conveying authority.[25] Being *under* authority for a pastoral carer means that he or she cannot offer care apart from the religious body that endorses that ministry and authorizes that it take place in a particular setting. There is no such thing as the private practice of pastoral care. The noun "pastor" and the adjective "pastoral" *mean* having authority because one is subject to or accountable to that authority. Lay or ordained ministers cannot just be themselves; they do what they do and are what they are as representatives. They inescapably represent the strengths and weaknesses of the community that in some way authorizes their ministry. In nonecclesial situations they also may represent the hospital or other agency that employs them or a professional association that certifies their competency.

In addition to being accountable to structures beyond themselves for what they are and do, pastoral carers *are themselves* authorities. Persons who have been educated in the theory and practice of the faith, whether ordained or not, possess an authority themselves. Mark's statement about Jesus in the synagogue at Capernaum, "as one having authority, and not as the scribes" (Mark 1:22) is not unlike what may be perceived about good pastors. They are experienced by those to whom they minister as having something within them that can inspire and support. Breda McGee's supervisor told her to go and see the patient in room 301 rather than to spend her time making beds. In terms of the carer's own self-understanding and experience this is what has been referred to as "pastoral identity." In terms of the way others respond to the carer, this is what is meant by "pastoral role." The fact that in the New Testament even Jesus' authority is sometimes defined negatively—"not as the scribes"—suggests something of the intangible quality of being a religious authority, of having both the role and identity of a pastor.

The way pastoral authority is expressed varies considerably from person to person. I believe that Richard Sennett's analysis of authority is clearly applicable to the ministry of pastoral care.[26] Not only the laity, but also many clergy have difficulty *being* authorities, that is, being accountable for what they say or being set apart from those over whom they have authority. They may express their authority paternalistically, alleging that what they do is for the good of the person over whom they exercise it. Sennett has called this the "authority of false love." They may also express it autonomously, as Sennett puts it, "without love" or without proper concern for the persons most affected by it.

Pastoral care also involves *conveying* authority to others. Historically, the term *pastor* has often involved a supervisory dimension and referred only to one in charge of a parish or other place of ministry. (I discuss this dimension in some detail in chapter 4.) Although conveying authority has been almost exclusively associated with the clergy in the church, there are many lay people involved in administrative and supervisory responsibilities in their primary employment who are increasingly taking such responsibilities for the pastoral work of the church. They convey authority to others just as do the ordained. I have found it useful to think of the pastor as a "person in-between," one who receives authority, exercises it, and conveys it to others. Conveying or delegating authority is difficult for many persons to do, particularly when the authority conveyed has to do with something that is personally important to the pastor. It is not unusual for someone to profess to convey authority to others but covertly to retain it by insisting that the one to whom it is conveyed "do it my way." On the other hand, those who delegate may become overconcerned about the problems of those to whom they have attempted to convey authority and not provide adequate attention to the task that needs to be accomplished.

Being under authority, being an authority, and conveying authority are all related to the pastoral carer's inner sense of pastoral identity. Moreover, her acceptance of a pastoral role is essential to functioning adequately in that role and in interpreting her role to others. Acceptance of that role and satisfactory practice in functioning in it is dependent on an evolving inner sense of identity with the pastoral role as integral to who one is.[27]

4. In discussing authority as a dimension of pastoral identity I have necessarily touched on the dimension of *accountability* in the meaning of "pastoral." As I suggested above, Tillich's distinction between intentional and unintentional carers can better be made today in terms of degrees of accountability. Clergy have a greater accountability for their ministry and a greater responsibility to deepen their ministry by reflecting upon it and learning from it. Use of the term "greater" suggests a continuum relationship between laity and clergy, on which clergy have a greater degree of involvement in and understanding of the theory and practice of their ministry. Laity have accountability for the same things, but to a lesser degree. The lesser degree of accountability is not from logical necessity, however, but from the historical circumstances of the importance given to clergy authority in the church. Moreover, the continuum image is a horizontal, not a vertical one. The clergy are not "above" the laity, nor do they perform their ministry apart from them. Moreover, that the clergy are imaged as "farther along" the continuum in the direction of professionalization has nothing to do with religiousness, depth of faith, or effective function. The image simply portrays the fact of the clergy's greater time involvement in study for and practice of their ministry.

In using the term "accountability," however, one must deal with the question, "accountability to what or whom?" There are three types of accountability applicable to both laity and clergy, but applicable to the clergy to a *greater degree*. First, the minister is understood as accountable to an ecclesial community which has authority to interpret how her or his particular ministry is an appropriate expression of God's calling. Second, the minister, clergy or laity, is also accountable to his or her peers in ministry and sometimes to those specializing in a particular type of ministry in order to maintain standards of good practice in the same way that other professionals are accountable to their peers. A third accountability is the accountability of the minister to himself or herself to advance in the practice of ministry—to become competent in caring and in understanding the faith tradition he or she represents.[28] All four of the dimensions of pastoral identity discussed in this section—attitude, ability, authority, and accountability—contribute to discerning of the distinctive mark of a Christian minister.

Identifying the Character of the Carer by Fostering

Fostering the Christian life and developing the mark of the Christian carer involve internalization, nurturing, and sustaining. Certainly some of this is involved in what I have said about pastoral identity. Here, however, the focus is on the "internalizing" of the Christ as he has been experienced and interpreted in the Christian community. Christ is internalized in much the same way a parent is internalized by a son or daughter. Many of the parent's values, commitments, and ways of approaching life become a part of who the daughter or son is. The Eucharist is the central Christian symbol of internalization. The Christian life is fostered by relationships within a community whose center and focus for being and celebration is Christ. The church is a community that nurtures the Christian in the experiential knowledge that he or she is remembered and that Christ is *for* him or *for* her.

The church has always strongly affirmed the relationship between the ministry of Christ and the ministry of the Christian church. In his exhaustive study of ministry, theologian Bernard Cooke has said:

> All Christian ministry finds its origin in the salvific ministry of Jesus himself; throughout history, Christian theology is united in recognizing this principle. There has also been agreement on the principle that all authentic Christian ministry involves a participation in Christ's ministerial mission and power, but there has been considerable disagreement as to the nature of this participation.[29]

An important part of the way participation in Christ's ministry has been discussed in Christian theology involves the relationship between the person and work of Christ. In my own development as a minister, a strong influence came from the lines of this simple hymn which affirms the unity of Christ's person and work:

> Though what I dream and what I do
>   In my weak days are always two,
> Help me oppressed by things undone,
>   O Thou whose deeds and dreams are one.[30]

As I reflected upon the words of the hymn it seemed to me to reflect the disunity of what I myself was and did and pointed to the unity or integration in the life and work of Christ. Some years later I found in Paul Tillich's theology a clue to interpreting the relationship between the unity and integrity of Christ and my own lack of unity. The details of this formulation may not be nearly as satisfying to others as they have been to me, but I present them in order to challenge pastoral carers to consider how their ministry may in some way be related to and continuous with the ministry of Christ.

Tillich's way of emphasizing the importance of Christ's integrity or oneness is to say that Jesus "is the bearer of the New Being in the totality of his being, not in any special expressions of it."[31] Tillich rejects the emphasis of different elements of the Christian story which result in "the separation of the words of Jesus from his being, the pietistic separation of his deeds from his being, and the orthodox separation of the suffering of Jesus from his being."[32] In contrast to this, Tillich argues that Jesus as the Christ must be understood holistically, as one whose words, actions, and being are all of a piece. Other Christian theologians and theological traditions may not emphasize Christ's unity as strongly or in the same way, but what Tillich says is not peculiar to him. It is in keeping with the central Christological affirmations of the church.

Our question here is: If Christ's person and work are one, and if the ministers of Christ are to be in some way like him or continuous with his ministry, how can these two affirmations be brought together in an understanding of the character of a Christian carer? One does not have to understand or agree with the philosophical underpinnings or the details of Paul Tillich's theology to appreciate the way he approaches the question of how the person and work of the minister might be patterned after that of Christ. Tillich recognized, even in the light of the Protestant principle that is critical of all formulations of what one should be and do, that the Christian cannot really avoid the question of how what one is and what one does are related to each other and to the person and work of the Christ.

What Tillich does is to bring together the apostle Paul's injunction in Philippians 2:5, "Let the same mind be in you that was in Christ Jesus," with the discussion of the form of God and the form of humanity that follows it. From this he concludes that human beings are asked to "take the form of the Christ," but that this can never mean copying concrete traits from the biblical picture. If these are imitated, they become ritualistic prescriptions or laws and distort the image of Jesus' unity, his identity, and his integrity.

Although what Christians do cannot appropriately express what they are in the way that it does with Jesus as the Christ, the Philippian injunction to take the form of Christ may be understood as asking them to participate in the new being by seeking the kind of unity of being and doing which the Christ exemplifies. This can be done within the specific contingencies of their lives. The form of Christ that Christians take is a never-completed quest for unity in what they believe, are, and do.

This image of "taking the form of Christ through a quest for unity" is an image of the character of the Christian minister that I believe is applicable for all members of the caring community, both clergy and laity. The question of an integrated doing and being is not ignored, but it is not something to be achieved. It is a guiding image or quest, something sought after with faith and an expectation of grace, something that may be fostered in the life of the Christian carer.

Some Final Reflections

In this chapter, I have attempted to address the issue of the character of the carers who represent the caring community in its ministry. It is a fascinating and difficult issue with which the Christian church has struggled since its beginning. If the ministry of the church is in some way a continuation of the ministry of Christ, what kind of expectations should it have of those who are Christ's representatives? There have been many different answers to that question. Some of them have resulted in claims about the holiness and authority of the clergy that were radically different from expectations for the laity. Others have emphasized the holiness and piety of all the people of God in a way that resulted in a separation from the world in which they lived. In a time when the communal contextual paradigm calls for recognition of individual, cultural, and gender differences and emphasizes the authority of the community rather than that of its leaders, how we are to perceive "a distinctive mark" that identifies the caring community's ministers is an important issue.

I shared the story of one lay carer, an Irish Catholic woman who was involved in the training of priests in pastoral caring. Even in that brief story one could see the way that her personality traits, the circumstances and events of her life, a call to ministry, and the expectation of her denominational tradition contributed to the shape of her ministry. I then applied David Duncombe's three modes of identifying and clarifying the meaning of Christian life to finding the distinctive mark of a Christian minister.

There have been many descriptive attempts to identify what the Christian life involves and what marks the minister as authentic. I presented several of these descriptive efforts and was chastened by Søren Kierkegaard's reminder that, descriptively, one can really not see the difference between the "knight of faith" and any other person. I turned, then, to Duncombe's other two modes of clarification, discernment and fostering.

I attempted to relate the process of discernment to the concept and experience of pastoral identity, what I believe has been the central focus of the clinical pastoral paradigm. I argued that the most important elements in a pastoral identity are a pastoral attitude, ability, authority, and accountability. Finally, I identified what Duncombe calls "fostering" with the term "quest," specifically a quest for the kind of unity between what Jesus was and did that he expressed in his life and work. Using part of Tillich's Christology, I suggested that the Christian minister, the pastoral carer, "took the form of Christ" through a quest for unity and integrity. The chapter may indeed identify more problems than answers for those problems.

Questions for Consideration

1. What do you see as the distinctive mark of the Christian minister, and what are the reasons for your point of view? Describe someone who, you believe, exhibits that mark.

2. How has your particular faith community differentiated between what was expected of the laity and what was expected from clergy? What discrepancies do you see here between your church's theory and its practice? In what way does it compromise in order to "get the work done," meet the budget, and so on?

3. In the light of Kierkegaard's picture of the "knight of faith," how is the Christian carer's mark open to description, and how does it defy description?

4. How is your ministry continuous with the ministry of Christ? In what ways do you make that connection or attempt to deny it? How do you use the Bible and other authorities in making your argument?

5. In recent years the American Association of Pastoral Counselors has extended the use of the modifier "pastoral" to the laity as well as the clergy. This chapter has also stretched the term to include lay carers as well as clergy. In the light of its historic and contemporary usage, is this stretching the term "pastoral" so much that it loses its meaning? What is the rationale for the position you take?

6. What is the meaning of the term "pastoral identity"? To what degree do you have that identity? What evidence do you have for that judgment?

4

Care Through Consultation on Caring

I'm a little older than some of you, and I think that some of the
experiences I've had have helped me understand. But that
doesn't keep me from understanding someone who's younger
and different from me. As long as I remember not to talk too
much and really listen to someone it works out.

—Lay pastoral carer

The first chapter explored the broad human meaning of care and
how it is expressed through hearing and remembering. The second
chapter attempted to show how care, something affirmed to be
both a need and an expression of all human beings, is affected by
the contexts in which care takes place. Knowledge that is claimed
to be universal can be oppressive knowledge unless it is attentive
to what is particular to a context, culture, or gender. Thus, care
must re-member as well as remember, that is, empower to change
structural rigidities as well as bring them to mind.

The preceding chapter focused on the person of the carer, what
he or she needs to be as well as do. It recognized the difficulties in
trying to do this with external criteria and suggested some more
elusive and intuitive criteria. This chapter broadens the meaning
of care to include the teaching and learning of it. Beginning with
the clinical pastoral paradigm, but more fully expressed in the
communal contextual, pastoral care involves the equipping of the
saints for ministry by a pastor who is a participant/consultant for
the ministry of all those involved in the community's caring.

A major problem in writing about learning to care is that reading about pastoral care in books is not the best way to learn how
to offer care to another. Neither is experience alone a very effective teacher. What has been learned in the last forty to fifty years
is that members of a caring community best learn pastoral care

87

by doing it and then reflecting upon what they have done in the company of others involved in the same ministry. Books such as this one are inevitably and appropriately secondary sources for learning and are used to add to the interpretation of experience provided by the actual setting for ministry. Heije Faber, a Dutch pastor/teacher who studied the pastoral care movement in America in the late '50s, was most impressed by the fact that American students learn pastoral care by first doing it without thorough training beforehand and, even more important, consider that initial lack of training as a strength, not a weakness, of the educational process.[1]

Although the classical and the clinical pastoral paradigms have generally operated on the assumption that ordained pastors and those being trained for ordination were the ones to whom the learning process was directed, the communal contextual paradigm requires that assumption to be challenged. In the communal contextual paradigm clergy, and those preparing for ordained ministry, are still primary learners of pastoral care, but the increasing numbers of laity who are involved in pastoral caring and who are interested in learning more and more deeply about the ministry have become an important part of those learning to care. Moreover, because of the involvement of the community in pastoral care, learning to be a pastor increasingly involves learning to teach it.

James C. Fenhagen has described as "a persistent heresy" the belief that the gifts necessary for the life of the church are centered in an ordained person. One of the most exciting phenomena in the church today, Fenhagen says, is the recovery of a "sense of 'giftedness' on the part of a large number of diverse people. We are discovering that we do indeed have evangelists, teachers, prophets, and healers in our midst, and they are beginning to discover what such gifts mean."[2]

The World Council of Churches and the Consultation on Church Union both deny a clergy-based concept of ministry. "All ministry, lay as well as those of bishop, presbyter, and deacon, are to be understood as at once personal, collegial, and communal. . . . Ministry is exercised by men and women who have been individually called and baptized, and in certain cases, also ordained."[3] Ordination is not synonymous with ministry but occurs only "in certain cases."

In another of his books, Fenhagen has argued that it "is more important for the ordained ministers in a congregation to enable others to identify and carry out their ministries than to do it themselves."[4] Similarly, Ronald H. Sunderland, who has been one of the pioneers in developing methods for educating laity in pastoral care, has insisted that pastoral supervision has become a basic tool for ministry by clergy and should not be confined to the few who choose to engage in postgraduate study. "Pastoral supervision is not a specialty," says Sunderland. "It is a fundamental task for which the church will need all pastors to be prepared." He is concerned that training clergy in supervision should not be delayed until pastors have gained parish experience. If it is not a part of seminary training in pastoral care, "there is the risk that they will as neophytes in ministry adopt a clergy-based concept of pastoral ministry which must then be unlearned."[5] Following Sunderland at this point, one of the concerns of this book is that its readers will not adopt "a clergy-based concept of pastoral ministry."

Although clergy quite often have more education in pastoral care than the lay carers for whom they are pastorally responsible, if they are leaders of a congregation, their freedom to specialize is limited. Within the congregational context they cannot become specialists—they must represent the whole ministry of the church. Although large congregations can have persons who specialize in one area of ministry or another, what the clergy are set aside for by the church that ordains them is to represent to the community and to those outside it the whole ministry of Christ.

Laity, in contrast, *are* freer to specialize in one dimension of ministry. Their representative function is more limited. They can specialize in pastoral care and do only that or specialize in community ministries or educational ministries. Thus, the clergyperson or clergy staff is teacher of ministry and representative of the "whole" ministry of the community of faith, whereas the laity are more often than not "specialists" in a particular ministry, such as pastoral care.

How do persons who believe they have been called to a ministry of pastoral care or who are considering such a call learn to express their care more effectively? In one sense, caring cannot be taught. If the capacity to care has been given by God to human beings as the primary means of expressing their relationality and responsibility for the world around them, then caring is not something that is brought in from "outside" the person like a new concept or idea. It is more like an artistic talent that is already there, but which can be developed to a much greater degree.

In a speech given at the Fifth Conference on Clinical Pastoral Education in 1945, Paul Tillich addressed this question of how it is possible to teach pastoral care when care is a universal human function. He emphasized that care cannot be monopolized or controlled by any profession, including the clergy. The difference between those who offer care professionally and all other human beings is not that the clergy exercise this function and others do not; the difference is that the clergy along with other professionals consciously exercise care, reflect upon it and learn from it, whereas others express their care "indirectly, casually, and mostly unconsciously."[6]

Although I do not believe that it was his intent, Tillich's differentiation between professionals and those who care without thinking much about it has tended to limit concerns for learning to care or learning to care more effectively to theological education for professional ministry. Theological educators, particularly those in the practical fields, have thought of their task as helping students *be* something, not just learn something. The strength of the professional emphasis in theological education has been in helping students see themselves as developing their professional personhood, as being involved in a process of making their experience a part of themselves and bringing that experience in relation to theories that will enhance future practice.

Education for laity in pastoral caring and in other dimensions of ministry has tended to minimize the development of the person in ministry, an accomplishment understood for the full-time minister as the development of the professional self. Lay training in ministry has tended to focus on teaching listening and responding skills and to offer information about responding to particular kinds of problems. It has tended to ignore or deemphasize the person of the minister. Thus, Tillich's distinction between those who offer care naturally and those who offer it intentionally has helped those of us who have specialized in pastoral care and theological education, but it has tended to place lay education in caring in a separate and lesser category.

Because the communal contextual paradigm views pastoral care not as a ministry of the ordained pastor alone but as a ministry of the community assisted by the ordained pastor, it requires that we go beyond Tillich's distinction and affirm intentionality of care for both laity and clergy. The difference between laity and clergy of the caring community is not that the clergy are intentional about their care and the laity are not. Instead, the difference may be identified at two points: level of involvement and teaching role. The clergy have a greater time involvement in ministry. The other difference is the clergy's having been called or set aside as teachers of pastoral care and of other dimensions of ministry. The distinction is similar to the one that has traditionally been made in Presbyterian polity. Both laity and clergy may be elders, but the clergy are set aside as having in addition to that the role of teacher. The distinction between laity and clergy in the pastoral care ministry is also similar to that used in professional associations between those qualified as practitioners and those practitioners who are also qualified to be supervisors. The supervisor or teacher continues to be a practitioner, but adds to that the function of teacher/supervisor.

Learning to Care:
Some Contributions of the Classical Paradigm

What does one need to learn in order to be effective in a ministry of pastoral care? The three paradigms for pastoral care offer different answers to that question, but the answers of the later paradigms complement and build upon what has been emphasized before rather than negating it. James Fenhagen has identified four ministry functions shared by both clergy and laity, the first two of which are classical in their emphasis on the Christian message. The first is telling a story. The people of God are sent into the world with a story to tell. Ministry begins when they *own* the Christian story—when they "hear it, internalize it, feel it, participate in it, and tell it."

Second, God's people "are sent into the world to bear witness to a particular view of what is of primary value. . . . Christian ministry involves a continuous clarification, in the light of the Gospel, of the values we ourselves hold, and a commitment to bear witness to these values at every point where decisions are made." Third, the people of God are participants and builders of community. This, Fenhagen says, "is a ministry of listening, of healing, and of caring." Fourth, they are "spiritual journeyers." "At the heart of ministry is self-conscious participation in the spiritual journey of the people of God. We cannot give to others what we have not found ourselves."[7]

Fenhagen's ministry functions are important to consider in learning the ministry of pastoral care, but they should not be viewed as sequential. It is an important part of learning pastoral care to learn, identify with, and tell the Christian story, but that learning and identification may take place concurrently with or subsequent to a ministry of listening, healing, and caring. The minister's attempts to offer care may contribute significantly to his or her learning and telling the story. What Fenhagen underscores for us is that the ministry of pastoral care cannot be simply *doing* something for another. It involves *being* something—being someone who is a reminder of the Christian story and tradition because one has made that tradition in some way a part of one-self. Pastoral carers, lay or clergy, must be in a process of learning the story and learning to represent it to others. The emphasis on being as well as doing is a central part of the clinical pastoral para-digm, but the emphasis on the message or story requires that we turn to the classical.

The contribution of the classical paradigm to learning pastoral care and achieving a Christian pastoral identity may be explored in a variety of sources. Unfortunately, many of them are out of print and can be found only in theological libraries. Two of the most important resources for identifying and understanding the classical pastoral care are John T. McNeil's *A History of the Cure of Souls*, published in 1951,[8] and Clebsch and Jaekle's *Pastoral Care in Historical Perspective*, published in 1964.[9] More recently, Thomas C. Oden has reminded us that "there has been a pervasive amne-sia toward the classical Christian past" which has resulted in "a bland sense of absent-mindedness and a growing naivete toward the wisdom of classical pastoral care."[10]

Oden is certainly correct that modern American pastoral work "has been stronger in personal and practical aspects than in his-torical and theological awareness" and that the "fabric of effective pastoral work involves the constant interweaving of scriptural wis-dom, historical awareness, constructive theological reasoning, sit-uational discernment, and personal empathy." Pastoral care, like any other dimension of ministry, needs to examine the concrete problems it addresses "in the light of scripture and tradition."[11] Not only the classical, but also the clinical pastoral and the com-munal contextual paradigms, contribute to effective education for pastoral caring. The important thing is that all three paradigms contribute to the answer through some form of "mutually critical correlation."[12] The relative authority of classic Christian and other sources must be worked out and placed into actual situations of ministry by particular caring communities.

In considering the authority for teaching pastoral care, some understanding of the patterns of leadership and authority in the New Testament is quite valuable. David Steele has noted that in the early community of Christians in Jerusalem the need for quick, definite, clear-cut decisions led the early church to give au-thority predominantly to individuals, apostles who had been with Jesus or those with charismatic gifts. Later, in the new churches established and nurtured by Paul, there was a greater need for community building. Authority, therefore, was given over more to the community itself than to outstanding individuals. In later epistles, the primary need was for stability and rootedness; therefore, in contrast to the earlier emphases upon individual and community leadership, authority was given more to scripture and tradition and to those who interpreted them. All three authority patterns are strongly based in scripture and the tradition of the church, and it is need that should determine which is given primary emphasis.[13]

Steele draws a useful parallel between the church of the later epistles and the church today. When those epistles, which have been called pastoral, were written persons with firsthand physical acquaintance with the Christ were no longer living. In these epistles, the prominent leadership functions, therefore, were *shepherding, eldership, overseeing,* and *teaching.* These functions, he says, continue to be the "building blocks of church leadership at any age." In considering the teaching and learning of pastoral care, the first two functions, shepherding and eldership, apply both to laity and clergy. The second two, overseeing and teaching, apply primarily to clergy.

The shepherding function is described in 1 Peter 5:2–3, but Paul spoke earlier of bearing one another's burdens (Gal. 6:2), of admonishing one another in wisdom (Col. 3:16), and of building one another up (1 Thess. 5:14–15). This is the personal or individual care dimension of ministry.

The eldership function involves age and maturity in the faith and being a representation of God to the people and of the people to one another. James 5:14, for example, presents the elder as a wise older person who brings grace and healing to the sick. Literal age, however, is less important than the minister's willingness to be identified as a representative of the church, carrying some of the church's meaning and authority as a part of his or her personality.

The function of oversight described in 1 Peter may be identified with the administrative dimensions of ministry and emphasizes care for the community as a whole. The need for pastoral guidance of this type apparently

> became evident only after the apostles—the charismatic leaders or ones who had direct knowledge of the Christ—had died out or moved on to another place. At that point an overseer was needed to be sure that the work begun by the apostles was continued and developed. One can surmise that the earliest pastoral supervisors were less likely to have been dynamic preachers of the Gospel than faithful deacons left behind to keep things going.[14]

The function of teaching, particularly the teaching of pastoral care, is related to all the other three ministry functions. Before exercising effective oversight, for example, the church leader must first teach people how to minister in the name of Christ. And, before the laity will open themselves up to be taught, the church leader will need to become the shepherd who cares and an effective elder or authority figure.[15] Whether ministry is expressed through shepherding, oversight, eldership, or teaching, Christian ministry has always been understood as being in some way an extension of the ministry of Christ.

In his exhaustive study of Christian ministry, theologian Bernard Cooke has said:

> All Christian ministry finds its origin in the salvific ministry of Jesus himself; throughout history, Christian theology is united in recognizing this principle. There has also been agreement on the principle that all authentic Christian ministry involves a participation in Christ's ministerial mission and power, but there has been considerable disagreement as to the nature of this participation.[16]

Hermeneutical problems prevent any simple identification of what occurs in ministry today with events recorded in the New Testament, but one can certainly suggest continuity with the ministry of Christ and the ministry of the early Christian church through the use of themes prominent in the New Testament. I point to two of them.

One important theme, found primarily in the Synoptic Gospels, is Jesus as a teller of parables. According to the New Testament scholar John Dominic Crossan, a parable is a story/event that breaks into and breaks down the most cherished assumptions of its hearers. Jesus "took the religious and cultural tradition of his hearers and contradicted it with Samaritans who were 'good guys,' not bad, or vineyard workers who 'unfairly' received more wages than they deserved."[17] By pointing to the unexpected meaning and importance in the ordinary events of life and ministry, the shepherd and overseer may challenge the assumptive world of the supervisee in the context of a relationship in which he or she and the supervisee can view that assumptive world together.

Another theme, found predominantly in the ministry of Paul, is the juxtaposition of the theological and the practical. Paul's epistles are a fascinating mix of profound theological argument and practical, sometimes petty, concerns of the persons and groups whom the apostle addressed. What is authoritative, in my judgment, is not Paul's practical solutions to the problems of his day, whether about marriage and divorce, competitiveness and interpersonal conflict, or whatever. What is authoritative in providing a model for ministry is Paul's commitment to viewing those concerns in the light of the person and work of the Christ. "Whatever the issue in human experience to be examined, a practical or technical solution is in itself inadequate. All that persons do and are is to be understood in the light of the God revealed in Jesus Christ."[18]

Learning to care, informed by the classical paradigm and its emphasis on the message, may involve instruction in a number of things, including those mentioned: the ministry of Jesus, the Christian tradition's understanding of ministry, and Paul's blending of theology and ethics. The important thing is that learning pastoral care is not simple instruction and experience in listening skills or the characteristics of particular human problems. It may indeed involve that, but it should also always have a component that informs and reinforms one on the major elements of the Christian story and tradition. The pastoral carers do not have to be articulate in their expression of that tradition in words, but they need to be committed to an ongoing process of learning it and becoming a part of it. I strongly affirm what Thomas Oden has said (cited above), that the "fabric of effective pastoral work involves the constant interweaving of scriptural wisdom, historical awareness, constructive theological reasoning, situational discernment, and personal empathy." Learning from the classical paradigm is an important part of that.

Learning to Care:
Some Contributions of the Clinical Pastoral Paradigm

How does one learn to be a pastoral carer? The answer to this question from the point of view of the clinical pastoral paradigm has been: "through competent pastoral supervision of acts of ministry." The classical paradigm has insisted that the "saints" be equipped with the story, that they be familiar and identified with it. The clinical pastoral paradigm insists that pastoral carers know not only the story but themselves and their relationships. It assumes that the message of God's care is inseparable from the messenger.

The clinical pastoral paradigm, particularly through the clinical pastoral education movement (C.P.E.), has made a more important function of supervision in ministry than supervision has been in any other profession. The C.P.E. movement has affirmed that supervision is more than enabling persons to carry out a task more effectively. It is ministry itself. Pastoral care is a larger category of which pastoral supervision is a subtype, but pastoral supervision is a ministry of pastoral care that is carried out by a minister called to the "teaching office" of the church.[19] The importance of *pastoral* as a modifier of supervision is in designating it as ministry, not simply a technique to accomplish a more important task, such as preaching, teaching, or parish visitation. Whether done individually or, more commonly, in a group setting, supervision that is pastoral is ministry itself. It is a major element in "equipping the saints."

A distinctive historical feature of clinical pastoral education as it has developed under the clinical pastoral paradigm is that it has taken place in a structure primarily concerned with service rather than education. Certainly, the training institution, whether a church or other agency, is concerned with education or it would not have opened itself to trainees of one kind or another, but its concern for education stops when education appears to conflict with service or, in the case of a for-profit corporation, when education conflicts with profitability. The supervisor is in a supervisory role because he or she and the students are working together in an authority structure designed to facilitate the provision of service. Thus, developing primarily in hierarchically structured health care institutions the *clinical pastoral* paradigm has understood "equipping the saints" as involving the pastor's role as supervisor.

The Three Relationships

Central in the clinical pastoral paradigm is learning by examining data from three primary relationships: those with authorities, those with peers, and those with persons for whom one is functioning in an authority role, such as parent or pastor. Much of what takes place in individual or group supervision influenced by the clinical pastoral paradigm can be understood as learning based on these three relational experiences. This pattern seems to have developed experientially, without much thought being given to its theoretical importance.

It may not be immediately obvious to the reader or, for that matter, to the supervisee how he or she is an authority. That fact itself is a matter to be worked with in the supervisory relationship. The supervisee, theological student, or lay carer is an authority by being placed in an authority role, namely that of a representative of the caring community or the chaplain's office. The way in which he or she functions within that role is a central issue in pastoral supervision. What does it feel like to "be" a minister when one is not fully prepared, educationally or experientially, for it? What are the effects on one's identity of being treated like a minister? The pastoral supervisor helps the supervisee examine these experiences and learn from them what ministry is like and what it may mean to accept the fact that one is seen as a minister.

That contemporary clinical experience is also related to the student's relational history insofar as that has been shared with the supervisee's supervisor and peers. The pastoral supervisor shares her assumption that contemporary relationships in the ministry setting and in the training group are significantly related to the supervisee's history. Exploring those relationships in depth, however, goes only as far as the supervisee is willing to explore those relationships as they are expressed currently or historically. He and the supervisor have developed ground rules for the exploration in an individual and/or group contract for learning. Neither party is expected to go beyond the learning contract that has been agreed on. A major part of the pastoral supervisor's role is suggesting connections between experiences of the supervisee and offering the opportunity for him to make similar connections.

One of the most important things that can be observed in clinical pastoral education is how persons both search for and retreat from peership, demand it and then seem uncomfortable when they have it. This observation has important practical and theoretical dimensions. Practically, it contributes significantly to the way supervision is carried out. The supervisor assumes that her supervisees are seeking peership with her in the practice and understanding of ministry. On the other hand she sees them retreat into dependency and ineptitude when the anxiety of being in the clinical situation increases. As supervisor, she points this out and attempts to explore the meaning of supervisee's affirmation of and search for peership and his subsequent retreat from it.[20]

The following brief vignette touches on a part of the retreat from peership that I have repeatedly observed and experienced.

> **Pastoral carer:** I felt completely lost in that room. I don't know what to say to someone who's facing that kind of suffering.
>
> **Supervisor/consultant:** What did you say you felt? "Lost" is the word I think you used. What did your lostness feel like?
>
> **Pastoral carer:** Alone and confused, wanting someone to take over the situation for me.
>
> **Supervisor/consultant:** It occurs to me that your feelings might be telling you and the patient that she's been heard and understood. Have you thought about how you might try to get that across to her?

Pastoral carer: No, I had hoped you would tell me.

Supervisor/consultant: What I am telling you is to value what you
were feeling and use it in the best way you can.

The clinical situation, exposing the student to the pain of
human life, challenges him and gets him in touch with the difficulty of the caring process. He does not know what to say and, his
inadequacy having been touched, he becomes more dependent
and longs not for a peer, but for someone who *knows* the right answer. The supervisor/consultant refuses to be that kind of authority and points the supervisee to the potential authority of his own
feelings. She notices what he apparently did not see, that his feelings gave him access to the deeper life of the patient and some of
what the patient was experiencing. Rather than being able to
function in a peer relation with the patient, the supervisee sought
an answer to distance himself from that peership. The supervi-
sor/consultant offered support through affirming the resources he
had within himself and refusing to be used only as an authority
on what to do.

Theoretically, the seeking of and retreat from peership can be
seen as an important developmental theme, appearing in various
forms in childhood, but also repeated again and again in adult life.
Persons seek "equality," but then become uncomfortable with it
and attempt instead to move to a power position above or below
the other, demanding from above on the basis of authority or from
below on the basis of need. Peership in human relations is a fragile
commodity. Theologically, the denial of peership can be understood as an expression of human sin. Human beings tend to feel
anxious in peership and attempt to move to a more clearly structured position in relation to others, apparently unable to trust relationships that are based more on choice than on demand. The
issue of the search and denial of peership is one of the most important insights growing out of the clinical pastoral paradigm. The
concern with how persons deal with peership, however, is an issue
more clearly related to the communal dimension of the communal
contextual paradigm and its impact on learning to care.

Learning to Care:
Some Contributions of
the Communal Contextual Paradigm

While emphasizing the importance of learning in community—
in a small group setting—the clinical pastoral paradigm has been

strongly individualistic. Its strength has been its ability to respond to the individual learning needs of the student and to meet him where he is. It has also focused primarily on the ordained minister or persons moving toward ordination. Moreover, its emphasis on the professionalization of supervision has tended to professionalize pastoral care and separate it from the laity. In contrast to this, the ministry document of the Church Uniting (Consultation on Church Union) affirms that all ministry will be *collegial* and *communal*. "Baptism and ordination alike associate the individual with others who share the same call. Ministry is inherently a shared responsibility. Thus no minister is independent or autonomous."[21]

Similarly, the World Council of Churches document *Baptism, Eucharist, and Ministry* views ordained ministry as *collegial* and *communal*. It sees a need for "a college of ordained ministers sharing in the common task of representing the concerns of the community." It also speaks of an "intimate relationship between the ordained ministry and the community," where "the exercise of the ordained ministry is rooted in the life of the community and requires the community's effective participation in the discovery of God's will and the guidance of the Spirit."[22]

Both of the documents quoted above are strongly expressive of the communal dimension of what I have called the communal contextual paradigm. Ministry is not primarily hierarchical, but communal and collegial. As the clinical pastoral paradigm has insisted, it has an inescapably personal dimension as well. The communal contextual paradigm goes beyond both of these to define pastoral care as a ministry of the caring community which is nurtured and facilitated by the pastor through her or his teaching office, not a ministry of the clergy alone.[23]

In the light of the discussion of "contexts for care" in a previous chapter, the teacher of pastoral care must be attentive to the particularities of the person receiving care and the contexts that help form who that person is. Writing from a feminist perspective, Lynn Rhodes has argued that authority in supervision should come from models of leadership that reflect

> values of partnership and teamwork. Friendship and solidarity are two images of life in a Christian community that are emerging from feminists. Both images require that leaders learn how to empower others and learn to work collaboratively. These forms of leadership are always consciously working on equalizing power dynamics. . . .
>
> In order for the context of supervision to be made explicit, an analysis of the sexist and patriarchal elements is necessary. The supervisor will need to ask what the context says about women,

about their roles in a specific church, and about their roles in the communities that inform that church's life. . . .

The supervisor's task is to provide contexts in which women have opportunities to work on issues of difference and exclusion.[24]

She further emphasizes that if the supervisor is male, it is very important that he clearly understand the importance of women being together in support groups. Perhaps most important, Rhodes encourages

all men who supervise women to study and work with other men in similar power situations to explore and examine their own sexism. One of the most explosive issues they need to explore is their understanding of sexual dynamics in collegial relationships. Men and women have had little experience in working closely together in relationships of mutuality, and especially not in work that demands much sharing of the intimacies of people's lives.[25]

Writing in a way that resonates with Rhodes's feminist perspective, Eldon Olson has insisted that the pastoral role

must be defined in terms of supportive mutuality, a mutuality in which the corporate body of the church ministers to its pastors. Any lay care ministry which is circumscribed by its pastoral author's energies is a violation of the credal confession of the communion of saints. Not only must the pastoral leader of lay care ministries eagerly allow and solicit mutuality from laypersons in a congregation, he or she must also participate in a fellowship of peers which supports and enriches a personal sense of self.[26]

Much earlier, Paul Tillich spoke of care as "essentially mutual." One who gives care also receives care. "In most acts of taking care of someone, it is possible for the person who is the object of care also to become a subject." Caring and being cared for, Tillich continues, "is one act, not two, and only because it is one act is real care possible." Without mutuality, Tillich believed, we turn persons into objects or cases and break "their self awareness as a person."[27]

Finally, William Lloyd Roberts writes about the character of pastoral supervision "in a small, affection-centered congregation" where the pastoral supervisor "is always and inevitably a participant-observer."[28] The pastor as supervisor "is always both a participant and observer in the midst of a community. Neither doing all the work nor watching it done are appropriate options for pastoral supervision." For Roberts, one of the important things this means is that the pastor "is a *consultant* who asks questions and makes suggestions."[29]

The writings of all of these authors suggest the importance of modifying the supervisory model that has been so important in the clinical pastoral paradigm because that model has not sufficiently recognized the peership involved in the image of mutual intercession. A paradigm shift to the communal contextual involves the dynamic relationship between supervision and consultation and examining what that relationship reveals about the members of the community. I touched on this in my discussion of the denial of peership as an important focus of supervision in the clinical pastoral paradigm. What I hope to do here is to develop this idea further by describing the tension between consultation and supervision created by the communal contextual paradigm.

In pastoral supervision, the supervisor has ultimate responsibility for the ministry being performed and, as part of his or her professional function, is required to oversee the work of the supervisee. This is the familiar position of a male pastor in a congregation or a chaplain supervisor in a health care institution. In contrast, in pastoral consultation, the consultant may be overseeing the same type of ministry but is not ultimately responsible for it. The person seeking consultation has freely chosen the consultative assistance and may accept or reject the consultation that has been offered at any time. In a supervisory contract, however, supervision is not voluntary. Whereas the need for supervision is associated with the early stages of ministry or other professions and often avoided after that, consultation can be appropriately associated with any stage of personal and professional development.

The influence of the communal contextual paradigm and observations about human resistance to peership have caused me increasingly to view all types of clinical pastoral education as a consultative process which takes place within a supervisory structure. It is consultative because it is entered into freely by the student. This freedom of entry is an essential assumption of the educational process even when a program is "required" by a seminary or other church structure or when supervision is required by a professional association. A primary focus of supervision is examining the choices a supervisee makes. The supervisee who denies the assumption of free entry for himself or herself and the supervisor who does not make use of that assumption can abort the whole learning process. Learning clinically is predicated on the student's responsibility for choosing to be there and all the subsequent choices related to that initial one. The task of the pastoral educator, whether in an institution or a parish, is to encourage self-evaluation in the light of the consultation of significant others. Essential to the process is the fact that whatever consultation is offered may be rejected by the student in the process of his or her self-evaluation. Then, of course, the rejection of the consultation can be examined for its meaning, but that too can be rejected.

The communal contextual paradigm represents a norm for human beings that is more peerlike than hierarchical. It recognizes the particularities of human beings and insists that they be recognized and respected in such a way that one gender or cultural context or other feature associated with power is not assumed to be superior or normative for another. In the light of this paradigm change and the earlier observation about the human tendency to deny peership, pastoral education programs may be viewed as, ultimately, consultative in that they are dependent on the supervisees' choosing to be there and on their subsequent choices about what they will do with the consultation they receive from their supervisor and their peers in the learning process. Further, the goal of the supervisory relationship is that it become consultative—that it will eventually take place without the constrictions of a supervisory structure.

In fact, however, most education takes place in institutions that are hierarchically structured. Clinical pastoral education takes place most often in a hierarchically structured health institution. Education for laity in pastoral caring takes place in parish or diocesan structures that have strong hierarchical elements. The setting of virtually every educational experience, therefore, creates a tension between implementation of tasks through chain of command and choice of and the carrying out of tasks for the purposes of education. Quite positively, this tension creates important learning opportunities for the supervisees or students. How do they deal with the conflict between the requirements of service and the need for learning? If learning can be viewed as a choice of the learner then, at best, it is a consultative process. It takes place, however, within a supervisory structure and so offers for both teacher and learner a tension between the supervisory and the consultative relationship. The student is free to choose what he or she hears or learns, but at the same time, with the same persons, is required to perform certain functions and to fulfill a particular role. The way this often contradictory experience is worked out within the structure of the relationship is the heart of the pastoral educational process as informed by the communal contextual paradigm.[30]

A pastor entrusted with facilitating the ministry of a caring community can best be understood as a consultant on caring. Except in the most dependent relationships of childhood, no one knows what is best for another person. "Freed from the burdensome task of knowing what is best for another, the consultant is able to open his or her own person and offer a variety of responses and impressions with the confidence that the consultee can pick and choose what is useful." The consultee, "when freed from the illusion that someone else knows what is best, is able to accept numerous responses from a variety of people with the confidence that his or her own person will utilize the feedback advantageously and select a course of action out of an inner wisdom. "Where this view is not accepted, dependency is experienced as inferiority, self-disclosure is fraught with anxiety, and the authority of the inner person is mistrusted. Reliance on an outward authority usually results."[31]

I believe that this view of consultation offers a powerful description of learning through discovering peership. The consultant and those consulted are assumed to be peers and are free to learn mutually from each other. In fact, however, this optimal relationship is strongly resisted. Peership is denied; struggles for position above or below ensue. Thus, the image of the consultant as an operational image for the pastor is, in my judgment, an essential one. A good pastor, a good pastoral teacher, is one who assumes peership with those whom he is leading or teaching. This peership will be resisted. The pastor will be placed above or below, but must assume peership and work with its denial so that all parties can learn from what is happening as the clinical pastoral operates under the impact of the communal contextual.

Learning to Care:
Three Methods of "Equipping the Saints"

There are many training programs for "equipping the saints" that have been developed under the impact of the communal contextual paradigm. I mention three of them here. The pastor who has this responsibility within an ecclesial or other context for care can profitably learn from and adapt these and other programs to her particular ministry context. Although a structured and competently organized program like the Stephen Ministries may be just the thing for some contexts for ministry, it may not be appropriate for others. The important thing is that the pastor find a way to carry out her responsibilities of consultation on caring in a way that fits her particular situation.

The Stephen Ministries were developed in the late '70s by Kenneth Haugk, a Missouri Synod Lutheran minister and psychologist. By the end of 1991, over three thousand congregations or other ministry groups had had members trained in the program. Beginning with a skill-training model from counseling psychology and a conservative Christian theology, the Stephen Ministries have added flexibility to an initially rigid training structure so that the program can be used and adapted by many different types of groups. What primarily is being marketed by the Stephen Ministries is the initial training program for leaders, support services provided by the staff in the St. Louis office, and printed and video instructional materials.

The pastoral care minister in a large church that has used the program for a number of years is enthusiastic about the basic structure provided by Stephen Ministries, but takes some pride in his adaptation of the program to fit his own style and theoretical interests and his particular congregation. He describes the training for his church's Stephen ministers as a combination of Stephen Ministries training, clinical pastoral education, and spiritual formation. In addition to himself, there are eight "Stephen leaders" in the congregation who have been through the two-week training event in St. Louis and who are committed to leadership of the program over a two-year period, focused on two hours per week on Wednesday evenings. These leaders work with the forty-five to fifty Stephen ministers presently active in this large congregation, who visit shut-ins and patients in hospitals and nursing homes. The training sessions are held in small groups of six to eight, led by the local Stephen staff ministers, which focus on both ministry experiences and the minister's self-understanding and personal growth.

Equipping Laypeople for Ministry is a program developed by Ronald H. Sunderland, a C.P.E. supervisor and former executive director of the Institute of Religion at the Texas Medical Center in Houston. Sunderland's original concern was to extend C.P.E.-type training beyond the theological students to a new market, the laity, offering his program in a series of week-long workshops for pastors and C.P.E. supervisors. While his materials are copyrighted, he has insisted that he wants to "give away" his workshop design to colleagues with the hope that they can use the design and materials in whatever way seems appropriate.

Sunderland's training materials are a series of verbatim interviews of pastoral care situations which he uses to engage his training groups and encourage them to develop similar materials of their own. The model is person-centered with a focus on developing pastoral skills. Perhaps because he sought to work within other institutions with other identities (the Institute of Religion and the Association for Clinical Pastoral Education), Equipping Laypeople for Ministry has not developed, like the Stephen Ministries, into an enduring institution. Sunderland's success has been in developing a viable program responsive to the conceptual paradigm of C.P.E. which has been adapted effectively to train the increasing numbers of lay ministers needed to work with AIDS patients. His recent work has focused on training groups of laity to work in "Care Teams" with people with AIDS. He is currently expanding the Care Team concept to provide respite support for families faced with Alzheimer's or related dementias, cancer, or pediatric diseases or disabilities.

The Ministry of Christian Listening includes elements similar to the Stephen Ministries and Equipping Laypeople for Ministry. Directed by another supervisor certified by the Association for Clinical Pastoral Education, Barbara Sheehan, S.P., it is a local program offered at the Catholic Center of the diocese of Covington, Kentucky. Although it is similar both to the Stephen Ministries and Equipping Laypeople for Ministry, it is more closely related to an Ignatian spirituality program called "The Art of Spiritual Companioning." According to its training staff, the Ministry of Christian Listening has been "designed for those persons who exhibit an ongoing adult spirituality and who themselves experience a call to enter a covenant relationship with others on their journey of spiritual growth." The program's purpose has been described as follows:

1. To develop listening skills appropriate for ministry
2. To learn to build healthy ministerial relationships
3. To become aware of spiritual dynamics operative in one's life
4. To grow in competence and confidence as a co-journeyer in a covenant relationship
5. To grow spiritually in relationship to a call to ministry

There is an application process for the program which requires the applicant's putting in writing his or her purpose for applying for the program, a statement of how the applicant has experienced a call to ministry, an autobiography that describes relationships with church and family, and a statement of the applicant's experience of prayer and images of God.

The program materials of the Ministry of Christian Listening suggest the following as "possible" criteria for acceptance into the program. (The word "possible" seems to indicate an awareness of the difficulties in trying to state rigid criteria for admission to this kind of educational experience.) The person who can benefit most from this program:

1. Has a positive and realistic self-image, with a flexibility and appropriate vulnerability that allows growth;

2. Demonstrates (as best one can in an interview) a flexibility and openness to different personalities and different styles;

3. Has clear goals for entering this ministry;

4. Demonstrates a sufficient integration within a believing community and family to enable support and ground for ministry;

5. Has at least a beginning awareness of and openness to a supervisory relationship;

6. Is realistic about his or her strengths, limitations, eagerness/fear about entering this ministry;

7. Has a pattern of growth in life and is open to continue this;

8. Demonstrates a moral and spiritual development consistent with a groundedness and a maturity that is adult;

9. Is capable of a consistent prayer life and has a reference for his or her own inner resources and strengths;

10. Does not evoke within the interviewer questions, suspicions, or concerns that cannot be identified.

The program itself goes on for thirteen weeks, beginning with a one-day retreat and continuing with weekly three-hour classes. The classes include a practicum where the participants work with an actual situation of a participant needing care, who is listened to by another participant and observed by members of a small group. There is a didactic component, with reading and lectures on topics relevant to human problems or to the personal and spiritual development of the participants. The emphasis is on the latter, indicating that the program is more focused on the growth in ministry of the participant than on the problems he or she might be called on to address. There is also weekly supervision of the participant's ministry, as well as a required period of prayer each day and questions for reflection during the week.

This program seems to me to bring together some of the most important elements of the C.P.E. method, linking them with a type of spiritual direction and concern for the character of the carers as discussed in the preceding chapter. The personal/spiritual development of the person and the learning of ministry are integrally related in the training process. In contrast to the pattern of Stephen Ministries and Equipping Laypeople, it is not a parochial program. It was first sponsored by a diocese, but now has more of the qualities of a C.P.E. program in that the participants come from a variety of ministry contexts and do their training with persons with whom they will not be otherwise involved. It is not a program provided by their church or place of ministry, but is something that participants seek, pay for, and use in their own way for development as ministers.

My concern here is to suggest that an ongoing experience of learning to care is important for every caring community, and the responsibility for involving members in it is the responsibility of the community's "teaching elder." In some cases it will be the ordained pastor's responsibility to provide the training. In other cases he or she can facilitate community members' securing their initial training elsewhere and having it supported and further nurtured in their own caring community or parish.

Learning to Care: A Continuum of Commitment

From the explorations I have made in various caring communities, one of the things that has become obvious is that among the members of these communities and, I imagine, in the parishes served by those who read this book, there is a continuum of commitment. Members of St. John's Church may be a long way from committing themselves to a thirteen-week course on Christian Listening that focuses on themselves as pastoral care ministers. A number of them, however, may be quite ready to visit in their parish and receive some training in how to do that more effectively. The goal of the teaching pastor is not only to get the work of visitation done but to be open to the development of a group of persons who are committed to the ministry of pastoral care and to their own personal growth in that ministry, at whatever level of commitment.

It is important to remember, however, that the pastor working in a parochial setting will probably begin to work with persons who have made a lesser degree of commitment. Many members of the community will continue on in the work of pastoral caring at the commitment level of "volunteer" for service. Others, however, will develop an increasing commitment to being ministers as well as doing those things that need to be done. Thus those who are learning to care in a particular community may appropriately be represented on a continuum of commitment and call to ministry. The continuum image is in no way intended to disparage the importance of those nearer to the volunteer end of the continuum. It simply recognizes the fact that some persons are at the point of relating their person and their ministry and some are not. Some will continue to do very effective work as volunteers in ministry. Others will have a vocation to *being* a minister grow out of their experience of representing the Christian community and its message through their acts of caring.

Some Final Reflections

This discussion of pastoral care as inclusive of the teaching and learning of care has raised some of the continuing issues in education in general and professional education in particular: the issues of how the experiential and the didactic are related; what the learner needs to know before he or she engages in practice; and how much theological or psychological theory needs to be brought into the process of learning to practice a profession or technical skill. The clinical pastoral paradigm has insisted that most of the necessary theory of how to do something can best be learned after trying to do it. Then what one needs to know will be more urgent and evident. Whether that principle holds in all situations of learning to care remains an ongoing question that teaching pastors will have to deal with in the way that most fits their style and situation of ministry.

Questions for Consideration

1. What is the place of ordination in your religious tradition? If baptism is the primary authorization for Christian ministry, what does the "in certain cases" phrase applied to ordination in the COCU paper refer to? How is ordination related to other authority-giving rites, such as certifying and consecrating? To what extent is ordination needed for the doing of pastoral care? for the teaching of it? Is the pastoral carer's image nearer to that of the priest who represents and intercedes or to that of the teacher of an important truth?

2. How do you understand the issue of generalization and specialization within ministry? Is it appropriate to associate specialization simply with specific focus, or does it necessarily imply education and training that is superior to the generalist? Can an ordained minister who specializes in pastoral care and counseling maintain his or her representative function as one who in some way represents the whole ministry of Christ?

3. How is what Paul Tillich referred to as "the unconscious capacity to care" nurtured and developed? How is it related to the experience of being cared for? Recall an experience of personal care and of pastoral care. How do you believe that those experiences influenced your understanding of the caring process?

4. As specifically related to the Christian message and our apprehension of it, in what way do you agree or disagree with Fenhagen's statement that "we cannot give . . . what we have not found"? What about Peter Bohler's injunction to John Wesley, "Preach faith till you have it."[32] Discuss both these statements in relation to the learning of care. To what degree and in what way does the pastoral carer need to be related to the Christian message?

5. What are the uses of the three primary human relationships in the learning of care? Reflect upon how you have been related to authorities, to peers, and to those with whom you have been an authority. How have those relationships been related to your family tradition and experience? How are they evident in your faith family or particular religious tradition?

6. Are the distinction and usage of the concepts of supervision and consultation made in this chapter relevant to ministry situations of which you are aware? What about the idea of "retreat from peership"? Does it indeed convey an important aspect of the human condition, or is it a false or relatively unimportant issue?

Part Three

Human Problems
as Contexts for Care

5

Limit and Loss—The Risks of Care

The days of our life are seventy years,
  or perhaps eighty, if we are strong;
even then their span is only toil and trouble;
  they are soon gone, and we fly away.

(Ps. 90:10)

What is your life? For you are a mist that appears for a little while and then vanishes.

(James 4:14)

Blessed are those who mourn, for they will be comforted.

(Matt. 5:4)

The first four chapters of this book dealt essentially with the persons who care and the communities of which they are a part. The next four chapters examine four fundamental human problems to which care is addressed. Continuing the understanding of "the problem" begun in chapter 2, all four of these problems will be interpreted as contexts for care. They are particular expressions of the human situation which the carer attempts to hear and remember in a way that is responsive both to the Christian message and to the persons receiving that message. Examining the pastoral caring response to persons experiencing the problem of limit and loss can contribute significantly to the understanding of human beings as relational with God and with other persons.

Limit and loss is the first, if not the most important, problem that members of the caring community encounter in their ministry. Learning to grieve and to respond to grief should be foremost in pastoral care, but it is important to broaden our view of grief to include many kinds of losses and the very fact of limit and loss itself. The fact that the lifetime of human beings is limited increases the value of life and challenges persons to live it as fully as possible. Limit and loss is more radically experienced in some lives because of the presence of developmental or circumstantial disability or the untimely death of significant others, and this accentuates the value and importance of the particular features of life that may have been lost. Moreover, the fact that the quality of life or the kind of life available to some is limited by bodily or mental disability can make those who are not so limited more aware of the value of the dimensions of life that are available to them.

I have argued that pastoral care today should involve contributions from all three pastoral care paradigms: the classical, which emphasizes the message of the Christian tradition; the clinical pastoral, which focuses on understanding the persons involved in giving and receiving the message of care; and the communal contextual, which broadens the clinical pastoral's focus beyond the pastor to include the caring community of both clergy and laity and which calls attention to the contextual factors affecting both the message of care and those bringing it and receiving it. A good pastor is involved in exploring and representing the Christian message about human limit and loss. She is concerned with the persons experiencing loss and with those, including herself, who are attempting to minister to them. The pastoral carer is also concerned with the particular contexts that affect how persons experience and deal with loss.

Limit and Loss in the Classical Paradigm

As one who both explores and represents the Christian message, the pastoral carer needs to be in touch with important dimensions of the Christian understanding of finitude and death, the fact of loss, and the hope for meaning and relationship in spite of loss. The question that the pastoral carer should be periodically addressing to himself is this: What does the Christian tradition have to say about the problem of human limit and loss? There is no final answer to this question or even a single answer, but it is one of the questions with which persons of faith should continually be in dialogue.[1]

A carer we shall call Susan, however, was resistive to the whole idea. A resident chaplain in a C.P.E. program, she described herself as a "practical person," interested in helping people, believing

she had a Christian calling to ministry, but not particularly concerned with thinking about what her faith tradition had to say
about life and death. After a particularly difficult death situation
in which she had been involved as a minister, Susan described her
feelings of frustration and anger as she listened to the family of
the deceased patient singing in the hospital chapel, "It's gonna be
all right! It's gonna be all right!" It's not going to be all right, she
thought. It's all wrong!

"What message do you have to offer?" the supervisor asked. "I
don't know," Susan replied. "I don't think I have one." "If you
don't think the family's message is right for you," said the supervisor, "I think you need to find one that you can represent." "I
don't like theology," Susan said; "it seems too far away from real
life." "Part of the reason you're here," said the supervisor, "is to
find a message that is not so far away. I'll be interested in what
you find that's right for you the next time we talk about this."
The human situation of limit and loss is a challenge to Susan and
the rest of us to engage the classical tradition enough to find a
message that will be "all right."

Undoubtedly, most important for pastoral carers who are committed both to explore and to represent the resources of the Christian faith is the Bible. Whatever means a person may use to be in
regular touch with the Bible as the central document of the faith,
they are likely to be of assistance in pastoral caring. Regular reading and study of the texts of the Common Lectionary can be a
meaningful way to be in dialogue with what the church is remembering, questioning, and celebrating at particular times of the
year. An important part of the pastor's role as teacher is to guide
lay carers in this enterprise. In the Bible, as Psalm 90 puts it, God
has set a reasonable limit of time for human creatures. Moreover,
finitude and mortality are not seen as intrinsically evil. The early
figures of the Old Testament died only when they were old and
"full of years." On the other hand, all suffering and death is also
seen as divine punishment for humankind's breaking of the
covenant with God.

For persons who are not involved in some regular group study
of the Bible, probably the best way to become acquainted with the
biblical view of a particular problem is to make use of responsible
secondary sources, such as Daniel Migliore's article on the Christian understanding of death in the *Dictionary of Pastoral Care and
Counseling*[2] or the articles on "The Kingdom of God and Life Ever-
lasting" in Hodgson and King's edited volumes, *Christian Theology:
An Introduction to Its Traditions and Tasks* and *Readings in Christian
Theology*.[3] If ministry does, indeed, begin when the ministers, lay

or ordained, *own* the Christian story, an ongoing dialogue with or in relationship to the story is essential for the pastoral carer.

In considering some of the classical paradigm's emphasis on the message of the Christian faith about limit and loss, one of the resources that has been helpful to me has been Jaroslav Pelikan's *The Shape of Death.* In this brief volume Pelikan has interpreted the way in which the early church fathers characterized life, death, and immortality. "The core of the Christian faith," he says, "is pessimism about life and optimism about God, and therefore hope for life in God. . . . Pessimism about man and optimism about God—nowhere do they come together more dramatically than in the Christian view of death."[4]

Pelikan uses five geometric figures to characterize the views of five of the church fathers about death. "The Christian answer to man's hope for immortality is both yes and no. Sometimes Christian thought has stressed the yes, less often the no, but both belong to the Christian answer." The first figure, the arc of existence, is associated with second-century church father Tatian, who argued against the preexistence and immortality of human beings by insisting that only God is without beginning. Any possibility of conquering death rests in God, not the immortality of the human being.

The circle, symbolizing immortality, represents the analogy between human life and the eternal life of God. This figure is associated with Clement of Alexandria, who presented parallels between Christian thought and the predominant Greek thought of his day in describing human life in the world as a pilgrimage between birth and death, the ultimate goal of which was the City of God. "I shall pray the Spirit of Christ to wing me to my Jerusalem."[5] This "shape" of death conflicts with the primary New Testament view of death, which denies any human immortality and presents resurrection as the only hope for dealing with the finality of death. It is, however, an important minority voice which cannot be ignored, and it is a shape that is still present today.

The third figure used to characterize a view of death is the triangle, which Pelikan associates with Cyprian, who like Tatian emphasized mortality more than immortality. The base of the triangle stands for those aspects of mortality which accentuate the continuity between human beings in their sharing the fate of death. The vertical dimensions of the triangle symbolize human relationship to God and human hope. The apex stands for the believer's hope for a divine intervention to grant life after death in Christ.

The parabola of eternity, associated with Origen, pictures death as God's way of bringing the soul back to Godself. Origen taught that the end and the beginning are alike, but in between the human being moves through time, existence, and death.

The final figure, the spiral, is associated with Irenaeus. It symbolizes history and counters those of Irenaeus's time who denied the historical reality of Christ. There must be a continuity between human history and the history of Christ. Otherwise death is the end of history. The death of a human being cannot be understood apart from the death of Adam and the death of Christ, but in Christ the human being can be formed into the shape of life rather than death.

Although these shapes represent a multiplicity of voices describing death in the Christian tradition, Pelikan argues that one figure, not a geometric figure but the figure of a cross, can bring them all together. The believer is signed with the cross at baptism and again at death. Disclosing God's capacity to know the meaning of human suffering and death, the cross encompasses the circle and describes the analogy between human life and eternal life in God. More radically than the triangle, the cross brings together the horizontal and the vertical lines in the shape of death. It "defines the lowest point and at the same time it delineates both the origin and destiny of the parabola of eternity." In Christ, the figure on the cross, "the spiral of history is fulfilled, and drawn clearly for all to see and, seeing, to believe."[6]

The value of hearing these voices from the church fathers struggling with death is that it can remind us that there is more than one voice today as well. The fact that Pelikan presents a variety of ways in which the classical tradition has interpreted limit and loss should open the pastoral carer to the variety of ways a person today may address the same issue. The struggle of the Christian carer today is not a new one or one for which there is a single right answer. Whether or not the figure of the cross can offer the Christian carer one shape or voice that unifies all the voices is a question that each person must decide.

One of the richest twentieth-century theological interpretations of the dimension of limit in the problem of limit and loss appears in Karl Barth's discussion of "man in his time." "To be man," Barth says, "is to live in time. . . . If this life of his is real, so too is his time as the stage on which he lives out his being." "Human life means to have been, to be, and to be about to be. Human life means to be temporal." "The time given to man tells him that he is not only the creature of God, but His covenant-partner. It speaks of God's faithfulness to Himself and His creature." But, says Barth, the time God gives is limited. "The span begins at a certain point, lasts for a certain period and finally comes to an end." "It is only . . . as allotted time, that time is his time." "For at a certain point life began. Now we are somewhere in the middle or before or after the middle. One day it will be over. This is how we are in time. This is our allotted time, and no other."[7]

Another twentieth-century theologian who addresses the problem of limit and loss is Eberhard Jungel, who describes death as "an event of relationlessness" in which the relationships of a person's life are completely broken off. The Christian hope of resurrection, however, involves the finite life of humankind's being made eternal. "Not by endless extension—there is no immortality of the soul—but through participation in the very life of God. Our life is *hidden* in his life."[8]

Daniel Migliore has said that human relationality makes us particularly vulnerable to the losses involved in death; that Christian confidence in the face of death is based not on human accomplishments or belief in immortality, but on the grace of God as revealed in Jesus Christ, from which nothing can separate us; and, finally, on that awareness of the incompleteness of the work of redemption, that God's final victory over evil is to come in the future.[9]

And finally, writing on "Eschatology and Pastoral Care," Jürgen Moltmann has said, "The soul is not immortal but the *spirit of God* is immortal, which already here, in this life, fills believers with the power of the Resurrection (Rom. 8:11)." Where God's life-giving Spirit is experienced, eternal life is experienced before death. "Wherever persons get close to the creative ground of lived life, death disappears and they experience continuance without perishing. . . . Death . . . is neither the separation of the soul from the body nor the end of body and soul but the transformation of the spirit of life, which fills body and soul, into the new, transfigured world-order of God."[10] Most important in this Christian message about death and about human limit and loss is that death is not a final separation.

In touching on some of the resources of the Christian tradition, I am doing what Susan was asked to do, namely, engage theology and the Bible and see what they have to say to the experience of limit and loss in the hospital. In one of Frederick Buechner's novels, the narrator and central character, Antonio Parr, experiences his own human limit at the grave of his sister. "I became aware," he says, that

> I didn't just have a body, I *was* a body. It was like walking into a closed door at night. The thud of it jolted me down to the roots of my hair. The body I was going to be dead. . . . You might say

that there at my sister's grave I finally lost my virtue, saw the unveil-
ing of middle-age's last and most intimate secret. There in Brooklyn
I was screwed by my own death."11

In a later book, Buechner relates this insight from the novel to
his own experience and the recognition that his death will be "a
nonevent which I will no longer have or be a self to participate in
it with," but in the light of that insight he is able to speak of trusting God with his own death.

> I begin . . . to see that death is not merely a biological necessity but
> a necessity too in terms of the mystery of salvation. We find by los-
> ing. We hold fast by letting go. We become something new by
> ceasing to be something old. This seems to be close to the heart of
> that mystery. I know more now than I ever did about the far side of
> death as the last letting-go of all, but I begin to know that I do not
> need to know and that I do not need to be afraid of not knowing.
> God knows. That is all that matters. . . . All's lost. All's found.12

In reviewing some of the Christian tradition's message about
death, one can see richness and variety. Not all these views will be
personally satisfying and in keeping with one's personal theological convictions. What is most important, however, is that one's
calling to ministry involve continuous *exploration of* or *dialogue
with* the Christian message. The sources I have turned to here are
challenging to me, but different resources from the classical paradigm may be more helpful to other Christian carers. If one is committed to care, then one must be familiar with the message that
informs that care and which the carer represents. One can offer
pastoral care effectively before he or she knows the message well,
but the dialogue with the message must be alive and continuing.

Limit and Loss in the Clinical Pastoral Paradigm

The clinical pastoral paradigm reminds the pastoral carer that if
the message of Christian care is to be heard and remembered, the
person representing the message is a major element in conveying it.
And it is not just the person of the pastor that is important. The relationship between the carer and the one cared for must also be attended to. Because of this emphasis on the person, the clinical
pastoral paradigm has made explicit use of psychological theory in
understanding the persons involved in the pastoral care relationship. Theology has, of course, always made use of psychology. The
difference made under the influence of the clinical pastoral paradigm is that psychological theories about the person have been

explicitly used. In trying to understand and interpret the problem of limit and loss, therefore, attention to some of the important psychological material on grief and loss is essential for the pastoral carer.

In her excellent popular book *Necessary Losses*, Judith Viorst comments that when we think of loss, "we think of loss through death of people we love. But loss is a far more encompassing theme in our life. For we lose not only through death, but also by leaving and being left, changing and letting go and moving on." A few of the "necessary losses" that Viorst points to are the facts that our mother is going to leave us, and we will leave her; that what hurts us cannot always be kissed and made better; that we will have to accept, in other people and ourselves, the mingling of love with hate, of the good with the bad; and that we are utterly powerless to offer ourselves or those we love protection from danger and pain, from the inroads of time, from the coming of age, and from the coming of death. "These losses are a part of life—universal, unavoidable, inexorable. And these losses are necessary because we grow by losing and leaving and letting go."[13]

The "capacity to master separation facilitates growth by permitting an openness to losing the familiar, be it people or their support. Separation mastery allows the individual to face the specter of ambiguity and aloneness that accompanies surrendering ideals, hopes or self images."[14] Similarly, Robert J. Lifton has suggested: "There is no love without loss. And there is no moving beyond loss without some experiencing of mourning. To be unable to mourn is to be unable to enter the great human cycle of death and rebirth."[15]

Mourning

Most simply defined, mourning is the period of time it takes to let go of what has been lost and to become accustomed to living without it. It is not a pathological phenomenon but a life-giving journey that may lead to a deepened sense of identity. In his classic paper, "Mourning and Melancholia," Freud presented the ideal that an important way of dealing with grief was to identify with the longed-for person. Thus the pain of permanent separation is diminished by internalizing a part of the lost person. It is similar to the way the child copes with the many small separations of parental unavailability by creating an internal representation of the caregiver's presence. The significance of separation for each person originates in the caregiving relationships of early life, which create a psychological foundation for later relational experience. This foundation has been called a variety of names, such as object constancy, a cohesive sense of self, and secure attachment. It is important for dealing with later separations and losses in life both for the value of the foundation itself and for understanding separation and loss through the study of how it develops.

The pattern for mourning may be seen in the child's natural drive toward separation from the mother. In her study of children separated from their families in World War II England, child psychoanalyst Anna Freud commented:

> The war acquires comparatively little significance for children so long as it only threatens their lives, disturbs their material comfort or cuts their food rations. It becomes enormously significant the moment it breaks up family life and uproots the first emotional attachments of the child within the family group. London children, therefore, were on the whole much less upset by bombing than by evacuation to the country as a protection against it.[16]

John Bowlby's trilogy, *Attachment and Loss*, deals with the fundamental nature of human relationality under the apparently more scientific rubric of "attachment." Bowlby, who early in his training was a student of Melanie Klein, sees human attachment as necessary for biological survival and continuous throughout life. He believes that it is at least of equal significance with feeding behavior and sexual behavior. Attachment behavior plays "a vital role" in human life "from the cradle to the grave."[17]

Also studying children separated from their mothers, Bowlby observed a three-stage reaction process. The infant (1) protests acutely; (2) falls into deep despair; and (3) finally gives up and becomes superficially adjusted to the separation, but detached. Infants who are repeatedly left and disappointed will do whatever they can do to adapt to what appears to be their abandonment and chronically unmet needs. Self-negation begins when the natural response to chronic frustration becomes too much to bear.[18]

Similar to Klein, but with a very different language, Bowlby also affirms the power of separation anxiety as a natural and inevitable response to the absence of an attachment figure. His own view is a variation of Freud's "signal theory," in which anxiety is essentially a warning of danger—in this case the leaving of the parenting one—and an announcement of a frustrated attachment, which is distressing in itself and not just a signal of something more dangerous.[19]

According to Bowlby the first phase of mourning involves a *numbing,* which includes a denial of the news of the loss. What Bowlby calls "defensive exclusion" enables the person experiencing the loss to direct her thoughts away from the unwanted situation.

During numbing there is a sense of estrangement, in which nothing seems real. Bowlby's second phase is *searching-yearning,* in which the bereaved person is preoccupied with thoughts of the lost one. Bowlby describes searching-yearning experiences in which the survivor of an intimate relationship pays significant attention to those parts of the environment in which the lost one was most likely to be found.[20]

The value of these theories is that they place limit, loss, and grief at the very beginning of the developmental process, as an integral part of it. Loss, therefore, cannot be viewed as simply an experience contradicting life—somehow an exception to the life process. It is a part of living from the beginning. Each person has some preparation for loss and grief.

The psychological theorist who has most effectively interpreted infantile mourning is Margaret Mahler. Mahler was a pediatrician who later became a psychoanalyst and who developed a separation theory that conceived of it as a process directed toward individuality and autonomy. She saw separation as part of a larger developmental process of psychological differentiation. In Mahler's theory the infant is at first self-absorbed. She calls this "normal autism." As the infant develops attachment to its mother, Mahler theorizes that there is a stage of symbiosis or a merger with the parent in which there are very poorly defined self and other boundaries. Gradually, however, the child develops a sense of psychological separation, and finally, at about two and a half to three years, achieves a state of object constancy. "The achievement of object constancy is thought to bring about an entire reorganization of the organism that affects all of development and is so fundamental that Mahler labels this stage 'the psychological birth of the infant.'"[21] Object constancy here means that the child is able to stay away from the parenting person for a significant time without losing faith that she or he is coming back and is not lost forever.

Mahler's theory has been convincingly criticized by Daniel Stern, who has presented a variety of evidence to show that even at birth the infant does not exist in the undifferentiated autistic state posited by Mahler. Stern's observations point to early differentiation and relationality that contrast significantly with Mahler's theory.[22] More important than debating whether Mahler's autism stage actually exists in infants, however, is affirming the value of her way of affirming the basic nature of human relationality. At the beginning the infant has a significantly diminished sense of the other and a relatively undefined sense of self. Through development, both awareness of one's self and of the other increases, as does differentiation between the two. For our specific purposes here, Mahler's theory of infantile mourning can be seen as preparation for a life of limit and loss. As a part of a theory of persons who are essentially relational, the process of differentiation that Mahler conceived can be usefully applied to other significant losses of relationship and the subsequent mourning that follows them.

Kerry P. Duncan, a pastoral counseling colleague in Atlanta, has used Mahler's theory to interpret a pastoral experience with a grieving member of his former parish, a woman in her mid-sixties, whom I will call Jean. Prior to the death of her husband, Tom, he and Jean lived together on a four-hundred-acre farm in central Georgia. They had been married for forty-one years. Together they had raised seven children. After Tom's death the pastor visited Jean at least twice a month for the next four and a half years and made notes on this relationship. As a part of his master of theology thesis, he interpreted Jean's experience in relation to Mahler's theory of infantile mourning.[23] I present a much abbreviated version of his report—partly in my words, partly in his—on what happened. I can only touch on some of the richness of this pastoral experience.

It was summer, the time to pick tomatoes, carrots, and beans. For years this had been their pattern. There was comfort in the routine of picking vegetables. It meant togetherness, not boredom. Pleasantries, compliments, and sweet words did not exist here. Doing meant more than words. Following one behind the other in the garden, they worked, one weeding, one picking the best for the table, leaving the rest for the birds. But today their togetherness would end.

A storm had come up, and lightning struck the barn. Inside it was enough hay to last the cows for half the winter and a '39 Ford pickup. Tom ran to the barn to get the truck out. Even for an experienced farmer it was hard to recognize the danger, because there were so few flames. When the blast came, Jean recognized that it meant death. He lived for a while, but within twenty-four hours he had fallen into a coma. Within a few hours of that he died. Jean did not deny Tom's death. What she experienced was a period of craziness, of being in a daze, and of being in a shell and isolated, as in Mahler's period of autism.

That period, however, did not last long. Gradually she became more aware of herself. Jean, like Mahler's infant, began to move toward an external preoccupation with Tom. She wore his flannel shirts and carried with her the aluminum cross Tom had normally kept in his pocket. At night she placed his pajamas neatly on the pillow beside her on the bed. In the morning she returned them to the drawer. What was happening was like Mahler's symbiotic phase, where the infant's need for the mother is absolute. Jean's boundaries, like the infant's, were blurred. She began to see more and more of Tom's traits in their son. "I knew he was not Tom," she said, "but I couldn't seem to help it. I saw Tom when I looked at my son. I feel guilty when I think about it. It's like when Tom died our son lost both his mama and his daddy."

This brief inclusion of her son into her feelings for her husband was a positive experience in that during this early stage of mourning it enabled Jean to make "me" and "not me" distinctions. Mahler notes that children who are able to reconstruct a symbiotic unity with a substitute mother—as, in effect, Jean did with her son, are better able to proceed toward individuation than those unable to do so.

The next phase of mourning involved Jean's exploring Tom's life history. She put old photographs in order and remembered with her pastor the good times—and some of the bad times—they had had together. She was beginning to see Tom separately from her and with a good deal of clarity. She was preoccupied with Tom's things, his pajamas and shirts, but at this point in the process they were more reminders than a way of clinging to an identity with him. Tom had been a diabetic, and their life together involved monitoring sugars, fats, and starches. At a family dinner with her children, Jean left the table and returned with a bowl of sugar. As she shared this with the pastor, she spoke of it as an increased awareness of her family and a loosening of her constant awareness of Tom.

Preacher, you know that thing underneath the sink? The trap?

Yeah.

Last night mine got backed up, and nothing would go down. You know what I did? I went out to his toolbox. He would have flipped if he'd seen me in his tools. Anyway, I got out one of his big wrenches, climbed up under there and fixed it.

You did?

Yeah, and you know what? It wasn't nearly as hard as I thought it would be.

Mahler describes the child as practicing her differentiation by autonomous functioning. Differentiation from the mother allows the child to relate to a variety of mother substitutes. Separation anxiety decreases, and the need to cling exclusively to the mother wanes. Sometimes the mother can try to push this process along, encouraging the child's separation. Jean's family tried to move her along in her mourning, but she resisted it. By now Jean was into her second year of mourning. Members of her church and of the community were disturbed that she was not yet over Tom's death, but viewing the process of mourning in terms of Mahler's theory, much of what she had done seemed natural and normal.

The final phase of the separation-differentiation process for Mahler occurs when the child begins experiencing extended periods away from the mother as well as a desire for a widening range of relationships. Jean began to take a more active interest in running the farm. She ordered some new cattle and changed the way the chickens were fed. She also bought a new tractor, commenting to the pastor that Tom would surely roll over if he could see the new John Deere in the barn. These periods of relative autonomy, however, were sometimes followed by feelings of guilt, frustration, and anger. It was like the child's experiencing anxiety about getting too far away from mother and needing to go back to the old ways for emotional refueling.

At the end of the pastor's report on his relationship with Jean, she was still resistive to many relationships in church and community. She had achieved a satisfactory degree of autonomy, but was very cautious about entering into much more than superficial relationships. The pain of the fact of loss was still too great.

I have shared the report of this pastoral relationship at this length for several reasons. First, it is simply and beautifully told, with care and great respect for the life experience of the person experiencing loss. Second, it also, quite obviously, had great importance for the pastor. He learned significantly about the way this person experienced loss and sought to relate this to a more general psychological theory that could aid him in preparing to meet other situations of grief. Third, although I have not presented that part of the thesis, it also stimulated the pastor to do some significant theological reflection on the experience of human loss. He sought to do what I am encouraging all pastoral carers to do—to bring their pastoral experience into dialogue with the best available psychological theory and with the classical theological themes of the Christian faith.

Influential Interpretations of Grief

One of the most important interpretations of grief for the clinical pastoral paradigm's concern with the person has been Erich Lindemann's pioneering study, "Symptomatology and Management of

Acute Grief," which was published in *The American Journal of Psychiatry* in September of 1944. The article affirmed grief as "work," something necessary for life rather than something to be avoided. In this he was following Freud's concept of "working through" a life problem and coming to a realistic insight about it and resolution of it. Lindemann described five things that he had observed in acute grief: (1) somatic distress; (2) preoccupation with the image of the deceased; (3) guilt; (4) anger; and (5) loss of customary patterns of conduct. On the basis of these observations, he theorized that there are discernable stages in the grief process that the grieving person and those who care for that person should be aware of. [24]

Granger Westberg's little book *Good Grief*, published in 1962, and at this writing still in print, is one of the books that established Lindemann's stages of grief as a part of popular, pastoral wisdom. Knowledge of these stages is still useful. Far from original when it was written and even less so now, *Good Grief* continues to sell, perhaps because people need to hear that grief can be good. Westberg's way of presenting the Lindemann stages is given below. Each sentence is the title of a brief chapter:

> We are in a state of shock. We express emotion. We feel depressed and very lonely. We may experience physical symptoms of distress. We may become panicky. We feel a sense of guilt about the loss. We are filled with hostility and resentment. We are unable to return to usual activities. Gradually hope comes through. We struggle to readjust to reality.[25]

A different, but complementary, perspective on grief was developed some twenty-five years after Lindemann's by Elisabeth Kübler-Ross in her pioneering studies of dying patients.[26] Lindemann's study of grief work concerned those who had lost someone close to them through death. Building on the work of another University of Chicago psychiatrist, C. Knight Aldrich,[27] Kübler-Ross studied the grief of the dying persons themselves. Some of the interesting difficulties Kübler-Ross had in undertaking her study at the University of Chicago hospitals in the 1960s are noted in her book. She found at first that there were no patients whom the medical and nursing staff would acknowledge as dying. Her allies in conducting the study, therefore, became the chaplains, who were more open than other staff members in acknowledging the fact of dying and discussing death with patients.

According to Kübler-Ross, the dying patient goes through the following stages: denial, anger, bargaining, depression, and acceptance. These stages, perhaps because there are fewer of them than

Lindemann's, have become even more familiar in popular and in pastoral literature. They have become the law, if not the gospel, about the way a person is supposed to die. Whether or not the stage theories of grief are accepted with that kind of rigidity, what is most evident is that pastors need to be persons who are "acquainted with grief"—with grief theory, but most of all with their own grief and with persons in grief. Loss and death may never be friends, but they should be very familiar acquaintances.

Two recent studies of grief have focused on grief that is "unrecognized and unsanctioned" or "disenfranchised."[28] Beginning with the now familiar assumptions that grief work is obligatory and that incomplete grief work results in dysfunction, the authors in these studies examine unauthorized grief and grievers. Whereas grief for family members has been strongly legitimated, the importance of grieving over the loss of close friends is seldom recognized as having potential intensity as well. The authors in these studies also call attention to the often overlooked need for grief work in children, homosexual and heterosexual persons living in out-of-wedlock intimacy, rape victims and adult survivors of child sexual abuse—particularly those who have kept the assault secret, AIDS victims who have hidden the nature of their illness, prenatal death, birth mothers who have given up their infants. The implication of these studies is that pastoral carers should be on the lookout for grief and grievers wherever they are.

Over twenty years ago in an issue of *The Journal of Pastoral Care*, I shared a statement of a rural preacher who was a student in a summer course on pastoral care. He was responding to a question about ministry in a situation of grief. As one might imagine, what he wrote reveals that he had not done well on some of the parts of the course that dealt with theory. When speaking out of his own experience, however, he makes a powerful statement about responding to grief. "It is not my policy," he wrote,

> to ask someone, lest [*sic*] prays when they have lost their loved one. For this very same person may have prayed more than I have ever prayed. In this case, I would rather be Silence. For I remember when my father die, many people come and say, "you have my deepest sympathy," but one person come to me without any words of sympathy or quotation of scripture to me. He sat with me. When I would stand up, he stood up. If I walk to the door, he would also walk to the door. I have never been so comforted and warmed by Christian love as I was at that moment. It reminded me of Jesus when Mary came to him weeping and said, Lord if you had been here my brother would not died. Jesus did not say a word, but

groaned in the spirit. Not many people at this time want someone
to pray for them but your present and Silence is the best expression
for pray at that time.[29]

Limit and Loss
in the Communal Contextual Paradigm

The clinical pastoral paradigm addresses the human problem of
limit and loss by focusing more on the grieving person than on
the Christian message about finitude and death. It offers comfort
through understanding that grief is a process and a "work" rather
than a pathology. At its best it offers the presence and silence of
the caring person in the face of grief. Its strengths, however, point
to some of its limits. In using stages to understand the grief
process of the individual it tends to lose some of the individuality
of the experience of loss—the way that it happens for each person
or culture. Much of the contextual element of specific griefs is
lost. Moreover, the clinical pastoral paradigm's focus on the individual person in grief and on the individual caring pastor tends to
ignore important communal dimensions in the facing of limit
and loss.

For example, as valuable as Kübler-Ross's work has been in understanding death and dying, her stages of grief have sometimes
become a rigid kind of orthodoxy both for health care personnel
and for friends and family of the dying. Stage theory as an interpretive scheme can reduce the anxiety associated with ambiguous
and unpredictable human processes, but when forcibly applied to
the realities of a person's life it may obscure rather than reveal the
character of the dying person. A valuable contextual critique and
corrective to rigidifying Kübler-Ross's tenets can be found in Larry
R. Churchill's "The Human Experience of Dying: The Moral Primacy of Stories Over Stages." Churchill argues that when "we become obsessed with these stages as normative protocol we are
treating dying as a technical problem."[30]

To put dying into stages is to place theory over personal meaning
and, in effect, deny dying persons the opportunity to tell what dying
means to them. Only the dying can say what their deaths mean and
how they should cope with them. Putting dying persons in stages
may help reduce our anxiety, but it distances ourselves from the
dying person and makes them less like persons to whom we can relate. "The notion of story," says Churchill, "is a corrective to this
heavy emphasis on stages. . . .'Story' is a category of interpretation
for the experience of dying which is logically prior to 'stage.'. . .

Stories are the primary texts; categorizations into stages are best seen as commentaries on these texts."[31]

Churchill acknowledges that the dying "do at times deny their diseases, become angry, depressed, and the rest. I do not deny the usefulness of these concepts," he says, "I simply refuse the powerful urge to make them foundations of our philosophy of care." More important than knowing that dying persons are bargaining is for them to be able to share with a caring person "what they are bargaining for, with what and with whom. . . . The fact that they are in a bargaining stage gives only a shell of an answer as to where the dying are." "It is the resulting disallowal and exclusion of the personal and idiosyncratic which makes the stage paradigm inadequate descriptively and conceptually . . . which makes the stage paradigm objectionable morally."[32]

Churchill concludes that "the notion of the dying as teachers and helpers reaffirms a communal framework for human meaning. . . . The emphasis on community is essential because it acknowledges our interdependence with the dying. The dying need to be part of a community, to be sure, but it is also true that the dying can teach and support the communities of which they are a part." [33]

It is also important to interpret grief work in the context of the family system. One person in a family cannot mourn and change without evoking mourning and change in all the relationships of the family. A former student and colleague, Louis Lothman, has examined the work of Ivan Borzormenyi-Nagy on denied mourning from a theological perspective and applied it to his own work on the pastoral counseling of families.[34] Nagy's normative picture of family relationships is one that emphasizes relational vulnerability and the capacity for mourning. He believes that mourning enables persons to relinquish their reliance on introjected images of parental figures and accept their own vulnerability. Nagy emphasizes that this is an intergenerational phenomenon and, although one generation may be more affected by the loss, family mourning is never limited to one generation alone. "Sensitivity to the systemic nature of mourning in families, either in the mutual engagement of mourning or the collective denial of it, is important for anyone who would recognize the communal dimensions of human life in offering care to families."[35] Although he insists that he is "not religious," Nagy's emphasis on the balance of fairness in the family makes his work more congenial with views of human relationality and vulnerability that come from the Christian tradition.

Louis Lothman's argument, based on a theological perspective developed from twentieth-century theologians Karl Barth, Reinhold

Niebuhr, Langdon Gilkey, and Jürgen Moltmann, is in keeping with the argument of this chapter that acceptance of limit and loss and the experience of mourning evoke an authentic human vulnerability and appear to lead to a richer human life and love. Insofar as mourning is aborted or blocked, however, it leads to destructive consequences in human persons and families. The pastoral carer, therefore, needs to become a midwife of mourning and a facilitator of the acceptance of human finitude and vulnerability.

The resources of a single pastoral carer to deal with the pain of human limit and loss, however, are usually not sufficient. A number of years ago, my mother, as a part of the completion of her grief work over my father's death and the acceptance of her identity as a widowed person, established a group at her church called "WHO." The name of the group stood for the group's motto and purpose, "We help others; we help ourselves." The group was directed by the members with a minimum of consultative help from the pastoral counseling minister of the church. The WHO group's focus was on getting persons like Jean, the Georgia farm widow, back into significant relationships again, through visitation and kind but persistent invitations to participate with others who had experienced a similar loss. As the brochure describing the group stated, "Those attending WHO have come through the experience of bereavement with a desire to fill the vacuum in life with service to human needs."

> Through the years of the WHO organization, it has been found true that as members feel stronger and more independent they move out into broader groups and embrace wider interests. During their stay they have shared their grief and faced the future, but above all they have shared the feeling of suddenly becoming half a person, which cuts across barriers of age and background. Members' ages run from about 35 to 70, but WHO has an axiom: the number of birthdays is not important; the age of grief is.[36]

There are WHO-type groups in many congregations. The structure is very loose. Those who come are called attenders rather than members. In that sense it is what some psychological theorists call an "open group." The choice to attend rather than the obligation of membership is emphasized. It is a ministry of those who have mourned to other mourners. It emphasizes common predicament and the authority of those who have experienced it to respond to others in a particular way. A specially trained clergyperson is used as a consultant on particular problems, offering some teaching on visitation and communication, but the attenders, using a minimal leadership structure, take major responsibility for the ministry that takes place.

Two pastoral events, one by an ordained minister and hospice chaplain the other by a lay pastoral carer, may illustrate what Churchill means when he speaks of the teaching and support that can be offered by the dying.

T. K. Lang describes his work as a hospice chaplain with Ann, a forty-two-year-old woman with whom he became acquainted some three weeks before her death. When he first entered her room he was told that he could not sit in a particular chair because it was occupied. Seeing no one there he asked, "By whom?" Ann answered matter-of-factly, "Death is sitting there all the time." Her creative self seemed to resonate with woodcuts from the Middle Ages that show a dying man surrounded by "friends and relatives praying for his soul, while under the bed demons with horns and claws awaited their chance to snatch the man from his faith and virtue into hell."[37]

As she came to know the chaplain, Ann expressed her fear of death but also affirmed the children and friends who supported and surrounded her with their caring. She also expressed her faith in God's care of her in the past and conviction of God's dependability in the future as well. Her expressions of her faith accompanied the handling of numerous practical questions having to do with disposition of various possessions and taking leave of her friends.

Ann planned a funeral service with those who were closest to her, choosing hymns, poems, and scripture. She asked her pastor of many years to conduct the service and requested that the chaplain speak at the graveside ceremony. Ann requested that all of her friends come to a party the evening of her funeral to celebrate her life and theirs.

During her last days Ann's friends filled her room with their everyday lives, making her a part of them. They assisted with her physical comfort, massaged her body with lotion. Chaplain Lang notes that the "cup of joy mixed with the cup of sorrow." It was quite natural when, in the midst of all these activities, he reminded them of the story of the woman who came to see Jesus bringing "an alabaster jar of ointment. She stood behind him at his feet, weeping, and began to bathe his feet with her tears and to dry them with her hair. Then she continued kissing his feet and anointing them with the ointment" (Luke 7:37–38).

Eventually, however, close to the end of her life, Ann had only her closest friends with her. Then, after having made sure that all the practicalities involved with death were taken care of, she asked the chaplain to hear her confession. She also wanted to "tie up loose ends and wind up the estate in relation to God." At the end of the liturgy, she received the absolution: "I do declare that your sins are forgiven. In the name of the Father, the Son, and the Holy Spirit. Peace be with you." Some days later she asked to receive Communion, the bread and the wine and the words: "The crucified and resurrected Jesus Christ has now given you his holy body and blood which he gave as atonement for all your sins. He strengthens you and keeps you in a true faith till the eternal life. Peace be with you."

Several days later she said goodbye to the chaplain and to two of her friends. She asked them to take her hands in theirs. They held hands in silence for a while. Then Ann asked them to let go of her hands, stretched her arms upward, and asked, "God, take me!" After that she asked for something to make her fall asleep. "I need rest," she said, "so that I gain the strength I need to die." That morning she slipped into a coma, and three days later she died. The funeral went as she had planned. So also did the garden party in her honor that followed the funeral.[38]

The AIDS ministry in Donna's church had been going on for more than four years. It began with the illness of Michael, one of the congregation's own members, when Donna and a few others recognized that the fearful illness was not something out there somewhere, but was a part of them, just as Michael was a part of them. The AIDS ministry is now the largest ministry group within the church, comprising some sixty members, and Donna has gone on to start similar ministries in other churches. She believes that the lay Care Teams are offered a gift by their sharing in the intimacy of the cared-for person's dying. "We lay people don't get this normally. Ordained clergy are sometimes invited in, but rarely lay people." To illustrate this, she shared the story of a particular pastoral relationship.

"The day before Gene died he said to me, 'Baby, give me your peace.'" Donna, a lay pastoral carer, shared her ministry to Gene and his ministry to her in this way:

> He was afraid to die yet because he just hadn't achieved the kind of peace that would let him forgive himself. AIDS patients fairly drip with feelings of guilt. They often seem to feel that nobody is a more terrible person than they are. As lay people we can say to them, "Who are you that you think that you can sin better than I can?" One of the most difficult things about being a Christian is learning to accept forgiveness. I said to Gene, "How dare you not forgive yourself when Christ has forgiven you?" That seemed to turn it around for him so that he could finally say, "Take me, Father."

"What this ministry teaches us," Donna said, as she told me about her ministry, "is to speak deeply about life and death.

Gene's family asked two of us who had cared for him to come up to Wisconsin for his funeral. It was in a large Roman Catholic church, and I was scared to death. I was sitting right on the aisle next to the casket, and when it was my turn to go up to the front and speak there I touched the casket, and I said, 'OK, Baby, it's time for you to give me some peace.' And you know, I felt it. I felt warm, and I was able to stand up there with a sense of urgency to tell those people about their son, my friend, and their neighbor. The gift of peace had come full circle."

There are many things that could be examined and interpreted in Donna's ministry to Gene, but perhaps the most striking one is her sense of authority as minister to a dying patient. This is not merely a ministry of emotional support and attending to the physical needs of a dying patient. Donna has done that, to be sure, and that has made it possible for her to "speak peace" to Gene. No one has said to her the words said to the ordained clergy, "Take thou authority. . . ," but the radical nature of the situation and her own faith seem to have gone together to give her the conviction that she has the authority to offer benediction. Something of the uncertainty of her ministerial role comes through in the feelings she remembers at the funeral service, which seemed to be, "Who am I to be speaking here?" But she reaches symbolically to the casket and regains her ministerial authority to speak to the congregation from her relationship to the patient. Pastoral care is not the work of the clergy alone. It is the work of the whole caring community and the members of that community who accept pastoral care as a central part of their calling as Christians.

Some Final Reflections

God knows "how we were made," knows our limitedness, and yet remembers us. God's surprising promise is that as "those who mourn" our limits and losses, we shall be comforted. Pastoral care, understood as hearing and remembering, is bifocal. It attends deeply to the particularities of human existence, the details of the specific problems experienced by persons needing care. But it also looks beyond the problem to question what the problem is saying about the direction and character of the person's life. Where is he or she as a person in relationship with other persons and with God? The pastoral carer hears and remembers who the troubled person is in the larger context of life and death in God's world, a reality the grieving person may have never known or may have forgotten.

The message that God knows and God remembers is most powerful in relation to the problem of limit and loss. It can make caring possible in spite of the fact of loss. Pastoral caring for persons experiencing their limits and facing the loss of life or other radical losses can make clear the importance of care when cure is not possible. It is offering the gift of presence and relationship "now and in the hour of our death."

Questions for Consideration

1. This chapter has touched on only a few resources from the Christian tradition that address this profound human problem. What resources from the tradition are most helpful for you? What supports your belief that God remembers and blesses those who mourn?

2. How are you, and how is the patient that you are caring for, dealing with the polarity of body and soul—what Buechner described as the discovery of not just having a body but being a body?

3. In what way, if any, is the theoretical connection between the separation involved in early childhood development and the separation involved in later limit and loss helpful in understanding the human relationality and what is involved in losing it?

4. How is mourning and the failure to mourn expressed by the individual, the family, and the larger society?

5. What are the relative values of stages and stories in the mourning process? How do both ways of thinking about the process of dying help or get in the way of our understanding the experience of loss?

6. What are the functions of the common-problem support group in caring for persons who have lost a significant other? How does a pastoral consultant contribute to the ministry of such a group?

6

Patience and Patienthood—
The Need for Care

Pacience, as Poets say, and Philosophers, is a great vertue: Pacience is the best medicine that is, for a sicke man, the most precious plaister that is, for any wounde: pacience comforteth the sadde, gladdeth the mournful, contenteth the poore, healeth the sicke, it easeth the afflicted, contenteth thy friendes, annoyeth thyne enimies, helpeth all men, hurteth no man, it is a great thynge to fynde one man that is pacient.

—John Florio, 1578[1]

Pastoral caring involves patience and an understanding of patienthood. I recall the words from patients and families, "You never seemed in a hurry," as perhaps the warmest expressions of appreciation I heard during my years as a hospital chaplain. This chapter, therefore, deals with the human problem of the need for care and for patience, particularly as these needs are experienced in times of illness, pain, and suffering. It looks for the "pastoral" meaning in the words "being patient" and "being a patient," and argues that patience in ministry to the sick is perhaps the most important dimension of hearing and remembering. The chapter also explores the way in which pastoral carers themselves are patients. How is patienthood accepted or denied, and how is the fact that human beings are "those who wait" related to where they are with others and with God?

The concepts of patience, patienthood, and compassion are all important in describing the essential features of a good pastor. The terms patience and patienthood are derived from the Latin word meaning to suffer or to endure, from which the term compassion

137

is also derived.[2] Compassion has been described as "the virtue by which we have a sympathetic consciousness of sharing the distress or suffering of another person and on that basis are inclined to offer assistance in alleviating and/or living through that suffering. . . . In virtually all periods of history there has been an expectation that the physician and other caregivers be compassionate in the face of the pain and suffering experienced by those to whom they administer health care."[3]

"A case can be made for seeing compassion as the center of pastoral care. Compassion makes caring specific. Compassion radicalizes caring, giving our caring root in the deepest places of God's being."[4] The pastoral task in the problem of patience and patienthood was touched on in the chapter on context: responding to what is specific and particular in the illness without losing what is generally human and without ignoring what the patient is besides being a patient. The question that this chapter raises is: How does one respond specifically to the patient's need for care, fully recognizing the uniqueness of what he is going through, but without using the particularity of the patient's situation to deny the carer's own patienthood? What should the carer be listening for? Can understanding more of the patient's situation help overcome the loneliness and separation he may be feeling? How can one carer be sensitive to how being a patient really is different, how the experience of illness, pain, and suffering have separated him from life as it was before the illness?

Patience and Patienthood
in the Classical Paradigm

Primary biblical authorization for the pastoral carer's visitation of the sick has come from the story of the Last Judgment in Matthew 25 and Jesus' words, "I was sick and you took care of me" (v. 36), but Jesus' entire healing ministry forms the basis for this concern. And the very early involvement of the community in this ministry may be seen in James 5:14: "Are any among you sick? They should call for the elders of the church and have them pray over them, anointing them with oil in the name of the Lord."

The classical message for the sick has most often involved the challenge of the body and soul relationship or the struggle between good and evil in the world. It has sometimes been a message that viewed illness as an opportunity for growth, and it has sometimes related the illness to sin and thus has seen it as a call to repentance. The message was important for both the cared-for and the carer in trying to find meaning in the illness. There is a wealth of literature addressing this issue. I give only two examples.

Luther's letter to Caspar Mueller in 1534 touches on some of the most familiar elements in the classical message:

> I am sorry that God has heaped more sickness upon you, for I am certain that by God's grace you are one of those rare birds who take the Word of God very seriously and are faithful to the Kingdom of Christ. I also know that your health and activity can be useful and comforting to us all. . . . But if God wishes you to be sick, his will is surely better than ours. After all, even that noblest and most innocent will of our Lord had to be subject to the higher and supremely good will of his dear Father. Let us be cheerful, or at least patient, in submitting to his will.[5]

Luther's message presented God as clearly involved in the patient's illness and saw that God's grace was somewhere present in it. The patient was affirmed as a man of faith who trusts God's word and one who is valuable to the community. It would seem that God would want him well, but God may have some reason for the illness that cannot now be understood. Therefore, the patient should take comfort in the fact of good having come from the suffering of Christ and be cheerful or at least patient.

Another useful example of the classical Christian message is given under the appropriate title, "Making the Most of Sickness," which may be found in Clebsch and Jaekle's *Pastoral Care in Historical Perspective*. It comes from Jeremy Taylor's seventeenth-century classic, *Holy Dying*. Clebsch and Jaekle comment that "Taylor was confident that sickness was sent by God for the edification and growth of the sufferer; the God who did nothing in vain meant illness to be a school of faith and virtue. Specific burdens and pains of disease taught their special lessons." Most important, they say, was that illness was understood to reveal the "precariousness of life and taught faith: the threat of the end of life reminded one that life was God's gracious gift." The sick person, therefore, was viewed as "God's attentive pupil."[6]

Taylor's own message is given under the section title "Of the Practice of Patience":

> Every man, when shot with an arrow from God's quiver, must then draw in all auxiliaries of reason, and know, that then is the time to try his strength, and to reduce the words of his religion into action, and consider, that if he behaves himself weakly and timorously, he suffers nevertheless of sickness; but if he returns to health, he carries along with him the mark of a coward and a fool; and if he descends

into his grave, he enters into the state of the faithless and unbeliev-
ers. Let him set his heart firm upon this resolution: "I must bear it
inevitably, and I will, by God's grace, do it nobly."[7]

One can see from this rendering of the classical message where
the influential image of "the good patient" might come from. A
lengthy interpretation of the person of the patient and his or her
experience of illness, pain, and suffering, using the psychological
theory that is so much a part of the clinical pastoral paradigm, follows this description.

Patience and Patienthood
in the Clinical Pastoral Paradigm

Medical ethicist Warren Thomas Reich has argued that the
"phases of compassion take their meaning from the leading questions that the caregiver asks himself/herself: What does this suffering require of me? What is a fitting response? How can I be the
sort of person who is responsive to the suffering of the one who is
before me, who is in my care?"[8] The clinical pastoral paradigm is
more concerned with the person giving and receiving the Christian message than with the message itself. This means that an attempt to understand the experience of the patient is of first order
importance. The pastoral carer who visits patients in hospital or
nursing home needs to have a good deal of knowledge of what it
feels like to be a patient. Fortunately, recent work in interpreting
the experience of illness has made that quite possible.

Susan Sontag has described illness as "the night-side of life," an
"onerous citizenship."

> Everyone who is born holds dual citizenship, in the kingdom of the
> well and in the kingdom of the sick. Although we all prefer to use
> only the good passport, sooner or later each of us is obliged, at
> least for a spell, to identify ourselves as citizens of that other place.[9]

In a book that can be a valuable resource for all those who attempt to care for those who are ill, Arthur Frank has written a series of letters to himself before he became ill. "I want to tell that
self," Frank says,

> to let yourself grieve your losses and to find people who will accept
> that grieving. . . . The losses you go through are real, and no one
> should take these away from you. They are a part of your experi-
> ence, and you are entitled to them. Illness can teach that every part
> of life is worth experiencing, even the losses. To grieve well is to

value what you have lost. When you value even the feeling of loss, you value life itself, and you begin to live again.[10]

Frank believes that the ill are responsible to express the experience of illness so that the rest of us can learn from it and that society has a reciprocal responsibility to see and hear what ill people express. "The question," Frank says, "is whether the rest of us can be responsible enough to see and hear what illness is, which ultimately means seeing and hearing what life is. . . . The mutual responsibilities of the ill to express and the healthy to hear meet in the recognition that our creativity depends on our frailty. Life without illness would not just be incomplete, it would be impossible. The paradox is that illness must remain painful, even to those who fully believe its necessity."[11]

Being a patient means dealing with pain. Pain may be defined as "acute or chronic physical, mental, or emotional distress associated with some disorder (injury or disease) or other unpleasant stimulus characterized by discomfort, which the mind perceives as an injury or threat of injury to one portion of the self . . . or to the self as a whole."[12] In a classic quotation from her essay "On Being Ill," novelist Virginia Woolf comments on the difficulty in communicating about pain and suffering:

> English, which can express the thoughts of Hamlet and the tragedy of Lear has no words for the shiver or the headache. . . . The merest schoolgirl, when she falls in love, has Shakespeare or Keats to speak her mind for her; but let a sufferer try to describe a pain in his head to a doctor and language at once runs dry. There is nothing ready made for him. He is forced to coin words himself and, taking his pain in one hand, and a lump of pure sound in the other (as perhaps the people of Babel did in the beginning), so to crush them together that a brand new word in the end drops out.[13]

Using Woolf's insight, philosopher Elaine Scarry speaks of physical pain as "unlike any other state of consciousness" in that it "has no referential content. It is not of or for anything. It is precisely because it takes no object that it, more than any other phenomenon, resists objectification in language."[14] Scarry offers a useful insight about the difficulties of understanding and responding to another person's pain.

> One might almost appear to be speaking about two wholly distinct orders of events. For the person whose pain it is, it is "effortlessly" grasped (that is, even with the most heroic effort it cannot *not* be grasped); while for the person outside the sufferer's body, what is

"effortless" is *not* grasping it (it is easy to remain wholly unaware of its existence); even with effort, . . . for the person in pain, so incontestably and unnegotiably present is it that "having pain" may come to be thought of as the most vibrant example of what it is to "have certainty," while for the other person it is so elusive that "hearing about pain" may exist as the primary model of what it is "to have doubt." Thus *pain comes unsharably into our midst as at once that which cannot be denied and that which cannot be confirmed.* (Italics mine.)[15]

Professor Wilbert George Patterson[16] of the University of Iowa follows a number of researchers and emphasizes the importance of distinguishing between acute, chronic, and terminal pain. It is helpful if pastoral carers can be aware of these differences. Acute pain, which lasts less than six months, is usually associated with some sort of injury, surgery, or disease. Patients are usually fearful of the consequences of their condition or anxious about the pain itself and what it means for their physical condition and style of life. Realistic reassurance that is specific and informative is usually helpful as well as the opportunity to verbalize their experience of pain.

Chronic pain is different in that it lasts longer than six months, and is more complex. Most of those who have studied chronic pain believe that it is not only a response to the nervous system but a learned behavior. It is a response that has been reinforced by various social and emotional factors. Another of the major writers on pain, Richard Sternbach, has said, "In acute pain the pain is a symptom of a disease, in chronic pain the pain itself is the disease."[17] In contrast to acute-pain patients, patients with chronic pain may not benefit significantly from talking about their pain. That attention, in fact, may simply reinforce the pain itself as a disease and a behavior. Instead, for chronic pain, prayer and medication, techniques of body relaxation, and other interventions aimed at reducing the domination of body over spirit and moving toward integration of the person as a unity of body and spirit seem to be most helpful.

Terminal pain is perceived by the sufferer as a signal of approaching death. It is a symbol of multidimensional loss of the physical, emotional, and spiritual aspects of the person's life. Its chief victims are the elderly, and sometimes the pain becomes a substitute for a more difficult-to-manage feeling of fear, anger, sadness, loneliness, shame, or guilt. The chaplain or other caring person may want to help the person with terminal pain explore what feeling is the most intense or what concern seems most dominant during the pain experience. Perhaps most important is some kind of truthful reassurance that the dying patient will not be abandoned as death draws near. The pastoral carer who is fully in touch with the Christian message of a God who remembers is best able to respond to this need.

Pastoral theologian Wayne Oates and his neurologist son, Charles E. Oates, note several typical ways that religious people respond to pain.[18] One of the most familiar to those who work in a hospital setting is *stoicism*, typically expressed by, "The Lord will not put on me more than I can bear." The stoic message is that one should endure pain free from passion, unsubdued by its grief.

An even more frequent response is *denial*. Based in Platonic and particularly Neoplatonic teachings about the unreality of the body, denial has a long history. Its familiar expression is, "If I had enough faith, I wouldn't be hurting this way." Various forms of mind-over-body religious expressions, such as Christian Science, institutionalize denial and under some circumstances may block pain. Pentecostal histrionics may relieve pain that has muscle tension and stress at its base. Hypnosis, religiously based or otherwise, may be particularly helpful with chronic pain by enabling the patient to alter pain perception, diminishing anxiety and depression and enabling him or her to become more functional and less dependent on others.

The name most often associated with the radical dimensions of denial is Robert J. Lifton,[19] whose research was originally focused on traumatic stress reactions related to war and later broadened to theory beyond that to offer a characterization of the world today. Writing about "the overall human struggle with pain," he sees many human beings suffering not so much with pain itself as from the diminished capacity to feel, what he calls "psychic numbing." "There is a close relationship," he says,

> between psychic numbing (including its acute form, "psychic closing off") and death-linked images of denial ("if I feel nothing, then death is not taking place") and interruption of identification ("I see you dying, but I am not related to you or to your death"). The survivor undergoes a radical but temporary diminution in his sense of actuality in order to avoid losing this sense completely and permanently; he undergoes a reversible form of symbolic death in order to avoid a permanent physical or psychic death.[20]

If it is not already obvious, it is important to assert here that there are some important positive features of denial. Most important is its "buying time" until the sufferer can take in or accept the full import of the suffering.

Continuing with the Oates categorization of responses to pain, there is also *magical thinking*—a blend of denial and stoicism. In such thinking everything is particular. There are no general laws or consistent causes and effects. The feeling, if not the verbal expression, is: I should be an exception and have no pain at all.

Most strongly based in the biblical tradition, however, is *realism*. Here pain and suffering are recognized as part of our creatureliness and limitedness as human beings.[21]

An older but still persuasive theoretical interpretation of pain and illness is that of psychologist David Bakan, who interweaves the concepts of disease, pain, and sacrifice as sources of knowledge about human being.[22] Although Darwinian theory sought to explain evolution without any notion of telos, or purpose, Bakan found the concept of telos essential for interpreting growth and development as well as illness and pain. According to his theory, organismic growth and development can take place only if there is a certain degree of telic or purposeful decentralization. At the same time, that very decentralization can result in illness and death.

"The human organism is both strongly individualistic, separated from other organisms, and strongly social, involved in a larger human telos." Bakan's thesis about pain is that pain is the psychic manifestation of telic decentralization. "Pain does not exist until there is an organism which has been individuated. . . . It is the characterizing experience of the human organism torn out of its larger telos."[23] Resonating with other writers about pain, Bakan comments that "actual experience of pain is utterly lonely, without words of its own to describe it." Experiences can be analyzed in terms of our distance from them. "If the distance associated with touch is something slightly greater than zero, the distance of pain is less than zero."[24]

Pain produces the outcry that evokes help by others. Having no other locus but the conscious ego, pain is almost literally the price the human being pays for the possession of a conscious ego. Medically, the most effective devices for the elimination of pain are those which eliminate consciousness entirely. Pain is the demand on the conscious ego to work to bring the decentralized part back into the unity of the organism. Phenomenologically, pain appears to the conscious ego as not a part of itself. The ego appears to be a victim of external forces.[25]

Bakan's theory is strongly influenced by his Jewish religious tradition and the relational psychology of the Old Testament. I find it to be persuasive in its capturing something of the dialectic of human existence or, as Paul Tillich might see it, the polarity of individualization and participation—the never-ending human struggle between individuality and relationality.

The Patient's Suffering

In this section, as well as in the preceding one, I am concerned with the pastoral carer's understanding more about the person of the patient and the way that he or she experiences illness. Although in the discussion of illness and pain I have necessarily touched on suffering as well, it is important here to note some of the contrasts that have been made between pain and suffering. Pastoral theologian James G. Emerson, for example, describes pain as something that happens to us. It is the result of being hit, hearing an unkind comment, being disappointed. It is the consequence of a loss, a death, a tragedy. Suffering, in contrast, "does not happen to us; we choose to suffer. Strange, even outrageous as that statement seems," says Emerson, what we choose to do with pain "is the key to understanding suffering and ministering to those who suffer. . . . Suffering . . . is a synonym for enduring." We may choose to die rather than *endure*, or we may choose to betray or blame another rather than assume a burden ourselves.[26]

Suffering involves the sufferer's choosing to endure. The Psalmist asks for a speedy response from God, but his words reveal that he also understands that suffering means enduring:

Hear my prayer, O Lord;
　let my cry come to you.
Do not hide your face from me
　in the day of my distress.
Incline your ear to me;
　answer me speedily in the day when I call.
For my days pass away like smoke,
　and my bones burn like a furnace.
My heart is stricken and withered like grass;
　I am too wasted to eat my bread.
Because of my loud groaning
　my bones cling to my skin.
I am like an owl of the wilderness,
　like a little owl of the waste places.
I lie awake;
　I am like a lonely bird on the housetop.
　　　　　　　　(Ps. 102:1–7)

Physician and medical ethicist Eric J. Cassell distinguishes between pain and suffering in a way similar to Emerson's.[27] He notes, "There can be pain (or other dire symptoms) without suffering and suffering without such symptoms." Suffering, he says, "is the distress brought about by the actual or perceived impending threat to the integrity or continuing existence of the whole person." Suffering "requires a sense of the future" when the future is understood as starting an instant from the present. "A threat, by definition, refers to the future. In fact, suffering is sometimes caused by the fear that a terrible pain will recur even though, at the time of the suffering, the person has no pain." A sufferer may say, for example, "If the pain keeps up, I won't be able to take it," at the same moment that she is tolerating the pain.

The idea of future disintegration, says Cassell, "requires an enduring sense of personal identity—the identity must be conceived of as continuing into the future. In addition, the person must have concern for the preservation of the identity, otherwise disintegration or loss of intactness would not be a threat."[28] The sufferer's fears involve not only the loss of the grand purpose of life, but specific day-to-day concerns about purposeful action, ordinary things like walking, seeing, and holding. There is an awareness that the ordinary, usual self will be lost.

In order to know and understand a suffering person, three kinds of information are required: (1) the natural facts of a person's life; (2) his or her values, or the contextual factors necessary to interpret those facts; and (3) aesthetic knowledge. Cassell has a particular understanding of aesthetic knowledge which he applies to understanding a patient. Taking a statement from philosopher Charles Hartshorne that life is a work of art, Cassell looks at a person's choices in life as a means of creation. The life created by those choices may be ugly or beautiful, profoundly moving or uninspiring, but it is important for the patient and for the helping person to look for and find a way of speaking about the aesthetic pattern that has been created by that life.[29]

Warren Thomas Reich describes three phases of suffering. The first phase is that of *mute suffering*. It involves being speechless in the face of one's own suffering. The muteness of the sufferer is a metaphor for the way that people are struck dumb by the force or unexpectedness of their suffering and, consequently, are unable to speak about it in a "language that will express their experience and their understanding of their suffering."[30] Reich believes that "an individual may experience mute suffering even when exercising the power of speech; for the significant muteness may lie in his or her inability to communicate with verbal, affective expression about the suffering itself."[31]

Following theologian Dorothee Soelle, Reich notes that a turning point comes when the sufferer is convinced that change is possible. For the sufferer can either adopt the attitude of stolid resignation to suffering ("that's the way things are") and apathy (not perceiving his or her own feelings about the horror of suffering) or can find a way to a new attitude of learning and changing. [32]

The second phase of suffering is *expressive suffering*, in which the sufferer seeks a language to express his or her suffering. That language, growing out of dialogue with a carer, leads the sufferer out of the phase of mute suffering and becomes a metaphor for the response to suffering. This language may be of three sorts: lament, story, and interpretation.

The first language to be heard from the sufferer is often a lament. The complaining quality of the lament can be an annoyance to the pastoral carer, but it is simply giving voice to one's suffering, and can clearly be beneficial. "The Psalms of lament, for example, are not lyrics of submissiveness but the sufferers' expression of their own innocence, of their desire to be heard, of their petition for a sustaining, caring presence. The voice of lament can play a crucial role in growth through and beyond suffering."[33]

Suffering's second and most familiar language is the story or narrative. The story grows out of relationship with a caring person and must be recounted in dialogue. Telling the story of one's suffering is a means of re-forming the mute experience of suffering. A suffering person tells his story in the hope that he will be able to reconstruct and thus re-create his painful and dislocating past, gain some distance from it or put it into perspective, and thus "possess" the experience as a way of putting the past behind him.[34]

The story is also told in order that the caring person may affirm the sufferer in the search for a new story, a story that will account for and justify a new self that might emerge from the suffering (pain, trauma) with wholeness or identity or pride or meaning or at least with hope.

The third language of expressive suffering is interpretive. It is articulated in the attempt to interpret and understand the suffering. The sufferer is a victim or a victor, a fighter or a survivor, somewhat like the wrestling Jacob who, having prevailed in his struggle, is given a new name.[35]

These recent interpretations of illness, pain, and suffering seem to me to contribute significantly to understanding the experience of patienthood, but there is an older interpretation of patienthood that is at the heart of the clinical pastoral paradigm. It is the experience and interpretation of his own illness, by Anton Boisen, founder of clinical pastoral education. Pastoral carers need to have some knowledge of how Boisen interpreted that illness.

First of all, he understood it as involving the significant disorganization of a person's world. Something has happened that has upset the foundations upon which that person's ordinary reasoning is based. Using his own experience, he looked deeply at what was happening to the person and sought its meaning without simply dismissing it as "sick" behavior.[36]

Second, the acuteness of the illness and pain may be a positive feature which reveals strength, struggle, and search. "The more sudden the onset and the more acute the disturbance, the more likely the patient is to recover, provided he can be protected from self-injury and from physical infection and exhaustion."[37]

Third, suffering is a remedial part of the illness. "As long as there is suffering," says Boisen, "there is hope. When hope departs pain and suffering also leave."[38]

Fourth, at its best the crisis of illness involves an appreciation of the seriousness of life's struggle and a search for meaning in it. "Most persons in these periods of crisis feel that their eyes have been opened to unsuspected meanings and possibilities in their lives."[39]

Fifth, acceptance of responsibility for oneself and one's illness brings suffering, but there is also the possibility of a positive resolution of the crisis which brings a person to a higher or more integrated level of being.[40]

Sixth, the person of the therapist, the chaplain or other caring professional, and the relationship between that person and the patient is the most important feature in the positive resolution of human crisis. "The fact is," said Boisen,

> that psychotherapy is far less dependent upon technique than it is upon the personal relationship between physician and patient. Wherever the patient has come to trust the physician enough to unburden himself of his problems and wherever the physician is ready to listen with intelligent sympathy, good results are likely to follow regardless of the correctness or incorrectness of the physician's particular theories or procedures.[41]

Much could be said about this person-centered view of illness extracted from Boisen's work. Most simply stated, its contribution is the affirmation of potential meaning in the most chaotic and confusing illness, the belief that the illness offers the patient a moral opportunity for change, and that a caring relationship is the most important facilitator of that change.

Patience and Patienthood
in the Communal Contextual Paradigm

First of all, there are perhaps as many meanings to illness as there are cultures. As a psychiatrist and ethnographer, Arthur

Kleinman has been concerned with the cultural meanings that mark the sick person, stamping him or her with significance often unwanted and neither easily warded off nor easily coped with. Meaning is inescapable, he says,

> although it may be ambiguous and although its consequences can be significantly modified by the affected person's place in the local cultural system. Persons vary in the resources available to them to resist or rework the cultural meanings of illness, which may present a problem to patient, family, and practitioner as difficult as the disease itself.[42]

Ethnic background and personality style also affect the experience and expression of pain. One of anthropologist A. L. Kroeber's interesting observations[43] was of one culture in which a woman would show virtually no distress during childbirth, while the woman's husband might stay in bed groaning as though he were in great pain while she bore the child, and in more extreme cases the husband would stay in bed with the baby to recover from the ordeal while the mother returned to the field to attend to the crops.

Variations in response to pain have been noted in studies of men wounded in combat as compared to civilians with comparable surgical wounds. Response to pain varied considerably, the wounded soldiers showing much less pain response, apparently responding more deeply to thankfulness at escaping the battlefield alive, whereas for the civilians the wounding of surgery was a calamitous event.[44] Attempting to take these cultural, contextual variations into account in responding to patients is one of the pastoral carer's important tasks, one in which she takes on the "mini-ethnographer" role and function to which I referred in chapter 2.

An interesting and useful contextual response to pain and suffering comes from Nel Noddings, the feminist ethicist discussed in the first chapter. Noddings has not been satisfied with the ways that men have addressed the problem of evil, including pain, in the world and proposes to substitute what she considers to be women's way. For her the fundamental human evils are combinations of physical and emotional pain—"pain that threatens our sense of being." Physical pain accompanied by hope of a happy outcome, such as in childbirth, she says, is not evil. Physical separation that induces emotional pain uncompensated by a sense of fulfillment, relief, or other positive effect is evil to the one who experiences it. Helplessness unrelieved by a sense of happy dependence is evil. Pain, helplessness, and separation are the basic human conditions, but they are not evil in themselves. Her characterization of evil is somewhat like Paul Tillich's characterization of existential anxiety. It is a given in human life and ultimately becomes destructive only when denied or when one attempts to escape it.[45]

Noddings seems to enjoy taking Christian theologians to task for their points of view, some of which can be seen in the discussion of the classical paradigm. She is highly critical, for example, of C. S. Lewis's *The Problem of Pain* and Lewis's conviction, which resonates with much of the classical Christian message, that evil and pain are redeemed by eventual conversion to good purposes. Similarly John Hick's argument in *Evil and the Love of God*, that there is no place in Christian thought for suffering and goodness being wasted, is offensive to her. Noddings insists that if we believe that God teaches us something or cures us of something through pain, then we may feel justified in inflicting pain on others in the hope of teaching or curing them. Instead, she argues, it is time to elevate the Law of Kindness to a position of equality with the Law of Justice.[46]

Her "answer to Job" is "a personal caring presence," which says, "I am here. Let me help you." This "answer," Noddings believes, does not turn attention away from those who need help and solace toward some eternal principle that should be grasped in order for a situation to be justified. Woman, in contrast to man, feeds Job and the friends who visit him, begs them not to fight among themselves, and counsels them on how to be reconciled to each other to achieve a better common fate. The fate she envisions is not the isolated man's awful fate of suffering in loneliness. It does not present an ontology of totally separate human beings but one of relationship in suffering. Obviously, in her struggle with Christian "answers" to evil and pain, Noddings has come up with what we might see as "answers" that might also be viewed as Christian.

Patience and Patienthood
in a Carer's Theological Journey

For most of her ministry Nora had served her church and her order as a teacher, but this year she herself was being taught and in a different way—as a C.P.E. student and chaplain at Grady, the big public teaching hospital in Atlanta. "I hadn't been at Grady for very long," she wrote, "when I began to feel overwhelmed by the enormous amount of grief and suffering which I witnessed and experienced myself."

But there was one experience in particular that was too much for me. I had been called to the Burn Unit to minister to the family of a mother and daughter who had been seriously burned in a house fire. As I approached the unit I noticed a strange smell which had a nauseating effect on me. I didn't know what it was at the time, but later I realized that it was the odor of burnt human flesh! As I came closer and looked into the room of one of the victims, I saw the body of a young girl, charred and swollen. It startled me so that I could barely move or speak. I had an urge to scream, but the sound caught in my throat, and I felt for a moment as if I might vomit. I began to cry. My body shook, and I turned away from the scene. One of the nurses came to me and put her arms around me as I continued crying. Her eyes, too, were filled with tears, and I heard a great deal of compassion in her voice. "I understand," she said, "I think I know how you feel." After awhile I said that I needed some space. The nurse agreed. I knew I could not deal with the family at this time, so I went down to the chapel and sat in silence. Later I cried and prayed, "Why, dear God! Why all of this senseless suffering? Where are you! Don't you care!" That evening after work I drove to Stone Mountain to allow the earth to heal the pain I felt. Remembering this experience in my "novice days" at Grady has urged me to continue my journey toward finding some meaning in the midst of this senseless human suffering.

Nora's pastoral encounter with suffering, shared with the caring community of her ministry group, started her on a spiritual and theological journey—a journey seeking to understand the "why" of human suffering and the ways of God. I believe that all pastoral carers who seriously address the problem of patience and patienthood must take a similar journey. All three paradigms for pastoral care are involved in describing the stops along the way, although as a theological journey the classical elements may seem the strongest. Each traveler may stop at different places and arrive at a somewhat different destination, but taking the journey is important for anyone who would actualize his or her compassion.[47]

Nora's journey began with the question of where God was in all the pain and suffering she had encountered in the hospital. How does God relate to the suffering of the world? Some of the stops along the way in her journey included, of course, Thomas Aquinas and his Aristotelian God who was incapable of suffering, but who permitted it in human beings; Gibran's *The Prophet* and the wise men of Stoa who felt themselves above true sorrow, but found that they knew no love either; Ivan in Dostoyevsky's *The Brothers Karamazov* who said, "If this great universe, with its wonderful realities and splendors, is bought at the cost of the tears of an innocent child, then I will politely refuse to accept such splendor from the hands of the Creator"; Yahweh's words in Exodus, "I have observed the misery of my people who are in Egypt; I have heard their cry on account of their taskmasters. Indeed, I know their sufferings; and I have come down to deliver them from the Egyptians"(Ex.3:7–8).

She stopped on the journey with Hosea and the root meaning of the Hebrew word for compassion, "to suffer with," and with the Ephesian writer who exhorted us to "be imitators of God . . . and live in love, as Christ loved us and gave himself up for us"(Eph. 5:1–2). She considered Elie Wiesel's God who hangs there on the gallows. When anyone suffers, God is there. Most different and uncomfortable for her was a serious consideration of Jürgen Moltmann's book, *The Crucified God*, where both Father and Son suffer, perhaps most radically in the Father's abandonment of the Son to the cross.

Most nearly satisfying, however, was Schillebeeckx, who managed to hold on to his Thomism and affirm that God is pure being, pure positivity. Negativity can gain no foothold in God. Schillebeeckx cannot believe with Moltmann that God could abandon his Son to the torture of the cross. This would make God less than what a normal human being is. The cross cannot be between God and God but between God and all that is opposed to God in the world. Human rationality fails before the suffering in the world, but God does not suffer. Instead, God keeps vigil with Jesus on the cross until the eschatalogical act of the resurrection. We are saved, says Schillebeeckx, not by the cross and suffering, but in spite of it.

That is a sketch of Nora's theological journey, from the pain and stench of the burn unit, through many ideas about God and suffering, and finally arriving close to home with a God of pure positivity whom she found first at the mountain and then in Schillebeeckx. For me, and I hope for most pastoral carers, Nora's story helps encourage a similar journey for all those who seek to offer compassion that is informed by the Christian message, a response to the person of the patient and the carer's own person, and a serious awareness of the contextual issues that affect the patient's understanding of his situation.

My own attempt to understand pain and suffering does not affirm God's pure positivity as Nora did, but holds to a belief in a negativity, a nonbeing that exists, not in God, but in the world God created and continues to love. It is a belief that brings me close to Luther and closer to the American philosopher and psychologist of religion, William James. Following the direction of theologians like Barth, Tillich, and Macquarrie, I believe that something has been introduced into creation by those creatures who slip away from God's divine purpose.

Nonbeing is, in my judgment, not a devil or a personality, but something objectively real that arises in the interaction between God and God's world. As Paul Fiddes puts it, it is something that happens when God "enters empathetically into creaturely experience." Suffering "cannot be simply something one does." Suffering "befalls the victim like a fate." Similarly, God suffers in falling victim to a strange and alienating experience that must meet a God who enters human experience. God encounters that which is most alien and yet most God's own because it springs from God's creation. "It is most alien in that it arises from the side of creation itself."[48]

Karl Barth's affirmation is that "God has negated the negative, saying no to nothingness by taking it in himself, so that there is always a 'yes' to man hidden under his no."[49] Christ has broken, judged, refuted, and destroyed *das Nichtige*.[50] *Das Nichtige*, according to Barth, exists solely because of the free will of the creature and the creature's lapsing from the good. Thus, God's will is indirectly the basis for that which is hostile to God. It came to be as that which God rejected when God elected good creation, but by saying "no" to it, God has given it objective reality.[51]

If God experiences hostile nonbeing when sharing in the life of the world, then the fall of nature, like that of the human being, must be a "strange factor" to God—practically inevitable, but not logically necessary. The whole of creation and not just humankind has some kind of free response to its creator and can turn away from God's creative purpose. This point is similar to that made by process theology, that evil arises from the capacity to refuse to conform to divine persuasion. As Whitehead states in his *Religion in the Making*, "So far as the conformity is incomplete, there is evil in the world."[52]

If God's suffering is to be like our suffering, then nonbeing must be something that happens to God in relation to the world, not just something that God actively undertakes. It is not only a feeling and an act, but an injury and a constraint. God's suffering is not, as process philosophy appears to hold, a creative involvement with negativity intended to yield tragic beauty. As Paul Fiddes puts it, "As supreme Personality, God determines his being as God 'for us,' and it is not our place to protest in an excess of metaphysical politeness that he need not have done so."[53]

God uses the death of Jesus Christ to define who God is. The experience of death that God endured in the death of Jesus is preserved in the life of God just as all experience in relation to the

world enriches God's being. "In the Christian story the risen one
remains the crucified one. As the image in the book of Revelation
reveals, the lamb in the midst of the throne has the marks of
slaughter upon him."[54]

In an article in *The Christian Century*, Professor Belden Lane has
used the same and other similar images in reflecting upon his experience with his mother's suffering in the last stages of bone cancer. "The grotesque," says Lane,

> is a daring exercise in summoning the absurd, making fun of what
> is feared. Its goal is to defeat—at least in the space of a long mo-
> ment's laughter—the power of darkness. It is an attempt to invoke
> and subdue the demonic aspects of the world. It reminds us of
> what used to be called the *via negativa*—the discovery of God's
> presence in brokenness, weakness, renunciation and despair.[55]

Some Final Reflections

The reader's theological journey in pastoral caring may be quite
different from Nora's and mine. My argument is not for the particular stops taken along the way, but for the importance of the
journey. In dealing with the human need for care, the fact of illness, and the experience of patienthood, elements from the classical, the clinical pastoral, and the communal contextual paradigms
will contribute to the journey that the carer takes, and in spite of
the difficulties along the way there may be unexpected moments
of grace. They may be like what happened to David.

The Elevator Man

He must have looked at my name tag [wrote David] and seen that I
was a chaplain. It was almost five in the morning. A little before
four I had been called to the emergency room where an eighteen-
year-old boy, an only child, had died, killed in a motorcycle crash. I
was there when the father and mother heard the news. The mother
fainted and hit her head on the emergency room floor. She was
taken into another room for treatment while I sat with the father.
When I left I felt drained of emotion except, perhaps, of anger. I
was reminded of Abraham and Isaac in Genesis 22. There God had
provided a ram, but where was the ram in this father's thicket? Why
didn't God provide a ram for him?

In my anger and despair, I heard someone say, "You a chaplain?
Ain't nothin' easy in this world."

It was the elevator man. "Who was it I was teaching about in my

Sunday school class?" he said. "You know the one who told the Israelites to turn from their evil ways."

Chaplain (only half aware of the question): That could have been a
number of people.

Elevator man (going on without hesitation): He wrote it out for
them, but the people wouldn't listen.

Chaplain: Was it Jeremiah?

Elevator man: You're right. That's who it was. You know, the people of Israel and the people nowadays aren't all that different.
We just don't listen. We keep right on doing bad and evil things
to ourselves.

To my surprise I realized that some of the anger and despair had
disappeared. I was beginning to feel peaceful. I remember wondering if this man could read my mind. He seemed, in his simple way,
to be talking to a part of me that I had lost.

Chaplain: The stories in the Bible could just as well be stories about
us.

Elevator man: You're right.

Chaplain: Those stories aren't about perfect people, but what I find
comforting about them is that God sticks by them. He sends to
them people who are there to keep reminding them of what
they have to do.

Elevator man: There are some strange stories in there, but nothing
stranger than what you'll see right here at Grady. Trouble is now
that the people won't listen now neither. They all say, "Repent!"
in their own modern tongue, but the good ones keeps dyin' and
the bad ones keeps doing bad like naughty children.

Chaplain: That's why we got to keep on trying, don't you think?

Elevator man: That's right. God's not finished with us. Gotta keep
reading the Bible, too. Those Israelites ain't all that different from
us.

Night elevator operators at Grady Hospital are not usually the
persons to whom one looks for wisdom and comfort in times of

despair, but perhaps the words of Paul apply at Grady as well as in Corinth: "Consider your own call, brothers and sisters: not many of you were wise by human standards, not many were powerful, not many were of noble birth. But God chose what is foolish in the world to shame the wise."

Questions for Consideration

1. What characteristics of pain seem most important for the pastoral carer to understand?

2. How does David Bakan's powerful theory of the polarity and paradox of pain and suffering relate or fail to relate to the life of a particular person whom you know? How did the struggle between relationality and individuality express itself in that person? To what Christian theological themes is that struggle related?

3. Do you believe with James Emerson that suffering involves choosing? What do you see as the "pastoral" message of that idea?

4. According to Eric J. Cassell, three kinds of information are required in order to understand the nature of a person's suffering: (1) the natural facts of a person's life; (2) his or her values or the contextual factors necessary to interpret those facts; and (3) aesthetic knowledge. How may these three kinds of information help the pastoral carer understand and minister to the sufferer?

5. Recall some of the apparently destructive "Christian" answers to pain and suffering that the Oateses and Nel Noddings identify. How have these answers functioned in the lives of patients, and what can contribute to the discovery of less destructive "answers"?

6. What are the steps along the way in your theological journey in response to suffering? What is your "answer to Job"? What are the problems with your answer from the point of view of Christian theology and pastoral care?

7

Abuse of Self and Others—
The Failure to Care

We must reach for the most complex psychopolitical understanding
of abuse and victimization without compromising our clear moral
vision regarding accountability.
—family therapist Virginia Goldner[1]

This chapter is about abuse: the failure of a person to care for her-
or himself and for others. The problems specifically addressed
under this rubric are the abuse of self through substance abuse
and addiction and the physical, sexual, or emotional abuse of others, persons over whom the abuser has power or control. To abuse
means literally "to take away from use," thus, to misuse or mis-
treat and, perhaps, to injure. The chapter, therefore, is concerned
with the misuse and mistreatment of persons, sometimes the
abuser himself or the abused herself. The argument of the chapter
is that shame is the most important concept for interpreting the
abuse of self and others. Moreover, similar to the assumption of
the two previous chapters about other problems, the assumption
of this one is that examining the problem of abuse can contribute
to an understanding of the ways in which persons deny or distort
their relationality with God and with other persons.

One of the important things that learning about the problem
of abuse offers to the Christian carer is a realistic confrontation
with the power of human destructiveness. The story of the father
who brought Jesus his son for healing after the disciples had failed
to help is a powerful illustration of the difficulty of resolving
many human problems. After Jesus healed the boy, his disciples
came to him privately and asked why they could not cast out the

159

evil spirit. Jesus' answer, as it has stayed with me from the King James Version, is, "This kind can come forth by nothing, but by prayer and fasting" (Mark 9:29). Abuses of self and others today are often "prayer and fasting" cases. Confronting these problems requires all the knowledge one can acquire and all the power and authority one can muster. It also requires time.

Faced with abuse of self and others, pastoral care as hearing and remembering takes on a somewhat different meaning. The hearing takes on a stronger historical focus. The pain of the present is important, but the pattern revealed by the past is even more important. The ongoing care of the pastor is most often expressed by remembering and confronting the abuser or the abused person with the fact that this has happened before and that the abuse is not to be minimized and denied. It must be addressed and addressed now with action or it will be repeated, and there will be serious or fatal consequences.

This chapter and the following one on the special relationships of the family are addressed more specifically to the ordained pastor than are the previous two. Care in situations that involve abusive behavior and for family dysfunction require more professional power and expertise than do situations of "limit and loss" and "patience and patienthood." This care also requires knowledge about the problem and knowledge about treatment resources available in the community. The ordained pastor is usually in a better position than the lay carer to offer the knowledge and the connections that can make those resources more easily available. Moreover, with problems of abuse and of family pain and dysfunction, what may be needed most is someone with the power of a professional role who can offer structure to the situation, enabling the persons involved to take action. The less structured care that is effective with grief and illness can be less effective with abuse, and may in fact add to the problem by inadvertently contributing to the denial of it.

Both dimensions of the problem of abuse—that is, abuse of self and abuse of others—are controversial. Those who work with abusers and the abused have strong opinions, advocate "strong medicine" to address the problem, and are often unwilling to think about the problem in ways other than those that have worked for them. This means that addressing the problem of abuse with some detachment, or without immediate commitment to a particular way of thinking about it—as this chapter will attempt to do—will be unacceptable to some of those who are deeply involved in it. With the problem of abuse, the pastor's empathy is an empathy of understanding more than feeling, and it often involves confrontation and challenge more than support. The pastor's primary responsibility is not to be caught up in the intensity of the abuse process or the ideology of abuse theory and treatment that says, dogmatically: This is the way it is and the only way it is. Whether the situation involves abuse of self or of others, it is the pastor's responsibility to be able to assess, evaluate, and connect the abusing person to an appropriate resource for help.

Understanding Abuse: Contributions from the Classical Paradigm

How is the problem of abuse related to the classical Christian tradition and message? Certainly, there are isolated biblical texts that deal with drunkenness, with rape, and with incest. The central message about abuse, however, lies elsewhere. It can be discerned when one begins with a dictionary definition of abuse as "misuse" or, perhaps, "injury," and places that in juxtaposition and in contrast with the kind of biblical understanding of humankind's purpose presented in chapter 1 of this book.

Humankind has been given dominion over all the earth. That dominion has been reinterpreted as care for the persons and things on the earth rather than as a statement of power over those persons and things. The human is pictured as a steward—one who cares for something in covenant with another. Human beings are entrusted by God with the responsibility of using wisely, developing, and nurturing what they have been given. In the Genesis story, Adam and Eve are a part of creation, but they have also been given responsibilities to care for it.

Douglas John Hall, who notes that the Bible as a whole contains some twenty-six references to the steward or to stewardship, believes that the "metaphor of the steward is sufficiently rich and inclusive in its original conception to be regarded an important symbol . . . for the whole anthropology of the biblical tradition."[2] Commenting on the Old Testament understanding of stewardship, Hall notes that "however important the steward may be in the scheme of things, he is neither ultimately authoritative nor irreplaceable. . . . He is strictly accountable to his lord, and he will certainly be deprived of his authority unless he upholds, in his actions and attitudes, the true character and wishes of this other one whom he is allowed and commanded to represent." Moreover, "from the one to whom much has been entrusted, even more will be demanded" (Luke 12:48).[3]

Within the biblical concept of stewardship, then, there is an emphasis on the positive nature of the relationship between the steward and the One for whom the steward carries out a task. Because of that relationship the steward is not just a servant, but a representative. There is an emphasis also on the responsibility of caring. It involves nurture and development, bringing that for which one is responsible into a better state than was present when the responsibility was given. Stewardship involves a significant relationship and a worthwhile purpose. Abuse of oneself or of others, then, involves denial of responsible relationship and failure to carry out one's given task.

The symbol for this failure appears in the familiar story in Genesis 3. Adam and Eve fail to fulfill their responsibility to care for and properly use what has been entrusted to them. This failure then resulted in an embarrassed self-awareness and a desire to hide themselves. They had become estranged from a proper relationship to their Creator and the creation that surrounded them. They had abused both their primary relationship and the task with which they had been entrusted, and, as the scripture points out, they were ashamed. Failure to honor one's stewardship or the failure to care and the shame that results from it is the major interpretive concept from the classical paradigm for understanding the problem of abuse.

The Old Testament has a good deal to say about shame, although not always relating it to abuse. Shame is understood objectively as the disgrace a sinner brings upon himself or herself (Lev. 20:17), or it may be the result of natural calamities such as barrenness (Gen. 30:23). It is sometimes viewed as divine judgment upon sinners (Ps. 44:9). A frequent expression is to "be put to shame" (Isa. 54:4, RSV) or "suffer disgrace" (NRSV). Subjectively, shame is experienced as a violation of one's honor and modesty (1 Cor. 11:6), or simply as a result of disappointment (Hos. 10:6).[4] Johannes Pedersen views shame simply as not having blessing. The source of shame is weakness, usually weakness in battle. Defeat "deprives the soul of its worth and shakes its self-confidence." "Where honour is the absolute maintenance of self, there shame must consist in being unable to maintain oneself." Nevertheless, Pedersen insists, "through prophets and psalms constantly rings the confidence that Yahweh will not let his faithful suffer shame."[5]

Gerhard von Rad's interpretation of the Adam and Eve story in Genesis 3 reflects the richness of this powerful and primitive human story. As he interprets it, Adam and Eve react to their taking of the forbidden fruit "not primarily with a spiritual feeling of guilt, but with bodily shame."[6] "Shame for our narrator," he says, "is the most elementary emotion of a guilty feeling at the deepest root of human existence, the sign of a breach that reaches to the lowest level of our physical being."

Another Old Testament scholar, Claus Westermann, points to three events in the narrative portion of the story: the opening of their eyes, the awareness, and the covering. Humankind's condition of other-awareness—knowledge and awakening from näiveté—is bought at the cost of painful self-awareness and shame. The aprons, the defense against nakedness, were an ineffective attempt to deal with shame. In fact, humankind's shame is uncoverable, but, interestingly, the struggle to cover that shame has a positive dimension in the creativity and color of the defenses that make up at least part of what we view as civilization.[7]

The biblical message about shame associates it with weakness and the failure to prove oneself worthy of trust. The human being is pictured as one who abuses or who may abuse what has been given into his care. Shame is bad, but, as Westermann's interpretation suggests, to be shameless is worse. It is to show oneself as not having taken in the values of one's community and culture. Whether dealing with one's shame or shamelessness, the human being is understood in the classical paradigm as one who may misuse oneself and others, hiding and denying what one has done. It is this condition that the pastoral carer must address in a situation of abuse.

Understanding Abuse: Contributions of the Clinical Pastoral Paradigm

Whereas the classical paradigm relates shame to the abuse of the human being's covenant to care, the clinical pastoral paradigm helps us in our understanding of shame and its relationship to abuse. The most persuasive interpreter of shame in the recent psychoanalytic tradition is Heinz Kohut, who places the origin of shame in the process of trying to meet relational needs early in life. This development is prototypical for later shame experiences. What the self needs relationally is *mirroring* and *idealizing*. Mirroring is associated with the human need for recognition. Idealizing is based on the relatively powerless child's need to feel as if she is part of something greater than herself. This at first has a grandiose quality, but later, if things go well, becomes realistic. When things do not go well in the developmental and continuing relational process, the grandiosity of the self leads to a paralyzing anxiety and the fragmentation of the self.

Kohut's understanding of empathy is the key to his theory. Empathy, for him, is not so much warmth or kindness as it is a disciplined, intuitive understanding of the other. It is the primary method by which we gain knowledge of persons. If things go well, the self learns the way in which empathic others experience the world and attempts to adopt this way of knowing other persons through what it experiences with them.[8] Human beings need the empathic response of others in the first few months of life in order that the self may be adequately structured. Similarly, empathy is needed throughout life in order that persons may be emotionally nourished. The normative human being is not the independent person, but the empathically related one.

With respect to shame as it appears in this prototypical situation of early life, the self asks for care, and for one reason or another fails to receive it or to receive enough of it. The result of not receiving it is shame at one's vulnerability and at the strength of one's need for care by the other. The first defense against that shame of exposure is a denial of the need, followed by a distancing of oneself from the other, and a compensatory turning back to the self as a substitute for the rejecting other person. Under optimum circumstances, when the rejection is not severe and consistent, the self may choose to endure the shame and maintain the relationship rather than denying the need and moving away. Under less than optimum circumstances, however, narcissistic grandiosity, which expresses by its action "I don't need anybody," is substituted for the experience of shame.

In Kohut's theory, shame is a response of the whole self to frustration and rejection rather than a struggle between conflicting parts of the personality. In order to survive and for the self to develop, the individual must internalize or "take in" significant others. When this process does not occur in a satisfactory way, the self turns to itself for nourishment.[9] Narcissism, the human phenomenon of the self's overconcern with itself, is the self's attempt to substitute self-care for care by a significant other who has been experienced as absent or inadequate.

The value of Kohut's theory for the pastor dealing with the problem of abuse is that it is a theory based in a relational understanding of human beings which resonates with a classical or biblical view. Moreover, it provides a valuable understanding of how the refusal to care or the failure to care may develop.

> It is the structural void in the self that the addict tries to fill—whether by sexual activity or by oral ingestion. And the structural void cannot be filled any better by oral ingestion than by any other forms of addictive behavior. It is the lack of self-esteem of the unmirrored self, the uncertainty about the very existence of the self,

the dreadful feeling of the fragmentation of the self that the addict tries to counteract by his addictive behavior.[10]

Jerome D. Levin, an addiction specialist who uses Kohut's theory in his work, says that the "alcoholic's pathological drinking serves to reduce tension and regulate self esteem in the absence of adequate intrapsychic resources to achieve such regulation." Moving from drinking to sobriety involves moving from an impulsive to a compulsive life-style. Compulsivity is a defense which performs a valuable positive function, defending against impulsive drinking behavior. In addiction, power and control are sought in fusion with an omnipotent self-object—alcohol; in recovery, they are sought in ritual, rigidity, and other defenses.[11]

The theory also provides a way of thinking about the shame experienced by an abused person. The breach of trust or misuse by one whom the abused person depended on activates the primitive feelings of dependence associated with early childhood—a time when the child was in fact almost completely dependent on a parenting person. Kohut speaks of "the lack of self-esteem of the unmirrored self" and "the uncertainty about the very existence of the self." In order to protect that person who is so important and upon whom the abused one is dependent, the shame and responsibility that should be taken by the abuser may be taken on by the abused person instead. The abusing person is temporarily protected from shame at the cost of the abused person's self-esteem. Although the pastor in a parish situation will not usually be involved in the treatment of an abused person, in his or her relationships with that person the pastor should be aware of the fragility of the abused person's self-esteem. The pastor should also know that much of the shame present may be misplaced and offer an informal caring relationship in which the abused person can recover some of her or his self-esteem.

Understanding Abuse: Contributions of the Communal Contextual Paradigm

The contribution of the communal contextual paradigm for pastoral care can be seen most clearly in our expanding awareness of the abuse of women and children and others with little power, the prevalence of which had simply not been acknowledged before. The beginning empowerment of those who have been ignored and oppressed allows practices that were assumed to be normative for everyone to be seen as part of a particular and arbitrary context rather than as the way things naturally are. For example, only when women were acknowledged to have a point of view that had as much validity as men's, did the physical, sexual, and emotional abuse of those with little or no power begin to be taken seriously.

Secrecy about the abuse, strongly supported by the power of shame, made exposure of the problem particularly difficult. Surely, anything so shameful could not possibly be true. Nevertheless, child sexual abuse has had a long history in American society. The necessary conditions for the accomplishment of abuse by trusted adults have existed in some, if not all, American homes for centuries. Until the ascendancy of psychology in the twentieth century, however, Americans failed to identify child victims of sexual abuse because such crimes were "hidden."

Laws prohibiting incest were slow to emerge. Disbelief that such behavior occurred and distrust of young victims marked the early opinions on the subject. Moreover, if the act did not cause pregnancy, the sexual act was not perceived as a concern of the law. On the other hand, children were perceived as accomplices whose testimony required corroboration in some form, preferably a confession by the defendant. If family members continued to stand by the accused, it was virtually impossible to convict.

Throughout the nineteenth century there was movement away from the assumption that sexual behavior could largely be regulated privately and toward a belief that females, defined in terms of their sexuality, were in jeopardy without public and legal assistance. "Early statutory rape law enforcement depended on proof of penetration and emission of semen. No lesser assaults were recognized. Courts seemed to care more about protecting young males from false accusations than protecting young females who were incapable of conceiving."[12]

In recent years, health professionals have identified a pattern of behavior adopted by child victims of sexual abuse and called it "child abuse accommodation syndrome." The syndrome is composed of five elements: (1) secrecy, which defines the circumstance in which the sexual abuse occurs; (2) helplessness, which defines the condition in which children are often given permission to avoid the attention of strangers, but are required to be obedient and affectionate with adults entrusted with their care; (3) entrapment and accommodation, which defines the child's initial response to sexual assault. Because she cannot escape or disclose the assaults without destroying the family and her security, she learns to accept the situation in order to survive; (4) delayed, unconvincing disclosure, often the child's response in a family conflict of authority; and (5) likely retraction of her disclosure if the assailant abandons her, calls her a liar, or if her mother becomes hysterical or does not believe her.[13]

The recent literature on the pastoral care of women has focused on the reality of male abuse of the less powerful and also brought out important insights about how the patriarchal system has involved women in that abuse. The thing that has been most surprising to male pastors or other counselors who have been told stories, particularly of sexual abuse of children, is the abused woman's anger at the mother for her complicity in the abuse. So often the mother tolerated the abuse or could not believe that it was happening because of her conscious or unconscious awareness of her own or her family's vulnerability if she attempted to stop the abuse. She was aware that she and her children might be turned out without any means of financial support—that their overall life situation might be worse than if nothing was done. The anger of the adult woman who was abused as a child, therefore, could be seen as focused on the social system that gave women little power or credibility as well as on the particular family member who was the abuser.

In their research for the book *Women's Ways of Knowing*, Mary Field Belenky and her colleagues note that they did not intend to be collecting information on sexual abuse, but found that in their interviewing "women spontaneously mention childhood and adolescent sexual trauma as an important factor affecting their learning and relationships to male authority." Of the seventy-five women interviewed, "38 percent of the women in schools and colleges and 65 percent of women contacted through the social agencies told us that they had been subject to either incest, rape, or sexual seduction by a male in authority over them. . . . Often the denial and silence that had been imposed upon them in the incestuous relationship carried over into present interactions with teachers who had power over them."[14]

Pastoral theologian and counselor Nancy Ramsey has reviewed some of the literature on sexual abuse and related it to three specific cases of such abuse. She notes some of the characteristics of abusing families, particularly having to do with shame. "Somewhat like the rape of an adult, abuse is an experience of utter vulnerability compounded by the fact that it is done to a child, who is even less able to cope. . . . The poignant absence of hope and gracelessness are consequences of shame many survivors describe. . . . Their pervasive shame begets a 'sickness of soul.'"[15]

The abused person is confronted with the destructive consequences of the sin of domination and betrayal, made even more powerful by the fact that the abuse was perpetrated by a trusted member of her family. Ramsey emphasizes the importance of the expression of anger, commenting that until women are able to express anger,

> they are hostage to it, and healing will not happen. Anger signals the necessity for change and a sufficient sense of self to know that what they experienced was wrong. . . . For some survivors, God and the church are so complicit in the experience of abuse that their understandable rage reduces the usual approaches to God to irrelevance.[16]

Ramsey argues that recovery involves making a sustaining relational connection with a therapist and, in most cases, members of a group of fellow sufferers. "The passage from identity as victim to a new self-understanding as a survivor is not unlike the hard but rewarding work of labor, especially when the image of labor includes a support team. . . . Recovery begins when the secret is disclosed and the shackles of silence [are] broken. A lifetime of silence has diminished the victim's sense of self and power to act."[17] The hearing and remembering of pastoral care may involve encouraging abused persons to recall painful memories in the context of a pastoral relationship or, perhaps more often, helping them find a group or other therapeutic setting where those memories may be shared and dealt with.

With respect to another kind of abuse of others, syndicated columnist Ellen Goodman has asserted that there is beginning to be a change in the public's mind about rape. There are only a few times when this sort of thing can actually be seen.

> This is one of those times. For as long as I can remember, a conviction of rape depended as much on the character of the woman involved as on the action of the man. Most often, the job of the defense lawyer was to prove that the woman had provoked or consented to the act—that it was sex, not assault.

Goodman discusses three Massachusetts cases of multiple rape in which there were three sets of convictions and notes how these verdicts reflect a change in public consciousness. She quotes the judgment in one of the cases:

> No longer will society accept the fact that a woman, even if she may initially act in a seductive or compromising manner, has waived her right to say no at any further time.

Goodman concludes that "it's time the verdict of those juries was fully transmitted to the culture from which violence emerges. If she says no, it means no."[18]

I have discussed the problem of abuse as a failure to care that is most likely related to the failure of care by the abuser's earliest caretakers. The classical paradigm offers a powerful symbol of this in the Genesis story of the Fall. The human beings misuse what they have been given to care for as stewards, and when their failure is exposed, they experience shame. An abused person also experiences shame, a misplaced shame which sometimes is protecting the abuser. It is also shame over being too weak to prevent the abuse.

The clinical pastoral paradigm's use of psychological theory places the failure to care or to care sufficiently in the early parent-child relationship. The abuser is one who attempts to deal with the shame of having not received what he sought in his primary relationships by abusing other relationships or turning his shame inward in the form of rage toward himself for his inadequacy and weakness. He may try to hide his shame in substance abuse or deny it by violating the boundaries of others in a futile attempt to get something that will make him feel satisfied, or, if a woman, by letting others repeatedly violate her boundaries.

The communal contextual paradigm makes us aware that this pattern of the failure in caring is not confined to individuals, but is expressed in social structure as well, in attitudes that encourage abuse of children, women, or other races and classes. Those in power tend to universalize their own behavior as normative rather than recognizing it as particular and contextual. A gender, race, or class that is in power holds on to that power by not being able to see things any other way or by a failure to experience shame over the way things are.

Pastoral Response to Abuse of Self

Although the pastor's *understanding* of abuse of self is significantly informed by all three paradigms, pastoral *response* is informed primarily by the clinical pastoral and the communal contextual paradigms.

Perhaps the most frequent human problem that confronts the pastor today is the abuse of self with alcohol or other drugs. For example, a leading member of the governing body of the parish is observed to be unpredictable in his attendance at important meetings and apparently unable to follow through with responsibilities he has undertaken for the church. The pastor calls this church leader, Joe Johnson, and asks if he can meet with him to discuss those responsibilities. When he stops by Mr. Johnson's house the next evening, the pastor discovers that Joe has been drinking heavily and has forgotten their appointment. Mr. Johnson apologizes profusely and asks to meet with the pastor the next afternoon. He keeps this appointment, and after a brief discussion of the responsibilities that he has undertaken and how he plans to meet them, the pastor asks him about his drinking.

> **Joe:** I don't think it's anything to worry about, Reverend. I've just been under a lot of pressure lately, and it helps me to unwind with a few drinks after work.

> **Pastor:** It does sound like you're worrying about something, Joe. Is it something you would like to discuss with me?

Without going any farther with the conversation between the pastor and Joe Johnson, it is important to consider how the pastor is thinking about Joe's abuse of himself with alcohol. His first responsibility as a carer is to express his care and to see whether Joe can talk about his feelings. The pastor leads from strength. He is not an expert on alcohol abuse. Joe may indeed be addicted, but the pastor begins with something with which he is familiar, people's feelings of hurt. He is familiar with that from his ministry in times of grief and illness. If Joe is able to share himself and his feelings and use the relationship with the pastor in a personal way, it may indicate that the alcohol abuse may be addressed indirectly by dealing with the pain Joe is feeling.

On the other hand, if the pastor's question about worry is met with denial of any problem, blame of others, the work situation, or something else, then the pastor may suspect that the abusive behavior—Joe's drinking—has been substituted for awareness of his feelings, and the addictive process must be addressed first. Certainly, I am oversimplifying a complex issue, but the first question a pastor needs to address is whether or not he or she can lead from the familiar point of working with human hurt. If not, it is important to begin the process of trying to refer Joe to the best available community resource for dealing with his problem. I say "begin," because the process will likely take some time. The pastor will probably want to tell Joe that he is concerned about his drinking and let Joe know that he intends to share that concern with Joe's wife, Jean. There he will repeat the process of seeing where Jean is with her feelings and consider referring her to a group, such as Al-Anon, for family members of abusers.

Most obvious in this brief discussion is the importance of the pastor's being aware of what resources for treatment are available in his community. If there is a for-profit treatment facility in the community, the pastor should know something about that facility's practices. Do its ethics balance appropriately with its need for patients? What other community resources are there, such as psychologists and psychiatrists with therapy groups for addiction-related problems? As I will develop further in the chapter on pastoral counseling, if the pastor is to refer as an appropriate expression of care, he or she needs to know what and to whom he or she is referring.

What theory does the pastor use to guide his pastoral relationship? The implications of what has been presented as the contribution of the three paradigms suggest that Joe's presenting himself drunk instead of being able to discuss his responsibilities to the church might first be interpreted by the pastor as a failure in stewardship resulting in shame. Family therapists Merle Fossum and Marilyn Mason have said that shame "exists passively without a name." "There are no words for the absence of an affirmation of self, as shame often is." The more active experience of shame, however, "does have words, like 'stupid,' 'weakling,' 'weird.'"[19]

The pastor simply does not know if Joe is feeling shame, but in the light of his failure to fulfill his responsibilities and being unable to keep an appointment with the pastor because of his drinking, it is not unreasonable to assume that he does. The pastor may wonder if Joe is feeling, to use Fossum and Mason's words, "stupid, weak, and weird." Does he appear to be blaming himself or others for what has happened? Are there nonverbal expressions of shame, such as averted eyes, lowered head, and slumped shoulders? Does it seem as if essential pieces of Joe's story are being left out, leaving the pastor confused and mystified? Joe may have come from a "shame-bound family" which promoted secrets and vague personal boundaries and unconsciously instilled shame in family members, binding them to perpetuate shame in themselves and others.[20] Or, on the other hand, does Joe appear to be "shame-less," completely denying that there is any problem at all? The pastoral encounter with Joe is inconclusive at this point. Joe is denying that there is a problem, but is doing so with more feeling than one would expect from a person in complete denial of a problem.

The pastor might wonder about the pain in Joe's present family and his family of origin. He should be open to Joe's talking about those family issues, but needs to be careful with any "poor old Joe" feelings he finds stirring in himself. He should also avoid getting involved in a lengthy discussion of Joe's drinking behavior, his drinking, or stopping drinking. If that is the way Joe continues to present himself and his problems, a referral to an addiction specialist is in order immediately. If he can talk about the more relational issues in his life, referral for treatment of substance abuse may be delayed or avoided.

Whether or not Joe appears to need immediate referral, the pastor is probably not the person to work with Joe on any deep or intensive level. Their other relationships in the work of the church may make this too difficult. The important thing is that the pastor make every effort to maintain his relationship with Joe—being available, confronting him with questions about his life situation, and letting Joe know that he will assist him in getting further help.

Fossum and Mason note that many of the characteristics that they identify with the shame-bound family they "first thought were specific to families with alcohol and drug addiction." In retrospect, they say, "it is clear that we were becoming acquainted with a much broader and more pervasive syndrome than anything limited to chemical addiction." The characteristic family could "be continued into subsequent generations independently of any active addiction." What they call the "shame-bound" family "is a stage for many forms of human pain and misery, not limited to chemical addiction."[21]

In addition to his thinking about Joe Johnson in terms of his shame and the possibility that he came from a family that was in some way "shame-bound," the pastor needs to be aware of two major views of addiction: the disease model and what has sometimes been described as the adaptive model. Although he or she need not be convinced of the validity of all the features of one model over against the other, the pastor does, however, need to be able to think critically and somewhat dispassionately about a problem. He should be able to consider the value of each model and relate that understanding to the particular pastoral situation. The disease model is more congenial with the clinical pastoral paradigm's focus on general theories of the person. The adaptive model is more contextual in its emphasis on differences among abusers of alcohol.

In the disease model, persons become susceptible to addiction either from a genetic predisposition or from psychological damage that occurred during childhood or, perhaps, from both. When a susceptible person is exposed to alcohol or other drugs and to environmental stress, addiction is likely to result. This in turn leads to socially destructive behavior and abuse of others as well as oneself.

The adaptive model starts with some kind of failure in nurture and care and inadequate environmental support. To this is added inborn physical or psychological disability. These problems, and the way that the person understands them, result in failure to achieve the levels of self-reliance, social acceptance, and self-confidence that are the basic expectations of society. In the light of this failure, the individual searches for alternative means of satisfaction or ways of adapting, such as the use of drugs, which offer a means of survival. The identity of an addict becomes more bearable than no identity at all.

The disease model assumes that the addicted person is sick. The adaptive model does not. Instead, it asserts that addicted persons are "responding adaptively within the limitations of their own abilities, perceptions, and environments." In the disease model, addiction is seen as the cause of a variety of problems. In the adaptive model the addiction is seen as a result of the same problems.[22] What is most important is that the pastor be able to think critically about the advantages and disadvantages of each model.

One of the most important advocates of the disease model, George Valliant, has argued for retaining the disease concept of alcohol on a strictly pragmatic basis. He compares those who argue against the disease model to those who argued that the Vietnam War was a good idea. Those theorists, he notes, had all the qualifications for making the judgments they made except one: none had spent much time in Vietnam. Valliant notes that none of the antidisease theorists have ever worked in an alcohol clinic. Again, arguing pragmatically, he likens alcoholics to people with high blood pressure. Alcoholics "who understand that they have a disease become more rather than less willing to take responsibility for self-care. That is why the self-help group, Alcoholics Anonymous, places such single-minded emphasis on the idea that alcoholism is a disease." Moreover, alcohol abuse often requires skilled medical attention during acute withdrawal. And because of addicted persons' increased likelihood of death from a variety of causes, they need a label that will allow them unprejudiced access to emergency rooms, detoxification clinics, and medical insurance.

Valliant believes the adaptive model only generates more denial in the already profoundly guilt-ridden alcoholic. Calling alcoholism a disease rather than a behavior disorder is a pragmatic device both to persuade the alcoholic to acknowledge the problem and to provide a ticket for admission to the health care system. The models of the social scientist and learning theorist can study the alcoholic, but Valliant believes that the disease model is needed to treat the individual.[23]

For pastoral carers, the disease model has an important positive value for church and clergy in that it contradicts the simple blaming of the alcoholic that has been associated with the clergy. The church has tended to split off or scapegoat the addicted person in an effort to simplify and personify evil and to distance itself from it. A major advantage of the disease model is that it reduces the church's tendency to objectify evil as external to itself.

On the other hand, the disease model has an important negative value in that it tends to externalize all concern with addiction onto addiction specialists and those recovering from addiction. Such externalization gives undue power to addiction specialists and for-profit hospitals specializing in addiction. It tends to take away any critical capacity that church and clergy may have in relation to the treatment process. Anyone who is not a specialist or not recovering is expected to yield his or her critical capacity to the ideology of the disease model and the addiction specialist. Because the disease model and twelve-steps groups have undoubtedly been effective with many people, that way of addressing the problem is often presented as the only way for all and becomes a kind of religious fundamentalism which allows for no critique of its methods. Any attempt at criticism is viewed as an expression of defense or denial.

The concept of "codependency" is thought to have evolved from the term, "co-alcoholic." It was first thought to be caused by the stress of living with an addicted person, but the phenomenon of codependency seemed to linger or escalate in families after the addicted family member was no longer using alcohol or other drugs. It was noticed that codependent spouses were often children of one or two alcoholic spouses and seemed to have reconstituted an earlier abusive childhood situation in their marriages. "Although it happened unconsciously, it was as if by reconstituting the earlier abuse situation the codependent spouse could now get (besides the security of the familiar) another chance to be 'perfect' or 'pleasing' enough to free himself or herself from the exaggerated shame, fear, pain, and anger that had been carried since childhood."[24]

Charlotte Davis Kasl describes a codependent person as "someone whose core identity is undeveloped or unknown, and who maintains a false identity built from dependent attachments to external sources—a partner, a spouse, family, appearances, work, or rules." "Codependency," she says, "is a disease of inequality in that any minority person who has to survive in a world defined by others will know more about those in power than about himself or herself."[25] According to the theory, because a codependent person has not developed a sufficient sense of self, she cannot really tell you how she is:

> She can only tell you how her husband, children, and cats are. She can't tell you how she *wants* something to be, but she can tell you

the rule for how it *should* be. Not having a center to resonate from, she takes her cues from the outside. . . . Because her spirit and soul have been profoundly neglected, she neglects her own inner self; indeed, it is unknown to her.[26]

Codependency has been a very powerful and important theory for many people. The concept and the language are given credit for freeing many persons from destructive relationships and allowing them to find an identity of their own. The problem is that it has become so popular that it seems to be used to describe virtually every human difficulty and to place it under the rubric of illness. "If society and everyone in it are addicted, self-destructing, infected with left-brain rationality, then people in recovery are the chosen few, an elite minority of enlightened, if irrational, self-actualizers with the wisdom to save the world."[27]

A good example of contextual critique of the codependency and recovery movement comes from feminist Harriet Goldhor Lerner, who expresses her fear that "the recovery movement (and it is indeed a movement, if not an epidemic)" is lulling us back into nurturing our weaknesses. "Recovery," says Lerner, "is a sort of compromise solution. It teaches women to move in the direction of 'more self' while it sanitizes and makes change safe, because the dominant group culture (never fond of 'those angry women') is not threatened by sick women meeting together to get well. . . . It is my expert opinion that women are competent, wise and not sick."[28]

Gail Unterberger, a pastoral counselor and seminary professor, has offered a similar critique of the twelve steps of Alcoholics Anonymous. She is concerned that the idea of community can take a back seat to the emphasis in AA on each person's individual journey. Another problem she sees in traditional twelve-steps groups is the image of a domineering, paternalistic God. She argues that the model is condescending to adult women and that "it hinders the development of the mature sense of self that addicted women often lack."

Unterberger expresses some of her concerns by developing a feminist revision of the twelve steps and encouraging other women to write their own rather than submitting to the twelve-step tradition. The fact that she offers this option seems to me to emphasize the importance of individuality as well as community, even though her major concern is with the latter. Although all twelve revised steps are provocative from a communal contextual perspective, one example may serve to give the direction of her revision. Where the original first step stated: "We admitted that we were powerless over alcohol—that our lives had become unmanageable," Unterberger's feminist revision substitutes: "We have a drinking problem that once had us." Her argument for the change is that powerlessness has always been women's particular handicap. "For men, admitting powerlessness indicates their readiness for God to move in and change them. Women, on the other hand, need to take an opposite tack; to stand up, affirm our will and empower ourselves."[29]

Pastoral Response to Abuse of Others

Although the pastor's *understanding* of abuse of others is significantly informed by all three paradigms, pastoral *response* to the abuse of others is informed almost exclusively by the communal contextual paradigm.

A young mother, Mary Martin, stops pastor Jenny Jones in the church hallway. Mary appears to have been crying. The pastor invites Mary into her office and asks:

Pastor: Those tears look like painful ones, Mary. Do you feel like telling me what they are about?

Mary: I don't know whether I can or not. I'm so ashamed. I suppose I should be angry, but I just feel betrayed and ashamed.

Pastor: Shame is terribly difficult to deal with, but it might help if you could tell me something about what's going on.

Mary: It's Mike, my husband. I just discovered that he's been exposing himself sexually to our five-year-old daughter. It's awful! I don't think any more than that has happened, but I don't know for sure.

How does the pastor respond to Ms. Martin's pain? She responds first by thinking about it. Her response might be essentially the same as Mary Martin's—"It's awful"—but she can be more helpful if she has a way of thinking about the problem and encouraging Ms. Martin to think about it before she acts. Moreover, like Joe Johnson's pastor, Jenny Jones also needs to lead from strength. She knows about pain and first must deal with Mary Martin's feelings and, perhaps, her own, if she is shocked by what she has heard. Ms. Martin needs to tell the story as she knows it, in the context of a trusting relationship. Pastor Jones is aware that shame "is terribly difficult to deal with," but beginning to address it rather than attempting to hide it indeed may help.

Dealing with some of the feelings is first and is important, but the pastor needs to know and do a number of other things. In anticipation of an event such as this one, she needs to have consulted with a lawyer about the abuse laws in her state and the requirements for reporting abuse. Both she and Joe Johnson's pastor should have a subcommittee of the parish governing board who are responsible for the church's counseling ministry. That committee should, among other things on its agenda, have discussed what should happen in the event of reported abuse. More of this aspect will be discussed in a later chapter.

The pastor needs to find out what Mary has done with the information on abuse and what she wants to do. Depending somewhat on the circumstances, Mary may need to talk with her pediatrician and use that resource for possible other referral for her daughter. Pastor Jones needs to help Mary begin to evaluate the possibility of further abuse and to consider where she is with her husband and some of the possible courses of action she may take. Unless there is clear danger of immediate further abuse, she should not take any precipitous action. The pastor works to stabilize the situation and work with deliberate speed. Depending on her relationship with Mike, the pastor will consider discussing the situation with him alone or with Mary. Prior to that interview, if at all possible, she should make use of a consultant who can help her assess her responsibilities and possible actions in the situation.

Again, this discussion risks oversimplification and is dealing with a case that is simpler to deal with than those which many pastors have to face. Most important is that pastors not work in isolation and that they have a plan for dealing with pastoral events such as this. The way Fossum and Mason describe a shame-bound family system and the way it may predispose its members to abuse others may be helpful. They use the metaphor of "the zipper" to describe what may happen in such a family. There is a boundary around the intellectual, emotional, and physical self that is closed by an "internal zipper" of self-respect and an "external zipper" of shame. "When individuals grow up in a shame-bound system, they grow up with unclear boundaries, with their zippers on the outside; they believe that they are indeed regulated by others and the outside world."[30]

Because such persons have been subject to victimization by others, "who can come up and unzip them at any time, taking them over and 'taking their stuff,'" they in turn may violate boundaries. Common "unzippings" of others range from mind reading—making interpretations of another's thoughts and feelings without checking them out with the person concerned—to parent-child incest. When the boundary is violated, the victim experiences shame. The perpetrator experiences shamelessness or denial.

In working with the perpetrators of these boundary violations, James N. Poling has noted that one of the most difficult issues for the therapist is, as one might expect, setting limits and appropriate boundaries. "It is obvious," he says, "that a man who molests a child does not know how to set limits on his own destructive behaviors, and does not respect the boundaries that other persons need in order to survive."[31] In their work with male adult sex offenders, Fossum and Mason found that these men had been deprived of nurturing touch in their childhood experiences. What they had been denied, "they had later taken; in the process they ended up violating others' boundaries. The denied or invaded touch resulted in that victim's 'taking' safe touch from some vulnerable young person."[32]

Understanding of the shame and shamelessness involved in abuse is important because it allows the pastor to act rather than just to react to what appears to be irrational and shameless behavior on the part of the abuser. A more active response, however, is required. Marie Fortune has offered some very helpful personal and ethical responses to sexual abuse. They include: righteous anger; compassion for and advocacy for the victim; holding the offender accountable; efforts toward prevention of future abuse.[33] The legal requirements for reporting sexual abuse vary from state to state. The minister needs to know the law in his or her state and have that interpreted for her or him from a legal perspective. The clergyperson also needs to sort out his or her own understanding of confidentiality and then gain some knowledge of how the law of that particular state has been recently interpreted.[34]

In another place Fortune has offered practical guidelines for pastoral carers dealing with abuse. I adapt them slightly for use here.

First of all, the pastor needs to be aware of his or her own comfort level with the issues of sexual assault, abuse, and sexuality. Everyone has biases and prejudices, and certain types of people with whom we do not work well; therefore, *do not hesitate to refer* people with whom you cannot work so that they may get help from a colleague.

Second, *when you observe symptoms or suspect abuse, ask*. Pastors are often reluctant to ask about things like abuse, suicidal feelings, or rape, apparently feeling that they should somehow know these things instinctively. It is important to deal with the shame, fear, and embarrassment that may prevent us asking directly for the information we need to help us help those within our pastoral care.

Third, *make a habit of routinely including questions about possible experiences of sexual violence early in any pastoral counseling interviews.* Again, it is easy to avoid such topics, but the fact that we have avoided them is part of the problem. Premarital counseling interviews may reveal some of the ways that a couple deals with conflict. Personal interviews with confirmands or other occasions of speaking with young people alone may provide opportunities to hear stories of abuse. Should this happen, the pastor should ask if the person has been to a rape crisis center or other source of aid. If she has not, find out if she wishes to contact someone who deals regularly with abuse or wishes to talk with you further about it. Respect her decision if she is not ready, but let her know that you, or other resources, are available.

Fourth, *make every effort to ask your questions in a matter-of-fact, normal, respectful tone of voice.* Your calmness and professional attitude can ease the feelings of shame and secrecy and may make disclosure possible at some future time. Some examples: "A lot of people have experienced a situation in which someone has abused or assaulted them. Has that happened to you?" "People troubled with anorexia [or some other symptom] have sometimes been sexually assaulted. I'm wondering if that's the case with you."

If there are no counseling centers nearby or readily accessible, the pastor may consider going to take some in-depth training in dealing with abuse or calling a center for advice when he or she needs consultation and guidance.[35]

In writing about what the church can do about sexual abuse, Peggy Halsey speaks first of the importance of breaking the silence. "We must make it clear," she says, "that we see the church as a refuge for people who are hurting and an entirely appropriate place for these issues to be addressed. We must find ways to demonstrate that the church is a place where people can feel confident [to] turn first, not last, for comfort and healing."[36]

James Poling, also writing from a religious perspective, is skeptical about the possibility of this. As an illustration, he points to the situation of a counselee, Karen, who knew her experience would be taboo in the church and "who was indirectly told to keep her silence." "Only a special community," Poling says, "could engage all of Karen's experience. That community was composed of Karen's physician, then her pastor and, later, her therapist. It was this special kind of community that could provide compassion and help her give voice to her pain. Still later, Karen selected a group of five persons who "became a counter-community to compensate for the deficiencies of her church and other social groups."[37]

Good pastoral care of victims requires theological reconstruction. It requires that we look with grave seriousness at victim blaming, at our premises and prejudices about violence and about sexuality, at our life experience and deepest feelings about women and men, at our beliefs about parents and children and family life.[38]

One of the places that theological reconstruction continues to be needed is in the understanding of forgiveness in relation to abuse of self and of others. The church and its leaders have been prone to encourage abused persons to forgive their abusers even in cases when forgiveness would involve denial of the anger necessary for healing. Dispensing forgiveness and encouraging its members to dispense it has been one of the ways that the church itself has abused persons. Elsewhere I have written about human forgiveness as a discovery, not a demand—a discovery that may become possible after a long period of recovery from shame.[39] More recently an article in *The Christian Century* dealt with forgiveness after violence in a way that is more relevant for victims of abuse. In that article, Richard P. Lord concluded that pastors or other well-intentioned Christians "have no right to insist that the victim establish a relationship with his or her victimizer to effect a reconciliation."

Richard Lord very helpfully deals with the fact that forgiving often implies excusing. If an abuser has a religious experience after the abuse has taken place, does this mean that "now we should act as though a crime wasn't committed"? In reflecting on his proclamation in worship, "Your sins are forgiven," the author, a pastor, imagines a battered wife thinking, Who gave you the right to forgive the one who beats me? and reminds us that forgiveness is "not a commodity that can be handed out" by the church or anyone else.[40]

A recent secular treatment of forgiveness by Sidney and Suzanne Simon says essentially the same thing psychologically about forgiveness that I attempted to say from a theological perspective, that forgiveness is not an act but a discovery. Below I adapt and interpret some of the very helpful implications of that thesis developed by the Simons:[41]

1. Forgiveness is not forgetting. We cannot forget, nor should we, because those experiences, even the pain they caused, have a great deal to teach us.

2. Forgiveness is not condoning. We are not saying that what was done to us was acceptable or "not so bad."

3. Forgiveness is not absolving those who have hurt us of all responsibility for their actions. They are still responsible for what they did and must deal with it themselves.

4. Forgiveness is not a form of self-sacrifice or swallowing our

true feelings and playing the martyr.

5. Perhaps most important, forgiveness is not a clear-cut, one-time decision. We can't simply decide that on today we are going to forgive. If it happens, it happens as a result of confronting painful past experiences and healing of old wounds.

What, then, is forgiveness?

1. It is a discovery, the by-product of an ongoing healing process. Failure to forgive is not a failure of will but happens because wounds have not yet healed.

2. Rather than being something we do, forgiveness is something that happens as a sign of positive self-esteem, when we are no longer building our identity around something that happened in the past. Our injuries are just a part of who we are, not all of us.

3. It is recognizing that we no longer need our hatred and resentments and no longer need to punish the people who hurt, wanting them to suffer as much as we did.

4. Realizing that punishing them does not heal us, forgiveness is putting to better use the energy once consumed by rage and resentment and moving on with life.

The Potential for Shame and Abuse in a Pastoral Relationship

I have already pointed to the potential for abuse in a pastor's or religious community's prematurely demanding forgiveness from an abused person. This is a destructive use of the church's or pastor's power in relationship with a person who has been hurt and abused. As Marie Fortune and others have suggested, there are times when pastoral care clearly calls for anger rather than forgiveness.

It is important to note, however, that there is in a pastoral relationship itself the potential for abuse simply because of the power differential between the participants. There is a type of shame inherent in the process of asking for help and in becoming dependent on the helping person. For example, a counselee with whom I had been working for some time expressed her experience of the therapeutic situation something like this: "I feel ashamed that you have seen me—that you know me as well as you do." Later in the same session her words, "I hate depending on you this much," expressed some of the rage and shame that result from the full recognition of human relatedness and the vulnerability that relatedness may produce.

Carl Schneider speaks of this vulnerability, as have many of the recent writers on shame, in terms of the psychotherapeutic relationship's involving asymmetrical disclosure and, consequently, asymmetrical power. The patient is "seen" when he is not himself and when he is vulnerable to intrusion. Depending somewhat on the initiative taken by the person needing help, the pastoral care relationship may be different. Nevertheless, as the incident above reveals, there are some significant similarities. In either pastoral care or counseling the pastor must be able to respect the patient or parishioner at a time when he may be unable to experience, maintain, or claim such self-respect.[42]

Anyone who has done a great deal of hospital visitation has probably experienced a related situation. The pastoral carer visits a patient when the patient is aware of his need. He "opens up" to the chaplain or pastor about some of his worries and concerns. Afterward, the pastoral carer goes away feeling as if she has done well, established trust with the patient, and is on the way to an important pastoral relationship. On the next visit, however, the carer is surprised to find that the patient acts as if he hardly knows the pastor. In contrast to the "open" way he related before, today he seems closed and distant. The pastoral carer goes away feeling confused. If, however, she were more aware of the function of shame in relationships where people "open up," she would not be too surprised. Probably, without being aware of it, she encouraged the patient to share more of himself than he was ready to share. Next time she may be more aware of the patient's need to protect himself from the shame of too much openness.

Most important for us here is underscoring the importance of the pastoral carer's being aware that persons who acknowledge their need for help are more than likely experiencing shame and vulnerability. Whereas they may be seeking help from the pastor because of abuse in the past, the situation they are now in has significant potential for abuse. One of the pastor's major responsibilities is seeing to it that no abuse takes place in that situation.[43]

Some Final Reflections

How does the pastor respond to Joe Johnson's self-destructive drinking behavior, to the sexual abuse of her child reported by Mary Martin, and to the many other abusive situations that may confront him or her? There is more than one way to answer that question, but all the possible ways can be guided by an understanding of care as hearing and remembering. All the possible responses should be focused on care for, not cure of the abuser and the abused. They should grow out of an understanding of the slowness of most of the change that takes place through a caring relationship rather than looking for immediate results.

The theological dimensions of a pastoral response to Johnson and to the Martin family may be found in the classical paradigm's focus on humankind's failure in stewardship—failure to care—and in the shame associated with that. The pastor is dealing with abused and abusing persons who, theologically or classically understood, are carers who failed to care or be cared for and who, therefore, must embark on the slow road of dealing with their own shame and the shame of others close to them.

Questions for Consideration

1. Why is it important for the pastor to think critically about abuse? In what way does a critical stance contribute to caring or inhibit it?

2. In what way are theological views of stewardship and shame relevant or irrelevant to the pastoral response to abuse?

3. Is abuse sickness or sin? Give the psychological and theological rationale for your answer.

4. Consider the relative merits and problems of the disease and adaptive models of addiction. How is this issue related to the theological question of the relationship between sin and sickness and the positive and negative features of the concept of patienthood?

5. How have church and clergy hindered persons' dealing with abuse situations? What kind of religious beliefs and resources seem to be helpful to abusing persons and families? What kinds seem to get in the way or be destructive?

6. Reflect on any changes that you are aware of in your attitude and understanding of rape and rape victims. How has recent public awareness of this kind of abuse affected your attitude and that of your church and community?

7. How might the profit-making dimension of the treatment resources in your community affect your decision on referral? What are some of the positive and negative features of the for-profit and the not-for-profit health corporation?

8

Special Relationships—
The Balances of Care

Often, like a child peering over the fence at somebody else's party, she gazes wistfully at other families and wonders what their secret is. They seem so close. Is it that they're more religious? Or stricter, or more lenient? Could it be the fact that they participate in sports? Read books together? Have some common hobby?

—Anne Tyler[1]

The concern of this chapter is what is commonly called pastoral care of the family. Like the previous chapters, this one assumes that human beings are relational with God and with other persons. More than the other chapters, however, it focuses the human relationality question around the issue of how a person can be fully relational without losing his or her individuality. The chapter is about the special relationships of human life, most often those of kinship, but sometimes relationships of friendship. It argues that the pastoral care of persons concerned with these special relationships involves assisting them in dealing with two fundamental balances of care: (1) care for themselves as individuals and care for the relationships that are most important to them; and (2) a balance of care among the generations closest to them: their own generation, the generation before, and the generation that comes after them.

Human Beings Are Relational,
but Some Relationships Are Special

As a relational human being, what guides me in my most important relationships with others? Although ethics makes use of general principles to guide human action, a principle applied within the context of my relationship to my spouse or my child has a different meaning than does the same principle applied in the relationship to a person whom I do not know in that special way. Our everyday experience tells us that although there are many ways in which these relationships are like all others, what is most important about them is that they are different from other relationships. In the case of special relations, general principles may not be adequate to describe the nature of justice, or love, or power.[2]

Ethical principles are usually based on the assumption that all persons are alike and can be appealed to in similar ways. What is most characteristic of special relations within the family, however, is the particularities that make them what they are. And those particularities are the histories of those persons and the voluntary obligations they have taken on in relation to their history with one another. "People are not interchangeable. . . . The kind and quality of the special relations I am in help shape the kind of person I am. The 'other' in a special relation . . . is in a real and inescapable sense a part of myself, and I in turn am a part of the other."[3]

The usual way to deal with the traditional New Testament text about how many times one should forgive one's "brother" is to interpret it so that it applies to the forgiveness of anyone, or, as the New Revised Standard Version says, "another member of the church," or "another disciple."

> Forgiving our brother or wife or child, however, is significantly different from forgiving any one who is not in that special kind of relationship with us. And the answer to that New Testament question, in the light of the concept of special relations, may differ depending upon which brother we are talking about. It depends not only on principle, but upon the story of our relationship.[4]

I experienced this issue most forcefully when as a parent I was trying to deal with the difficult to impossible problem of trying to be "fair" to my children, assuming naively that I could apply family rules dispassionately to each one. I found it both impossible and inappropriate to be dispassionate. The nature of special relationships is that they involve both reason and passion. The story of the particular relationship and family is involved in the decision about the right thing to do in a special relationship.

Kinship and Friendship

It is not only family members who are involved with us in special relationships. Friendships are also special. Psychologist Lillian

Rubin points out how friendships "facilitate our separation from the family and encourage our developing individuality by providing the contact and comfort needed for the transition from child-in-the-family to person-in-the-world."[5] Rubin contrasts friendship and kinship by telling the story of attending the wedding of her best friend's son. Although she and her friend were "like sisters," closer than most sisters, when she went to the wedding things were different. There were clearly marked places for family members, but no places reserved for "best friends." Rubin shares her feeling of being left out and how that feeling seems to illustrate the ad hoc quality of friendship, that there is no official recognition of this significant relationship.

In spite of that lack of official recognition for friendship, I have found in doing pastoral counseling that one of the most important things to determine in assessing the ability of a person to cope with life successfully in a painful or tragic circumstance is the existence and quality of his or her friendships. In trying to do that, one needs a practical definition of who is to be understood as a friend in the "special relationship" sense. The practical description I have used is that "a friend is someone you feel trusting of, comfortable with, and somehow better after you've been with him or her."

Contrasting kinship and friendship, Rubin notes that kinship relationships rest on bonds forged in earliest childhood years and have a quality that touches the deepest layers of inner life and most primitive emotions. They are, therefore, more likely to be more up and down, more tumultuous than friendships. "Friends *choose* to do what kin are *obliged* to do. . . . Friends accept each other so long as they both remain essentially the same as they were when they met. . . . If they change or grow in different or incompatible ways, the friendship most likely will be lost." Friends usually seem to be more understanding than kin, but, says Rubin, "we pay a price for that understanding," a lack of a sense of entitlement or claim on a secure and committed relationship. "We can fully dissociate from the friend; we can divorce the mate, but the sibling is ours for life, even if we never see him or her again."[6]

The kinship relationship and its givenness has a power to it that makes it special even when active interaction is absent. The marriage relationship, and perhaps the committed sexual relationship and the relationship of persons bound together in a committed and ritualized nonsexual relationship are somewhere in between kinship and friendship. The relationship is ritualized or affirmed by a larger, more public community, but unlike kinship it can simply be dissolved by choice. Although they are different, all three kinds of relationships are or can be special, that is, be understood as special cases of human relationality which involve story as well as principle.[7]

Contributions to the Balances of Care from the Classical Paradigm

In many ways it is difficult to find the message that the classical paradigm offers for the pastoral care of the family. What the biblical tradition says about the special relationships of the family are so obviously bound to an ancient culture that some of the most literal interpreters of scripture have difficulty in accepting their authority for today. The Bible presents stories of incest, adultery, and, even in the midst of patriarchal domination, marital conflict. These stories demonstrate that the human concern with family issues is far from a modern one, but the kind of guidance they give for family living today seems questionable. The task for the pastoral carer is to search for the central features of the Bible's message about the family and to try to focus on that center rather than the peripheral elements that are also in view.

There is also the strong affirmation in the biblical materials that whatever the scripture may be saying about the special relationships of the family, part of the Bible's central message is that these relationships are not ultimately important. The strong Old Testament condemnation of idolatry—"You shall have no other gods before me"(Ex. 20:3)—may surely be understood in our day to be inclusive of the idolatry of the family. Jesus' concern with the family in the Synoptic Gospels is less characterized by his prohibition of divorce than the single-mindedness of his religious vocation at the expense of his kinship family.

> While he was still speaking to the crowds, his mother and his brothers were standing outside, wanting to speak to him. Someone told him, "Look, your mother and your brothers are standing outside, wanting to speak to you." But to the one who had told him this, Jesus replied, "Who is my mother, and who are my brothers?" And pointing to his disciples, he said, "Here are my mother and my brothers! For whoever does the will of my Father in heaven is my brother and sister and mother." (Matt. 12:46–50)

Although special relationships, most often those of the family, are not ultimate, their "generational character" is an important expression of human relationality. In our book on the family, Brian Childs and I developed a norm for family living and a way of thinking about the pastoral care of the family which we called "generational care."[8] Our initial concern in doing this was to get away from a norm for family living that emphasized one particular form for the family. We proposed a functional rather than a structural norm—a three-generational caring relationship. Although I do not claim that this way of viewing family life is genuinely cross-cultural, it does help guard against assuming that one particular cultural form of family living can adequately describe what a family ought to be.

The calling to live as "generational" persons is expressed in a number of places, particularly in the Old Testament commandment to honor our fathers and mothers; the message in the teachings of Jesus on the importance of and the limits to family loyalty; and the concern with the nature of the Christian household expressed in the New Testament epistles. The biblical tradition tells us to "honor" our fathers and mothers, but to guard against idealizing them or any other human relationship. The biblical phrase "These are the generations of . . ." emphasizes humanity's place and responsibility within the sequence of history. To be a human being is to care for one's fathers and mothers and children.

There are fewer resources in the postbiblical history of Christianity about the care of the family than about the human problems that I have previously discussed. That, I believe, is because commitment to the Christian message often meant a turn away from the family, and thus family matters were viewed as secondary pastoral concerns. One interesting classical example of care for marriage and family issues, however, can be seen in Martin Luther's reinterpretation of Christian vocation as inclusive of marriage. At a time of religious and social change, Luther addressed such matters in his letters of spiritual counsel. He did this, however, with some anxiety. "When I began to write about married life," he noted in a letter in 1524, "I was afraid that what has occurred would happen, namely, that I would have more trouble on this account than with all the rest of my work."[9]

Luther's approach to marriage and the family was a very practical one. He sought to get marriage and sexuality out of the control of the church, to interpret sexuality on the one hand as a matter of nature rather than grace and to view marriage on the other hand as a civil, not a religious, issue since it involved both Christian and non-Christian. He believed that one should not make marriage and sexuality a matter of central concern, so that one could get on with the more important matter of salvation.

That point of view can be seen in the letters that Luther wrote to priests and nuns who had abandoned their vows of celibacy but who had difficulty in overcoming their inhibitions about sexuality and marriage. He not only encouraged marriage for such persons but interpreted the classical Christian message as God's "compelling" persons to marry. "This cannot be restrained either by vows or by laws. For it is God's law and doing." Whoever chooses to live alone "undertakes an impossible task and takes it upon himself to run counter to God's Word." It takes a bold man, Luther said, "to take a wife. What you need above all else, then, is to be encouraged, admonished, urged, incited, and made bold. . . . Stop thinking about it and go to it right merrily. Your body demands it. God wills it and drives you to it. There is nothing that you can do about it."[10]

Another interpreter of historical Christian resources with respect to sexuality and marriage was mid-twentieth-century church historian Roland H. Bainton. Bainton identified three classical views of the church toward marriage: the sacramental, the romantic, and the companionable. A more recent book by William Johnson Everett also deals with classical Christian views, but interprets Christianity's view of the family as basically ambivalent: on one hand honoring it; on the other, seeing it as an impediment to the holy life. "Nature and grace point to two different vantage points for approaching marriage," he says, and each Christian tradition "finds its own way of relating the two." In contrast to Bainton, Everett identifies four major ways in which the relation of nature and grace in marriage have been worked out: sacrament, covenant, vocation, and communion.[11] It seems valuable to me to consider Bainton's and Everett's views together.

The *sacramental* view, according to Bainton, stresses marriage as a religious relationship and an exclusive life commitment. "The term sacramental is applied to this position because of the strongly religious emphasis rather than because of the specific doctrine that marriage is a visible sign of an inward and spiritual grace. . . . The Epistle to the Ephesians (5:32) compares the relation of husband and wife to that of Christ and the Church and adds that this is a *mysterion*. The Latin incorrectly rendered this Greek word as *sacramentum*."[12] Nevertheless, this view emphasizes God's grace working through nature and marriage as an order of creation. The sacramental view places greater emphasis on expectations of the church and less on the natural dynamics of love, and tends toward reduction of marriage to an institutional form.

In strong contrast to the sacramental view of marriage was the *romantic* view of love and sexuality. "During the early church and Middle Ages the prevailing view of sex was disparaging. Marriage was sacramental, lifelong, primarily for progeny, unromantic, and rating below virginity." An attempted corrective of this was the romantic view in which there was an idealization of woman and of love itself. The romantic view, according to Bainton, appears to originate "in the Neoplatonic aspiration for union with the divine. The woman simply takes the place of the ineffable *nous*."[13] In many ways the romantic view of sexuality and marriage has been an antichurch, but not necessarily an anti-Christian, view. It strongly emphasizes individual passion in contrast to institutional stability.

Bainton's third Christian attitude toward marriage was the *companionable* which, in contrast to the romantic view's finding the religious in the beloved, was concerned that love for the spouse not in any way cool one's desire for Christ. By putting God first, men and women were able to labor together without particular consciousness of their biological differences. John Milton, who suffered with an unhappy marriage to a young woman unable to be a companion, began his discussion of marriage and divorce by saying that

> the first command of God was not, "Be fruitful and multiply" (the favorite text for the Catholic sacramental view), nor was it that "to marry is better than to burn" (the chief proof text of the Lutherans), but rather this, "It is not good for man to be alone." In God's intention a meet and happy conversation is the chiefest and noblest end of marriage.[14]

Bainton's conclusion is that the sacramental, the romantic, and the companionable are all important elements in a Christian marriage.

Everett's three symbols for marriage besides the sacramental complement Bainton's view. They have elements of the romantic and the companionable, but add other elements as well. *Covenant*, the primary biblical symbol for divine-human relationship, was only later applied to marriage. It is sometimes unconditional, sometimes conditional. Covenant is almost inescapably related to the legal concept of contract because, although the entry into it generally appears to be free, once having entered it freedom appears to be significantly limited. Covenant involves binding oneself for the creation of a higher purpose and as a model of God's ordering a new and distinct community among other communities. Because the covenant symbol for marriage is based on God's covenant with God's people, however, it is by analogy more clearly applicable to the parent-child relationship than to marriage, if the latter is understood as a relationship of peers.

Marriage as *vocation* begins with God's gracious call rather than, as in the sacramental view, being an order of creation. Marriage as a process of nature is clearly subordinate to the grace that comes through response to God's call to renew the creation. Married people and families are to serve God by carrying out their vocations. Marriage and the family facilitate this by stabilizing and supporting those involved. The equality of the couple can be seen in their common call to discipleship, but (as in Luther and in Barth) the roles that they carry out in that call may be static, socially determined, and apparently less affected by grace than the model itself suggests.

The symbol of *communion* stresses the resonance of two natures and the mutual participation both in a world they hold in common and in the qualities each has as a person. It brings together the romantic and the companionable, and has its origin in mystical experience. In communion, which Everett believes is the most appropriate symbol of marriage for today, grace operates through given structures of personality. "In taking nature seriously," he says, "it stands close to sacrament, but lacks the external or permanent symbolic structure typical of sacrament" and is less likely to stress the influence of church over nature. Rather than trying to transform the couple directly or approach them as members of a community, the communion model "tries to give them the power to reveal themselves to each other so that in the resonance between their real selves they might be transformed to higher levels of living."[15]

As was also the case in dealing with the other major human problems, what I have chosen as relevant contributions from the classical paradigm for pastoral care is in many ways quite arbitrary. In considering what the classical Christian message about special relationships might be, it is essential to make some judgment about what part of the message can offer guidance today and what part seems so bound to circumstances of the past that its relevance is marginal. In focusing on the concept of generational care I have made such a judgment, and I would challenge others to explore the implications of that concept or claim another concept from the tradition as more relevant. The material from Luther, Bainton, and Everett is intended to illustrate that in spite of the Christian tradition's relative lack of interest in family relationships, many of the elements within the classical Christian tradition can be resources for pastoral care today.

Contributions to the Balances of Care from the Clinical Pastoral Paradigm

The clinical pastoral paradigm's focus on the person rather than the message and its explicit use of psychological resources has contributed a number of important things to the care of persons concerned with special relationships. I touch on only a few of them. Psychoanalysis affirmed the centrality of human sexuality and emphasized the power and potential destructiveness of family relationships, including how they can be carried over from the past into the present. Family therapy, seeking an alternative to psychoanalysis' focus on freeing the individual from bondage to the family, has emphasized instead the way that family members are related to one another systemically, rather than historically. Some family therapists have been particularly concerned with communication within the family system. Others have emphasized the importance of family structure. And still others have focused on how the individual could be empowered to be an individual in spite of the power of the family system.

More recently, American psychotherapists have begun to shake off some of the influence both of Freudian psychoanalysis and of the family-system theorists to affirm the importance of both the individual and family relationality through the use of British object relations theory. My concern here is not to survey the contributions of these various theories. Instead I make use of a number of them by focusing on the central human issue of how a person can be a unique, individual self and at the same time be fully related to others in special relationships. The key to answering this question may be found in the meanings of *intimacy* and *closeness*. I use the work of three theorists to interpret the meaning of these concepts.

Peter Berger discusses special relationships in terms of persons developing a common world of meaning. Interestingly, he turns to the Yahwist account of creation in the book of Genesis and its picture of God's giving to humankind the task of naming the animals. This, Berger believes, symbolizes the essentially human task of ordering the world in meaningful relationship to oneself.

> The plausibility and stability of the world, as socially defined, is dependent upon the strength and continuity of significant relationships in which conversation about this world can be continually carried on. . . . The reality of the world is sustained through conversation with significant others.[16]

Special relationships are sustained through conversations in which "two strangers come together and redefine themselves." Berger describes the participants in the marriage relationship as "strangers," because "unlike marriage candidates in many previous societies, those who marry in our society typically come "from different areas of conversation." Contrasting present society with a more stable ancient one, he notes that unlike an earlier situation in which "the establishment of the new marriage simply added to the differentiation and complexity of an already existing social world, marriage partners in today's society are embarked on the often difficult task of constructing for themselves the little world in which they will live."[17] For Berger, the intimacy and closeness involved in special relationships are best facilitated by the construction of a common world through conversation.

Family therapists Lyman and Adele Wynne have focused on the meaning of intimacy in special relationships. They understand intimacy as a "*subjective relational experience* in which the core components are *trusting self-disclosure* and *communicated empathy*." Perhaps their most important contention is that intimacy "recurs most reliably, not when it is demanded as a primary or continuous experience, but when it emerges spontaneously within a context of basic, well-functioning relational processes." Self-disclosure in itself does not necessarily create intimacy. "An intimacy experience has not taken place, in our definition, until there is empathic feedback, that is until acceptance and acknowledgement are communicated, verbally or nonverbally, as an indication that this trust is justified."[18]

What seems most relevant for pastoral care out of this view is the Wynnes' conviction that preoccupation with intimacy as a goal "interferes with its attainment and also distracts, at the very least, from attention to other forms of relatedness." Intimacy can be experienced in brief, unidimensional encounters with relative strangers, but such "highly sporadic, intimate disclosures in 'one-time only' relationships are possible *because* of the unlikelihood of a further relationship and the attendant opportunities for betrayal." Intimacy in ongoing, special relationships is of a different order.

Intimacy involves relational processes that unfold sequentially. (1) There is the process of attachment/caregiving or complementary affectional bonding, the prototype for which is the parent-child relationship. (2) There is the communicating process in which there is a common focus of attention and the exchange of meanings and messages. (3) Joint problem-solving and the sharing of everyday tasks is the next relational process. (4) The final subprocess is mutuality, understood as the integration of the preceding processes into an enduring pattern of relatedness. It is important to note that mutuality "incorporates both distancing, or disengagement, and constructive re-engagement." These processes unfold sequentially, but are circular rather than linear in relationship to one another. Even after mutuality has been attained, "relatedness usefully returns to focus upon earlier processes for various periods of time." Until attachment/caregiving is incorporated into a relationship, that relationship "is not likely to become enduring and reliable."[19]

The Wynnes argue that in spite of the centrality given by Western culture to "being intimate," intimacy is not itself a primary relational process. It is secondary to more basic relational processes. Moreover, "although mutuality optimizes the likehood of intimacy," intimacy can occur before mutuality has developed, for example, in the problem-solving activities of preadolescents in the chum stage of development. Intimate experience is "a *supplementary*, but not essential, process for strengthening the bonding that has been crucial for the survival of the human species throughout the ages."(Italics mine.)[20]

Berger emphasizes the creation of a conversational world together as the key element in special relationships. The Wynnes emphasize the primacy of caretaking in developing intimacy. Psychotherapists Tom and Pat Malone negate neither of those views but develop the meaning of intimacy by contrasting it to closeness.[21] According to the Malones, who incidentally are father and son, the fundamental problem of relationship is, *How can I be myself when I am in relationship to another person?* Psychic health, they believe, is "the ability to maintain the self in relationships." In contrast to this kind of relational health, the neurotic person is one who has to accommodate and alter who he or she is in order to stay, even uncomfortably, in relationship. The psychotic is one who can find no way to be who he or she is in relationship to another. You are being intimate, say the Malones, "when you can be in your own personal space while you are also in the space you share with another." It is possible, they continue, "to be in this shared space when you are alone. The other then is there in your thoughts and feelings . . . [when] you are aware of them as you are of yourself."[22]

The majority of interactive impasses encountered in couples, say the Malones,

> come out of the confusion between their closeness and their lack of intimacy. Each is aware of the other, not himself or herself. When they do become aware of themselves, the pendulum swings to the other extreme; they are not related to the other. They move back into their personal space, away from the shared space. . . . Correcting this imbalance is not just an issue for therapy. . . . The same imbalance exists in most of us.[23]

Whereas closeness and intimacy are enhancers of experience, *neurosis* is a synonym for *nonexperience*. "The latter comes when, out of our own needs, we modify our own personhoods to 'take care of' the other. . . . 'Taking care of' others is almost always the opposite of caring for them. Caring enhances and enlivens both; 'taking care of' diminishes both." "'Taking care of' is close, not intimate; it is like providing a service. It is a necessary part of life, and when chosen it can be done healthily (be in the true sense a 'service'), but it does not build or change relationship." Closeness "affirms and sustains relationship," whereas intimacy "changes relationship."[24]

The central issue in personal life is what I have called the balance of care and what the Malones would see as the balancing of closeness and intimacy. "Without closeness, intimacy would be chaotic. Without intimacy, closeness would and does insidiously deteriorate into role playing and boredom."[25] "Whereas the prototype of closeness is the personal experience (in which I am more aware of the other person than I am of myself), in the sexual experience both persons are much more aware of themselves than they are of the other. . . . Intimacy depends on my ability to experience being *me* and *I* simultaneously; being who I am in relationship, sensitively aware of the other person." Such an experience is profoundly sexual, but not necessarily genital. "The essence of intimacy is the awareness one has of one's *self* in the immediate presence of another person to whom one is closely related."[26]

Although one can know the constructed image of another person from years of relationship, this may actually interfere with "knowing" the person as he or she is at this particular moment. "You cannot 'know' *others* even if they are willing to tell you, even if you are feeling close to them when they are telling you. Only when *you* are intimate do you know, because you know then what *you* are feeling and experiencing." The only personal information that can tell you about the other is "what you know and experience *in your own person*" about them.[27]

> In intimacy, the strangeness in the *other* allows and even provokes the new and strange we find in ourselves. This is why the intimate experience is so energizing: it changes the relationship, but, more important, it increases our awareness of ourselves. It allows us to change. To realize our search for this difference, this strangeness, helps us to understand experiential pairing, and why in it we seek the other face of ourselves.

It is usually easier to be intimate with a stranger than with someone we know very well because

> the strangeness is readily available; the lack of familiarity frees us from our already knowing, our judging and prejudging. The most

exciting and powerful intimate experiences, however, occur when we feel the same strangeness with familiar persons. We are most intimate when we are able to be strange with the person to whom we are closest.[28]

Berger's common conversational world, the Wynnes' fundamental nature of the primary caring relationship, and the Malones' interpretation of intimacy and closeness, all three contribute to the understanding of the balances of care in special relationships. It is important to have a common world to share with a special other person, to experience one's own caring and being cared for, and to discover that I can be most fully myself when I am with another. These are important expressions of the clinical pastoral paradigm's emphasis on the person.

Contributions to the Balances of Care from the Communal Contextual Paradigm

The impact of the communal contextual paradigm on intimacy and closeness in special relationships is changing so rapidly that my attempt to speak to it here will be quite limited. The most important point to make is that the pastoral carers today must look to the communal contextual for critique of their assumptions about what is normative for special relationships. The carer must "hang loose" with judgments about what is universal and what is particular in patterns of family life, particularly about what *ought* to be. Nevertheless, such judgments must be made and pastoral care informed by them. The norm of seeking the balances of care in family living is flexible, informed by all three paradigms. Here, in pointing to contributions of the communal contextual paradigm to pastoral care, I focus briefly on only two theorists.

In chapter 2, I used the work of feminist family therapist Deborah Luepnitz to point out how attention to the contextual contributes to a "re-membering" of persons "embodied with both capacities and incapacities, living within the idioms of gender, culture, race, and class, enhanced and inhibited by unconscious process, making choices in historical time."[29] She described her concern as a therapist as helping "both women and men appropriate their powers to preserve themselves, to prize interdependence, to be freely for-others, to live fearless and principled lives, to have the capacities for critical thought, political resistance, and sexual ecstasy." In re-membering, Luepnitz wants to bring together the "remembering" associated with psychoanalysis with the "restructuring" associated with family therapy in order to

change the roles and functions of the family members and lead to
new insight and understanding of them.

Luepnitz reminds us that the closely bonded nuclear family that
has been the norm for today "is not a historical constant, nor is the
intense interest in children's needs a constant. . . . The contemporary family . . . derives its structure from the bourgeois family of
eighteenth- and nineteenth-century Europe. It is this family that introduced the pattern I have called *patriarchal but father-absent.*"[30]
The father's absence from the home and the family's increasing
isolation from the community had by the contemporary period
almost guaranteed that the child would be the primary focus of
the home. Sometimes the child would be the emotional resupplier
of the parents, sometimes the scapegoat, and sometimes the child
would become the ally of one parent against the other. In contrast
to the historians who say that the nuclear family replaced the village in modern life, Luepnitz says it is the child who has replaced
the village and that "this excessive burden helps explain why children feel that they must take care of their parents emotionally,
and often develop symptoms in response to stress."[31]

Luepnitz believes that the concept of the unconscious in psychoanalytic theory is needed to account for human intractability,
but that relational, rather than drive-based, psychoanalysis is
more valuable for dealing with family issues. Psychoanalysis also
helps understand that what is learned very early in one's history is
relatively unchangeable. Thus "it is nearly impossible to change
the ways one experiences and pursues intimacy—much to the
chagrin of contemporary couples and therapists." Psychoanalytic
theory helps to "account for the intransigence, for the unyielding
qualities of gender. It tells us that gender is neither so permanent
and monolithic as a biological explanation would have it, nor so
amenable to change as social learning theorists—including many
overly optimistic feminists—would have it."[32]

What object-relations family therapy is seeking, informed by
the contextual understanding of feminism, is the creation of

> a new father, a man who will not be the tired nightly visitor, who
> will be more than a therapist-appointed expert, more than a coach
> to his irresolute wife, more than her backup, more than the separa-
> tor of mothers and children, but an authentic presence, a tender
> and engaged parent, a knower of children in the way that mothers
> have been knowers of children.[33]

The therapist or pastor who takes the contextual issues identified
by Luepnitz and other feminist therapists into account will "seek
to help the family solve its problems not merely in any way, but

in a way that will leave the family less patriarchal and less father-absent."[34]

Nancy Boyd-Franklin is an African American family therapist who argues that there is no such thing as *the* black family. Rather, the cultural diversity among black families is too often overlooked and misunderstood. This is something that it is important for pastors to remember not only about African American families, but about all races and cultures different from their own. African American culture, according to Boyd-Franklin, represents a unique ethnic and racial experience because of the African legacy, the experience of slavery, racism, and discrimination, and the victim system. Moreover, there are many myths about black families in the social science literature that have painted a pejorative picture of family function. In working with black families in particular, it is important to focus on empowerment as a central part of any treatment plan.[35]

What Boyd-Franklin advocates for therapists working with African American families can be valuable for pastors working with other types of families different from their own. They first need to explore their own culture and family, including beliefs, values, and biases. This can be done with genograms and other historical research. Speaking about her work in training family therapists in cultural and racial sensitivity, Boyd-Franklin says that exploring and sharing of their own cultures is "the most exciting and vibrant way to dispel stereotypes and to convey the notion of cultural diversity. As each trainee presents her or his own family, the concept that there is no such thing as *the* black family, *the* Jewish, Irish, Italian, or Hispanic family becomes extremely clear."[36]

Intercultural and interracial study of the family is important in assisting pastors in their understanding of what is universal and what is particular in patterns of family life, particularly about what *ought* to be. The structure of adequately functioning families varies greatly. Rather than being overly troubled that a family structure differs from his or her own, the pastor can helpfully inquire about and discuss the balances of care among the generations of the family and the balance between care for oneself and care for others to whom one is specially related. Let us move now to a practical discussion of how pastors may address the balances of care in the families for whom they care.

Pastoral Care as Addressing the Balances:
Prior to Family Pain

Pastoral care for the special relationships of life, most often those of marriage and family, occurs at two points: prior to the occurrence of family pain and after it has happened. The care prior to occurrence takes place through the day-to-day encounters with persons in families and other special relationships as the pastor hears, remembers, and responds to parishioners sharing their special relationships with her or him. Pastors do this by learning to think relationally, by thinking not just of the individuals they know, but of those persons in a network of relationships. One does not have to know a great deal about those relationships, but trying to remember parishioners relationally in terms of things that one has observed or heard about those relationships contributes significantly to the care that can take place when pain occurs.

Although as a teacher and clinical supervisor my work is different from that of a parish minister, one of the dimensions of my work with students is knowing something of their network of significant relationships. My opportunity for doing this is in the classroom or in informal conversations. In the classroom I encourage the telling of stories, which are often about the family. Outside the classroom I listen for stories that enable me to picture relationships. On one occasion one of my graduate students said that she would have to leave class early because of the death of her grandmother. "I think you remember my grandmother," she said, smiling. And indeed I did. I remembered a story and my feelings about the story. A mix of sadness and joy came through in the expression on my face. "I'm grateful for your grandmother," I said, and the student told me briefly about the circumstances of the death. I shared an association about the importance of grandmothers in my family, and we went on into the classroom, our care having been given to each other. Pastors who hear and remember have many moments like that.

In addition to the informal hearing and remembering that are a part of pastoral care for parishioners' special relationships, the pastor's teaching and preaching is an important part of creating conditions where care can take place. The way the pastor understands and interprets special relationships in classroom and pulpit makes possible significant pastoral relationships in troubled times or may let people know that the pastor and, perhaps, the church are not available to them in their particular family situation. How the caring community and the pastor understand and celebrate festivals associated with the family opens or closes the doors for care at other times. The strong emphasis on the intact, happy, nuclear family at holiday times creates barriers for those whose families or special relationships are not like that. The Christian community's and the pastor's task is to point to and interpret the importance of care in special relationships but not to overemphasize the form in which that care should take place.

One opportunity for addressing the balances of care prior to the occurrence of family pain is found in the pastor's helping to prepare a couple for marriage. That situation offers an example of the kinds of care and concern that can be expressed prior to any discernible difficulty in family relationships. The community's care is involved in the way it establishes and carries out policies for how weddings should be conducted in that particular church. The pastor is involved in a series of interviews that deal both with the wedding and with the marriage that it celebrates.

Just how much the pastor can offer in interviews with the couple to be married depends somewhat on the way that the pastor is approached in asking for services and the specific situation of the couple. If the couple is simply asking the pastor to "do a wedding," what can be offered may be quite limited. Even in that situation, however, there should be certain requirements for preparation time prior to the ceremony.

If the couple is "not asking for much," the pastor will probably have only two sessions with the couple prior to the wedding rehearsal and ceremony. One session is needed for the pastor to get acquainted with the couple as adults who have made an important decision about their lives. The pastor needs to know if what they have in mind for a marriage service fits with the view of marriage of the Christian community that the pastor represents. If it does not, and if discussion and negotiation do not change their view, then it is not likely that the pastor can perform the marriage service for them. A second session is needed to fulfill three purposes: to further the pastor's understanding of the couple and where they are in their lives; to interpret more to them of the meaning of the wedding ritual that will be used; and to further develop some sort of relationship between the couple and the pastor and church. The importance of the last of these purposes is that it can pave the way for future pastoral care with this pastor or, more likely, another. (What I have said thus far might be modified somewhat if the pastor knows one or both members of the couple very well. Even if this is the case, however, the pastor is getting to know them in a way that he or she probably has not known them before.)

In circumstances where the pastor has a bit more time and the couple seem to be open to the pastor's looking at their proposed marriage with them, what is indicated is an elaboration of the three purposes identified for the limited situation: further acquaintance with the couple; further acquaintance of the couple with the church and its traditions; and using the premarital situation to strengthen the relationship between couple and church.

One of the reasons a couple may choose to use the pastor to help them look at their situation prior to their marriage is that marital choice today appears to involve so much responsibility. In the days of family-arranged marriages, there was someone else to blame if the marriage did not go well. Today so little is arranged by others that everything appears to rest on the adequacy of the couple's choice. As Brian Childs and I put it in our family book, "In a time of relative freedom sexually and extensive career preparation, when the determinisms of family expectations, sexual and social needs are less, few people 'have to get married.' Instead, they 'have to choose to.'"[37] The responsibility of that choice is often a heavy one. In the case of a remarriage, a person often knows so much about what can go wrong and how bad it can be that the positive features of marriage may be obscured. Most couples need help in accepting the human paradox, that knowing a great deal about another in a relationship does not resolve the ambiguity in the relationship.

Although the importance of what a couple can learn in premarriage interviews has for some time been "oversold" by the church, what can be offered by the premarriage situation in terms of a significant relationship has not been sufficiently discussed. A major function of premarital pastoral care is relieving some of the anxiety about the responsibility of marital choice "through relationship with a parental figure who has nothing at stake in the success of the marriage." Although Childs and I made this emphasis in our book, I would now qualify the statement somewhat. Of course, the pastor has something at stake in becoming related to the couple and performing their marriage service, but if she has too much at stake—if the marriage has to succeed because of the pastor's involvement—the couple loses the value of a parental figure who can look at the relationship in a matter-of-fact way. The pastor should be uninvolved enough to say, "You seem surprised and disappointed that there's something wrong with your relationship," and in doing so suggest some of the natural ambiguity in human relationships.[38]

What does the pastor "do" in a premarriage situation? Usually, where the couple are not asking specific questions about the character of their relationship, the sessions should be fairly well balanced between acquaintance with the "marrying church" and the "marrying couple." An article by the late Kenneth Mitchell and Herbert Anderson has been extremely helpful to me in working with couples and in interpreting this work to theological students.[39] Premarital couples, even those who are looking for some counseling help from the pastor, are usually reluctant to examine their own relationship. What can be done, almost immediately without much resistance, is to get the couple to look at the marital relationships in the prior generation of their families and, in doing so, to surface assumptions about what marriage is and what the couple's particular marriage is likely to be.

Mitchell and Anderson suggest a variety of methods for looking at the prior generation, such as discussion of family myths and traditions as well as the roles of various family members and the explicit and implicit rules for family behavior in the respective families. With classes, but also occasionally with couples in pre-marriage sessions, I have asked them to write or tell a story about a particular time in their family that reveals something about what living in that family was like. Discussion of such stories can reveal their assumptions about marriage and the family without being directly critical of their present relationship.

As suggested by the Wynnes' concern with patterns of care, premarital couples accomplish much by discerning the patterns of care that exist or existed in the prior generation.

> How did the various members of the couples' families care for each other? What kind of expectations about care and loyalty were generated? How may these expectations of the prior generation conflict with the expectations of intimacy with one's intended spouse? What negative and positive images of caring in the marriage relationship does the couple have? Much of this can be elicited through the discussion of a genogram or detailed family history, whichever seems more congenial with the pastor's way of structuring a conversation. Most important to remember is that this is not simply gathering information for information's sake but enabling the couple to see how influential the parental generation is in their relationship to each other.[40]

Then, to claim the church's blessing for a marriage requires caring enough to understand some of the ways that the church has attempted to relate marriage to a life of faith. This is another way of caring for the prior generation. It requires acquaintance with some of the views of sexuality and the family discussed earlier as a part of the classical paradigm. What religious views of marriage have influenced the couple's coming to the pastor and church for its blessing? Having some familiarity with this material and the interpretive data associated with the marriage rituals can assist the pastor in further acquainting the couple with the church as a parental generation that is assisting them in marrying or contemplating marriage.

Thus far I have focused the concerns of the premarital interview away from the couple's own relationship and toward the relationships within their families' prior generation and, to some degree, on their own relationship to the parental generation. What has increasingly become important to me, however, is also spending some time in directing the couple's concern to the future generation. This concern clearly grows out of the image of caring for our generations. Both the physical fact and the symbolic meaning of creating children together expresses most clearly the commitment to care for and to invest in the future. Whatever the result of the couple's decision to have or not to have children, there appears to be a powerful human need in most couples to express who they are through the nurturing of a child. There are certainly exceptions to this, but these exceptions are always significant in the life of the person making the decision and for the other member of the couple.

I have observed more anxiety in a couple's discussion of this issue with me and with each other than in any discussion that may have occurred about their sexual intimacy with each other. As parenting is delayed due to extended career preparation, the anxiety about whether or not the woman can have a healthy child and, if she can, whether she should, becomes more intense. Pastors who fail to discuss the issue of children with the couples to whom they offer care and guidance are failing to recognize an important part of what each person is as a human being. To make a caring decision about how one participates in the generation that comes after one is an important part of what it means to be human and, explicitly or implicitly, an expression of faith.

I continue to think of the pastor's premarital work as "providing an interpretive bridge between the couple's present life situation, their families of origin, and the way that the church has historically offered blessing to a marriage."[41] A portion of the structure for premarital pastoral care presented in the Patton and Childs book on Christian marriage can, perhaps, be useful to pastors preparing for or reevaluating this portion of their ministry.[42]

Pastoral Care as Addressing the Balances:
At a Time of Family Pain

How does a pastor with little or no training in marriage and family counseling assist members of a parish or other persons who have turned to her for help with the pain that may occur in special relationships?

To begin, the pastor is called on to remember two things: (1) that she is not a family therapist; and (2) that she does not have to be in order to be useful to a family and its individual members. The pastor's task is not to *cure* but to provide a structure in which she can convey her *care* to each member of the family in the presence of the other members. Although pastors need to be reminded that they are not family therapists and are not expected to cure, they also need to be reminded that they can make use of many things that they already know about families and relationships—including their own—in order to be helpful to a family that is out of balance.

I am using the term "out of balance" to follow through on the interpretation of the family and other special relationships that has consumed most of this chapter. I am also using it as a common-sense diagnostic term—a generic way that the pastor and the family can understand and think about the family's pain without using explicitly psychological diagnostic categories. I am certainly not claiming that all families are alike or that there is only one family problem to be dealt with. What I am saying, however, is that for a person like the average pastor, who is not trained in family therapy, understanding, interpreting, and intervening in family pain in terms of an imbalance can be a productive approach. The pastor who has understood and interpreted the balances of care as a part of her religious tradition as well as a part of psychological theory can engage a family in dialogue about their balances of care. That engagement or dialogue about the balances can, in most cases, help move the family in the direction of a more nearly adequate balance of care. Again, the question is, how does this take place?

It takes place, first of all, by the pastor's getting the family together. A significant part of what the pastor offers a troubled family is her care, interest in, and sense of responsibility for each member of the family. If the family are members of the faith community that the pastor represents and serves, the pastor has already been given permission to care actively for each member of the family system. And, if the family are not members of that community, the pastor has probably been consulted at least partially because of what she represents. Thus, she has been given authority to care and to structure the situation of care.

In the majority of the situations with which the pastor deals, "getting the family together" means making every possible effort to see the marital couple together in the first interview and avoiding situations in which the person seeking help talks about the spouse or other family members without those persons being present. Caring individually for family members apart from the others can take place later on, but the first expression of care for the family is recognizing and valuing the whole family by relating to them together. The problem may first be presented as if it were one person's alone; for example, a child is doing poorly at school, or a husband has become so overinvolved in work that he is no longer available to his wife. Whatever the presenting problem, the pastor's efforts should be directed toward first seeing the couple together or, when the presenting problem focuses on a child, seeing all the members of the family together.

The pastor who has gathered family members into her office or other suitable place needs to remember that whatever she may have learned about the importance of "being with" in pastoral care still holds. It is usually true, however, that family members are so strongly related to one another that the pastor will have to be very active in order to be with the individual members when they are in one another's presence. A pastoral carer who is working with an individual can afford to be more passive and focus her care on listening. When a pastor works with more than one person, although being with and listening are never negated, she needs to be much more active in structuring the interview. This is particularly true for the relatively untrained pastor: the less training, the more structure. The pastoral family interview may be likened to a classroom in which the teacher is clearly in charge, where he is encouraging each member of the class to talk and at the same time using his authority to encourage the others to listen.

The family having been gathered, the basic method of the family care interview is to talk individually with each member of the family in the presence of the others. This in effect respects the commitment and loyalties that the family members have, but at the same time affirms separation and individuality. It illustrates the balance of care between self and others and the concern with all of the generations of the family.

Other than the central concern with the balance of care in the family, the most important assumption for the pastor to hold in the process of engaging the family is that the whole family is troubled, not just one of the members. It is the whole family's behavior that is a problem or that causes pain. It is the whole family or both members of the couple that are out of balance. If this assumption is undermined, the ineffective family pattern will more than likely be reconfirmed rather than having the possibility of being changed.

The way the pastor structures a situation in which the whole family or as many as possible are together and the questions or comments that she makes during the process of the interview are often referred to as interventions. Intervention is a useful concept because of its literal meaning, "coming between." The pastor in her dialogue is, in fact, moving in between or among the relationships within the family system. The intervention is not a cure for what is dysfunctional in the family, but it changes the pattern of relationships within the family. The family act differently when there is a nonfamily member in their midst. In the case of a pastoral family interview, the purpose of the intervention is to help the family become more aware of how they usually interact with one another. If they can see a pattern, they will have a choice to make changes in it.

The pastor, as one who actively structures what goes on in the interview, asks a question—makes an intervention—such as, "What hurts?" "What's going on?" or "What's not working in the family?" Or the pastor may begin the interview by sharing her first awareness of the problem, saying something like this: "George spoke to me after church last Sunday and said that the family was experiencing a lot of tension, and I wanted to come by and see if my talking about it with you would help." (Note that the pastor does not present the problem as it was presented to her, but redefines it as a family problem in the first statement she makes. If the initial statement begins to reinterpret what is going on as belonging to the family, something useful will have already been offered to the family.)

To whom is the first question to the family addressed? Family therapists differ in their approaches, although there is some unanimity that the identified patient or problem should not be addressed first in order that the concept of family pain rather than individual problem can be conveyed. The statement or question about the family pain or problem may be addressed to the whole family to see who will respond first. It may be addressed to one family member, either the one with most concern about the family's getting some help or, perhaps, to the one who seems least concerned or involved. With the latter approach there is more likelihood that what is happening in the whole family will be addressed, rather than the presenting problem that has been identified by the most concerned family member.

As she has done in the pastoral care of individuals dealing with other human problems, the pastor looks for and responds to the pain of each person within the system, but not so much that she loses touch with what else seems to be going on with the other members of the family. Although the pastor is an outsider to the family system, she can, in effect, be an insider to the individuals within it by her sensitivity to their feelings. What is perhaps most important is that the pastor actively structure the dialogue so that it takes place between the family member and the pastor. Particularly for a pastor with limited training, this is the only way that she can maintain control of the interview and take at least some steps to break up the dysfunctional pattern of interaction within the family.

A useful structure for a pastoral family interview involves raising the same question with each member of the family successively and attempting to have a similar dialogue with each on the same question or issue. A useful second question might be structured around the issue of how long each family member has been aware of the pain and their observations of how it affects each member. A third question might involve getting opinions from each on what they think should be done to deal with the family's problem.

Although only three specific interventions have been mentioned here, many things go on in the process of making them. The concepts used for describing families in the literature may be useful in the process. Thus, some of what may happen can be interpreted as an increased awareness of such factors as family roles, boundaries, secrets, customs, patterns of communication, or rules. The more useful and, I think, more familiar concepts for the relatively untrained pastor, however, are the balances of care—how the family members are dealing with relationships to their generations and how they are balancing needs for closeness and for the experience of being a unique individual. Interpreting to the family what the pastor observes about these issues is most always useful in helping family members become aware of things that they had taken for granted. The assumption here is that awareness of the way things are makes change possible. Experiencing the pastor as one who does not see the family in the same way the family does suggests that there are alternative ways of being.

Some issues relevant for working with couples and families will be discussed in the chapter on pastoral counseling that follows. What is most important is that the pastor uses that with which she already has some experience—responding to the pain of individuals by letting them know that they are heard and will be remembered. The difference with a couple or family, however, is that in order to do this the pastor usually has to be very active in structuring so that one voice can be heard at a time and so that it can also be overheard.

This discussion of pastoral family intervention is applicable to meetings both with couples and with parents and children. In meeting only with a couple, however, several things need to be emphasized further. In couples interviews the pastor may need to be even more active in structuring the dialogue so that it takes place, primarily, between the pastor and one member of the couple in turn. The questions to the couple may be the same or similar to those used in a family interview. They should deal with the problem as each person, in turn, sees it. How long has the problem been going on? What are each person's hopes or plans for changing the situation? Perhaps the most important thing in a couples interview with a pastor is the opportunity for each person to share his or her pain in the situation. Secondarily, it is the opportunity to "overhear" the spouse share her or his pain. People can "overhear" much more effectively than they can hear; therefore the interview is structured so that the overhearing can take place.

Some Final Reflections

Throughout the process of pastoral intervention it is important to remember that one's worth as a pastor depends on caring, not curing. Any healing that occurs is more gift than specific goal. On the other hand, pastoral intervention almost inevitably allows the family to experience things differently and, in relation to a caring pastor representing a caring community, to feel enough freedom and support to try something new. Even if that does not happen, there can be real satisfaction for family members in knowing that the pastor has tried to understand what is going on rather than just assuming that someone is to blame for it.

Questions for Consideration

1. How are kinship and friendship similar and different in your family of origin? How would you define friendship and identify your own network of friends?

2. Discuss your understanding of the concept of generational care from the points of view of ethics and of pastoral care. To what extent do you think that responsibility to care for the future generation is applicable to persons without children of their own as well as for those with children and grandchildren?

3. Relate caretaking and intimacy in the views of the Wynnes and the Malones respectively. How are they complementary or opposed? Consider the similarities and differences in a special relationship with which you are familiar.

4. What symbols for marriage are most meaningful to you? Discuss their use in premarital and other types of ministry. In what way do your marriage symbols affect the kind of wedding ritual you use and the way that you intervene in marital and family pain?

5. What is or what do you think will be the contribution of your family of origin to your function as a pastoral carer? How does your own family of origin affect or how do you anticipate your separation or differentiation from your family of origin will affect the way you deal with family relationships that come within your care?

6. In contemplating intervention into the life of a troubled family, what gives you the most anxiety? Where do you anticipate your strengths in engaging them will be? What are most likely to be your weaknesses? What can be done to deal with your anxiety and compensate for your limitations?

Part Four

The Pastor as
Counselor and Theologian

9

Pastoral Counseling: A Ministry
of Availability and Introduction

> There is a desperate need for counseling. It is not a procedure to
> be undertaken lightly. God did not see fit to make the human
> soul less complex than the human body.
>
> —Seward Hiltner[1]

"Pastoral counseling is a specialized type of pastoral care offered
in response to individuals, couples or families who are experiencing and able to articulate the pain in their lives and willing to seek
pastoral help in order to deal with it."[2] Pastoral counseling in a
parish or other setting that does not offer counseling as its primary ministry is a ministry of *availability* and *introduction*. Its
essence is the pastor's being there and helping persons to make
connections with other carers. This chapter is primarily about pastoral counseling when it is only a part of the ministry offered by a
caring community.

Elsewhere I have argued that pastoral counseling is a ministry
of the church or, perhaps more accurately, a dimension of the
church's unified ministry in the name of Christ.[3] Although there
are an increasing number of persons who specialize in the ministry of pastoral counseling, pastoral counseling is not itself a profession but a function performed by persons whose profession is
ministry. The definition of a particular type of counseling as "pastoral" has "more to do with the person and accountability of the
counselor than with the methods adopted for the counseling. The
primary criterion for determining that a method is pastoral is that

it be consistent with what ministry is and that it be appropriately related to the need of the person seeking help."[4]

A pastoral counselor is representative of an image of life and its meaning affirmed by his or her religious community. The pastoral counselor offers a relationship in which that understanding of life and faith can be explored. In the light of the central image affirmed in this book, pastoral counseling may be seen as a relationship empowered by a faith in a God who remembers us and who, through a remembering community, offers us the grace of remembering God's love for us in Christ. Like the other, less structured, types of pastoral care, pastoral counseling, at its best, employs elements of all three paradigms for pastoral care in its practice.

Pastoral Counseling in the Classical Paradigm

Thomas C. Oden's book *Pastoral Counsel* is a rich and fascinating resource for rediscovering the power of the classical Christian message for pastoral caring. At least partly because pastors who are interested in counseling have had the reputation of being like the Athenians described in the book of Acts, who "would spend their time in nothing but telling or hearing something new" (Acts 17:21), Oden wants to remind us that long before "psychology was a distinct profession, pastors engaged in activities that required psychological wisdom."[5] It is important to remember, however, that, contrary to Oden's attempt to find Carl Rogers's "necessary and sufficient conditions for successful psychotherapy" in the church fathers, it is with the message of God's hearing and remembering that the classical tradition informs us, not with the method.

The persistent theme in the Synoptic Gospels of the importance of listening, of getting the message, and the contrasts made between those who are prepared and those who are not, offers a powerful image for the pastoral counselor. The theme appears repeatedly, but the image may be focused in the text in Luke 8:18, which the New Revised Standard Version translates as "pay attention to how you listen." *Blepete* is an imperative which literally means "see" how you listen. The Greek word denotes sense perception, being able to see as distinct from blindness. It seems to call on all the senses for full awareness of the message being conveyed.[6] In the same spirit, the pastoral counselor sees how she listens and remembers, seeking the connection between the counselee's particular life situation and the message that the pastor represents. Beyond that, what is called for in pastoral counseling today is not Rogers's "necessary and sufficient conditions," but a pastor who is available and who is able to introduce the counselee to others who care.

Pastoral Counseling in the Clinical Pastoral Paradigm

What pastoral counseling has derived from the clinical pastoral paradigm is the emphasis on the person and the relationship and the use of both psychological and theological resources to deepen its understanding of counselor and counselee and the relationship between them. What the pastor offers in counseling to his parishioner is what I have called "relational humanness."[7] He may or may not solve the problem that is the immediate concern of the counselee in consulting with him. What he offers, nevertheless, is a personal presence and availability, a relationship in which the parishioner can share his pain and experience empathetic understanding by one who, to use the image of the preceding section, sees how he listens. Even though the counseling may involve only one session together, good pastoral counseling involves a meeting of persons, not just the presentation of and listening to a problem. This understanding of what happens in pastoral care and counseling is a contribution of the clinical pastoral paradigm, the insistence that not only the message of care, but the person of the carer is important, as are the relationships in which the care takes place.

One who is not a specialist in counseling needs to remember that the brief contact which a parishioner makes with a pastor can be quite significant and can facilitate the forming of a longer-term helping relationship with another professional if that is needed. Certainly it is important for pastors to secure additional training in counseling when that is possible, but it is perhaps even more important that they not underrate what they have to offer without that training. I recall doing a workshop on supervision some years ago with some priests and bishops of the Episcopal Church. At one point I presented a case of a priest who was facing a multitude of difficulties. The case was presented as a problem for the group to discuss and explore ways to handle. When I raised the "What would you do?" question, a crusty old bishop with no training in counseling responded without hesitation, "I'd be there!" And I am sure that no one in the group had any question about the value of his presence. The bishop believed in what he was and what he represented. Any good pastor should have a similar conviction and not be intimidated by a lack of training.

The other side of that valuing of one's person and what one represents is the pastor's awareness that ministry is not to be identified with healing or success in problem solving. And the pastor, without defensiveness about not knowing how to do something, needs to be able to offer care without claiming the ability to cure. As I argued in the preceding chapter, a pastor does not need to be a family therapist to meet with troubled families and respond to their pain. She needs to know that there may be value to the family in their meeting, but she should not claim or expect too much from what happens in that meeting. Significant healing may occur, but the care, not the cure, is what the pastor can offer.

Pastoral Counseling in the Communal Contextual Paradigm

The effect of the communal contextual paradigm on pastoral counseling is still in its beginning phase. The effect of the communal dimension of the communal contextual involves, first of all, the recognition that pastoral counseling is not a private practice but a ministry authorized by a community of faith.[8] Moreover, it involves an awareness that pastoral counseling is increasingly being done by nonordained persons who in fact have a pastoral accountability and who are not just persons with religious faith who are trained in counseling. The difference between a pastoral counselor and a so-called religious or Christian counselor is that the pastoral counselor's primary accountability is to a community of faith. Should he or she have the specialized training for it, the pastoral counselor's secondary responsibility is to a professional association of other pastoral counselors, not to a secular professional group. One does not have to be ordained to be a pastoral counselor. The communal dimension of the paradigm emphasizes this inclusiveness—but one does have to have that primary accountability to a community of faith.

The accountability issue may appear to be related only to persons whose ministry is specialized in the area of counseling and psychotherapy and not to be important for the parish minister. That is not the case. The parish minister has an important accountability to the community of faith for the counseling that he or she does. Pastoral counseling in a parish situation requires that the community, not the pastor alone, be responsible for it. (What I say here is applicable to both ordained and nonordained ministers doing counseling.)

I want to underscore the importance of the parish minister's accountability because I have observed in meeting with groups of ministers over the years that many pastors carry out their pastoral counseling in secret. No group within the church knows how much and what kind of counseling they are doing and what percentage of their time is devoted to this ministry. The pastor needs to report how much of his time is spent in this way, any money received for these services or given away to persons in need, the types of situations with which he may be dealing, and any consultation he is receiving and from whom. The confidentiality that is so important in any kind of counseling does not have to be compromised by the pastor's reporting regularly to a duly authorized committee of the parish that is responsible for the pastoral counseling ministry and is periodically advised as to how much counseling the pastor is doing and how much of this is an outreach ministry for persons not members of the congregation.

One way for a new pastor to begin her pastoral counseling is to ask the governing body of the church, session, administrative board, or whatever, to form a small, temporary committee to assist the pastor in the ministry of pastoral counseling and referral. (I suggest that the initial committee be an ad hoc rather than a standing committee so that the new pastor, when she comes to know the members of the congregation, has some freedom to seek change in the membership of the committee.) The formation of this committee immediately says that the pastor's counseling ministry is not secret. An important part of the committee's initial work is to advise the pastor of the "network of care" available in the community, the best available persons to help in certain situations.

After the initial work of the counseling committee to get the pastor started, it can be used to consult and advise on a variety of situations. Should the pastor have a fund available to help people financially in certain situations? The committee can make recommendations on this or set policies so that every situation will not bring on a new decision. What kinds of situations have legal implications for pastor and congregation? The committee can advise and suggest resources. The committee can support and advise without in any way breaching the pastor's confidential relationship with persons. Perhaps most importantly, the committee provides the pastor a sense that she is not working alone and that pastoral counseling is not a secret part of her ministry. It is the caring community that is providing it, not the pastor alone.

The contextual dimension of the communal contextual paradigm is changing the understanding of pastoral counseling in many ways, some of which have already been discussed in other chapters, for example, the increasing attention given to issues such as professional power, gender, race, and culture in the counseling situation. Perhaps the two most important points at which pastoral counseling has been affected are: (1) questioning the tendency of counseling theory and practice to universalize its understanding of persons, while ignoring, on one hand, biases in their generalizations and, on the other hand, factors such as gender, race, and culture; (2) critical analysis of the use and misuse of power in professional relationships, such as those of pastoral counseling.

Although a significant number of doctoral dissertations have been written on these topics, the theories of pastoral counseling that specifically address issues of race, gender, and other contextual issues are, at this writing, just beginning to be published. They are already, however, beginning to impact our understanding of the counseling process, particularly with respect to assessment or diagnosis and at the point of goal or possible outcome of the counseling process. Pastoral counselors are becoming aware of the fact that the major theories of the person have been constructed with male images of the dominant culture as normative for health. This orientation has resulted in prejudicial diagnoses and lowered expectations of persons who are different from that norm.

Because so much of the assessment process associated with counseling has been focused on factors "inside" the person, to address that bias a great deal of attention now must be centered on factors "outside" the person that are affecting his or her function. What is most important for pastoral counselors of either sex or any race, class, or culture, and is particularly important for males of the dominant culture, is that they continually review and reflect upon their own values and biases.

Elaine Pinderhughes illustrates what this type of reflection by a male counselor might be like:

> I want women to have equal chances, but I still have trouble when they have authority over me. . . . As a White male, I believe in the rightness of their cause but when they're very strong and come after me, I feel threatened. . . . There is dissonance for me in terms of being committed to feminism, recognizing the injustices that have been perpetrated against women on the one hand, and what that plays out to be in my own life.[9]

What are the apparent or possible effects of the counselor's values and biases on persons who are different? How has the counselor's socialization process affected him in similar and in different ways from that of the counselee, and how might that be affecting the relationship? The task for pastoral counseling is not to give up the search for common characteristics of human beings, but to distrust assumptions about what is common or normative for human beings until the counselor's biases are explored and understood.

With respect to the issue of power in the pastoral counseling relationship, what is most important is recognition of its potential for abuse. The pastoral counseling relationship has an explicitly acknowledged dependency relationship as a part of its structure. In contrast to pastoral care, in pastoral counseling the counselee has openly said in some way, "I need help." The counselee has acknowledged weakness and vulnerability with respect to at least some points in her life and has given the pastoral counselor the power to help her deal with this need for change. The dependency involved in this relationship is not a bad thing. In fact it can be very positive, a temporary "regression in the service of the ego," as some psychoanalysts have called it. Being dependent, being cared for, can nurture one into the strength needed to face the challenges of life.

However, the dependency and vulnerability of the counselee can be destructive when the pastor's power is misused or abused, and it must be recognized how easily the gratification inherent in the power of the counseling role turns that relationship into a "forum for the unfolding of power dynamics."[10] The opportunity for the abuse of power often presents itself in the human tendency to relate to persons in the present as if they were persons from the past. Because the pastor is a representative of other significant authority figures such as parents or teachers, parishioners and counselees often relate to him or her on the basis of their experience with other authority figures who were important to them. A parishioner may feel that she is "in love" with her pastor or may feel rejected by him because of prior rejecting experiences. The pastor needs to take this phenomenon seriously and be sure that he does not in some way use the counselee to meet his own needs.

The pastor who is relatively untrained in counseling and psychotherapeutic practice should deal with this transference phenomenon by concentrating on the practical dimensions of the problem as presented by the counselee and setting limits on the time spent with the counseling. Familiarity with Karen Lebacqz's work on the power dynamics in professional ethics and her recent study of *Sex in the Parish* are essential for all those who do pastoral counseling, particularly for those whose training and resources for consultation are limited.[11] These are a few of the issues that the communal contextual paradigm has helped focus for pastoral counseling.

Pastoral Counseling as a Ministry of Availability

The emergence of the American Association of Pastoral Counselors (A.A.P.C.) in the early 1960s was a significant factor in the further development of modern pastoral counseling. The major concern of the A.A.P.C. has been the development of pastoral counseling as a specialized ministry which takes place, by and large, in pastoral counseling centers separate from the regular structures of a parish and is carried out by ministers who regularly perform few of the traditional duties of ministry. Many of these pastoral counseling specialists are better trained for doing dynamic psychotherapy and marriage and family therapy than are psychotherapists from other professions, such as medicine, psychology, and social work.[12] The development of specialization in pastoral counseling frees the minister who is not a specialist in counseling to develop a specialization of his or her own. The pastoral nonspecialist in counseling and psychotherapy can and should specialize in short-term counseling relationships which help the counselee put the presenting problem in a larger perspective and become aware of some of the resources available for dealing with it.[13] The minister who is not a specialist in counseling or psychotherapy should be a specialist in *availability* and *introduction*.

Availability is usually defined as the condition of being available, which in turn means that something or someone can be got, had, or reached—is handy and accessible. The comfortable practicality of that dimension of availability should be coupled with the awareness that it is derived from the word "value." Although pastoral availability does not mean that pastors should have no boundaries or limits to their responsiveness to those who ask for their help, knowing that the pastor and what she represents to them is indeed available is of great value to persons needing care. Experience shows that generally those who have trouble allowing themselves to be available to people are the most likely to have unrealistic demands for attention placed on them.

Some of the depth and importance of this practical-seeming concept of availability can be seen in looking briefly at philosopher Gabriel Marcel's concept of *disponibilité*, which is generally translated as availability. Although there is no English word that adequately translates the French, *disponibilité* means spiritual availability, openness to the other, readiness to respond, forthrightness.[14]

Another translator and interpreter of Marcel's work, Joe McCown, says that *disponibilité*, which can be translated as at the disposal of, or availability, has in Marcel's work a "surplus of meaning." It is an attitude of turning toward the other in which one's self is present.[15]

> It is an undeniable fact, though it is hard to describe in intelligible terms, that there are some people who reveal themselves as "present"—that is to say at our disposal. There is a way of listening which is a way of giving, and another way of listening which is a way of refusing, of refusing oneself.[16]

Disponibilité is also associated with receiving and welcoming and, what is perhaps Marcel's central concept, "creative fidelity." "Creative fidelity consists in maintaining ourselves actively in a state of permeability, and we see here a sort of mysterious exchange between the free act and the gift in response to it."[17] Availability as receiving and welcoming is also related to the concept of hospitality as it has been used by Henri J. M. Nouwen and Thomas W. Ogletree.[18] It is important here to juxtapose the usable, practical, operational meaning of the concept of availability with its deeper, mystical, philosophical dimensions, because both are essential to ministry.[19]

How is the pastor's availability expressed? To move from the mystical quality of Marcel's concept to a very practical one, it is expressed through structuring. Structuring, as the term suggests, emphasizes the structure or context of the pastoral counseling. Seward Hiltner, in his 1949 book on pastoral counseling, used the term "precounseling" for what is here termed structuring and in many mental health settings is known as the "intake" process. Whatever the terminology, it is one of the most important and most frequently neglected elements in the pastoral counseling process. The emphasis in a great deal of counseling training on what is and is not a good verbal response to what a counselee says has contributed to this neglect. Structuring and evaluation, which are done early in the counseling process, are intended to broaden the focus of the counseling or develop the context in which it takes place. Structuring and evaluating help to determine whether the counselee's concern is one that can better be addressed with the pastor or with another helping person. In structuring, the pastor is also assisting persons in recognizing their need for help and affirming their humanness in asking for it. This recognition helps to shift the focus of the counseling from being solely on the problem to a beginning awareness of the value of a helping relationship.

One of the most useful structuring tools for the pastor is what I call the "magic questions."[20] These questions, used in some form by all the mental health disciplines, are: "What are you looking for?" "Why now?" and, "Why with me?" The pastor needs to give the parishioner or counselee an opportunity to ventilate his or her concerns and thereby reduce the anxiety associated with them; but in order to understand how those concerns might be dealt with, the "magic questions" are needed to order the data in an understandable way. The first question allows both parties in the relationship to deal, not with everything, but with something in particular. The second question can enable the counselee to focus the concern further. The problem probably did not always exist, but began at some time and therefore can end. The third question emphasizes the importance of the relationship in pastoral counseling, but also begins to put some realistic limits on what might be expected of the pastor.

Another important concept in the structuring or precounseling process is "the unit of care." Can the concern that the counselee brings be dealt with most effectively individually, with both husband and wife present, or with all those present who live in the household? The pastor is generally better equipped to determine this than the person asking for help. Clinical training and supervision can assist the pastor in taking responsibility for this dimension of structuring. As was suggested in the last chapter, having the appropriate persons involved in the counseling process is often more important than what is said in the interview.

Within the context of pastoral counseling, evaluation or diagnosis means not losing touch with the larger issues in the lives of persons in the process of attending to their specific concerns. At the least this involves maintaining awareness of the kind of picture that a person paints of himself or herself and finding appropriate ways to share that in the counseling process. The pastor has a special interest in and commitment to religious concerns,[21] but his or her ongoing diagnostic concern is in formulating ways to allow persons to see the larger picture of themselves in relation to religious and other issues, not in classifying them in a particular way.

The most important ability of a pastoral counselor is the capacity to offer an honest, caring relationship. It is that relationship which provides the counselee a direct and personal connection to the religious community and the values it represents. The pastor may or may not know a great deal about the problem that the counselee presents. In most cases, the counselee has enough knowledge to deal with the problem. What he or she usually needs, therefore, is a context (relationship) within which the resources necessary to deal with the problem can be mobilized. Pastoral counseling, normatively, offers relationship to a person who is representative of religious faith and who is disciplined and honest in his or her caring.

The pastoral counselor's relational skill is expressed in the counseling process through hearing and understanding the counselee's story as it is presented and in beginning to reinterpret it in terms that present the counselee as one with significant responsibility for the events of his or her life. Both dimensions of the process are equally important. What the counselee says must be understood accurately enough to affirm the value of who he or she is as a person, but it also must be enriched through the communication of the pastor's understanding of the counselee. Moreover, the pastor's role and function as representative of the story of faith enables him or her to reinterpret the counselee's story in the light of the faith's understanding of who a person related to God really is. The interpretive function in pastoral counseling is clearly relational. It is not bringing symbols and stories from outside the relationship, but as Charles Gerkin has suggested, it is a fusion of the horizons of pastoral counselor, the counselee, and the community of faith.[22]

Pastoral Counseling as a Ministry of Introduction

For many years I have been impressed with the value of Wayne Oates's concept of "the pastor as a minister of introduction." The minister introduces people to God, but "as the Christian pastor becomes *durably related* [I have italicized this marvelous phrase] to persons" the pastor "introduces them to each other and to persons who can enable them to help themselves by providing them with the rich resources that friendship, professional skills, and clinical experience can afford them."[23] The ministry of introduction, Oates says, "takes the unsightly, seemingly valueless, and even detrimental stuff of human suffering and turns it into a whole new world of significant and committed persons for the one who is in distress." Oates was concerned, as am I today, about irresponsible referrals which sometimes appear to be getting rid of someone the pastor does not know what to do with and who makes the pastor feel inadequate. It is important, therefore, to reinterpret referral in a way that reveals it as a positive ministry— a ministry of introduction.

I once directed a pastoral counseling center in a large church where the senior pastor had served for many years. Among the referrals I received from him were young adults whom he had baptized as infants. He was "durably related" to the majority of his congregation. When these persons came to see me, it was clear that they were still significantly related to the pastor. They often told me some of the things he had said to them. More often they spoke of what he had meant to them when they were younger. It was also clear that, because of the way he had introduced them to me— told them something about me and my work—they almost always had positive expectations of what would happen. Neither the pastor nor the person referred seemed to be concerned by the fact that the pastor saw them only once and suggested that they see me for further counseling. There was no competitiveness. I was an extension of this pastor's ministry and proud to be understood in that way. It made my work easier.

Not all pastors can stay forty years in one church and know their people this well, but all pastors can be aware that they cannot care for their congregation alone. They need other pastoral carers within the congregation and professional carers in the community whose work they know and to whom they can introduce persons needing care. One of the first pastoral responsibilities of a minister moving into a new community is learning the person-helping resources of that community. The community agency directory, if there is one, may be a place to start, but the pastor needs to know much more than names and phone numbers. She needs to know persons in those agencies so that referral may be an introduction to a person.

Usually more valuable than a directory is the network of knowledge of helping persons known to the congregation and the congregation's own concern that the pastor not have to work alone. Wayne Oates has called this pastoral exploration of the network of care in a particular community "making friends with fellow shepherds."[24] As the pastor does become acquainted, she becomes a minister of introduction to them for persons who need their help. She is also indirectly reminding the professional persons in the community that the church can be a caring community for persons in need and that a good pastor can be a valuable associate in care.

The ministry of introduction, moreover, is a ministry of introducing persons to persons. Only secondarily is it making them aware of agencies. In order to introduce or refer effectively, the pastor needs to know the person to whom she is sending a counselee. If the person to whom the counselee is referred works in an agency, the pastor needs to know something about it and its policies and advise the counselee—if this is the case—that the person to whom he is being referred may not be able to be his primary counselor. What is important, however, is that the pastor know that the professional person to whom she is referring a parishioner or counselee will see the person initially and be able to interpret what is to be done to respond to the counselee's need. A ministry of introduction is always person to person, and if the pastor finds that for some reason or other that has not been the case, she can take steps to see that the impersonality that the counselee has encountered will not happen again.

A pastor introduces parishioners or counselees to other professional persons because of (1) lack of time; (2) training that is insufficient or inappropriate for the situation at hand; and (3) too much involvement with the counselee or the counselee's family to allow the pastor to function professionally as well as personally.[25]

As a minister of availability as well as introduction, the pastor has time to see everyone once. Availability, however, does not mean that the pastor is obligated to continue with a counseling relationship at the cost of neglecting other significant ministerial and personal responsibilities. A pastor who has an advisory committee to consult about his counseling can use that committee to advise him on policies of time allotment. Certainly, counselees should know before a session begins or, at least, early in the session that the pastor may not be with them personally beyond the first session and may introduce them to another helping person.

The issue of level or degree of training is also important. Good pastoral care requires that it be handled well. Wayne Oates comments that when "a pastor says: 'There is nothing I can do to help you,' he has literally pronounced doom upon the person, for he represents God to the person."[26] It is certainly possible that the person seeking help sees the pastor as her last hope, not the first stop along the way to what she needs. The pastor who says or somehow conveys the message, "There is nothing I can do" is conveying doom, even though it is merely the pastor's own self-esteem that is requiring him to imply to the counselee that, although he is competent to handle most everything, this situation is even too tough for him. One of the more important things a pastor can learn to do is to acknowledge limitations in a matter-of-fact, rather than an emergency, way. As a minister of availability, he is open to seeing and hearing almost anything, but he is not obligated by call or covenant to know how to deal with everything. Again, the cliché is important to remember. The pastor's task is to care, not cure. If sometimes healing comes from a pastoral relationship, it is a gift or grace, not something to be demanded by either party in the relationship.

One of the important things I learned from the work of interpersonal psychiatrist Harry Stack Sullivan was the importance of "matter-of-factness." The characteristics of the helping person that Sullivan emphasized are quite valuable for a pastor, who may be called on to be the first available resource for almost anything. Those characteristics are: *sensitivity, security,* and *realness.*[27] The pastor needs to be sensitive to the counselee's level of anxiety, not overreacting to it, but taking it as a natural thing for a person seeking help to be experiencing. The pastor's own calmness can help the counselee reduce his anxiety. That calmness and the ability to convey that she is comfortable in her availability to the counselee helps to convey security. Realness is conveyed by straight talk about the problem and about the pastor's limitations in dealing with it. It is important that the pastor not be so intimidated by what she does not know about a particular kind of problem that she cannot make use of what she does know. What she does know is who and what is available in the community to deal with the problem.

The issue of too much involvement with the counselee to work with him on an extended basis usually works out quite naturally. The pastor and the counselee are most often aware that they or their family members are related in a number of ways other than through the counseling. The pastor, therefore, can easily point out that another person would have more objectivity in looking at the situation with the counselee. Probably both the pastor and the counselee feel that because of the other ways that they are related, the pastor's knowing all the details of the counselee's problem might make their relationships outside of counseling more difficult. Usually, however, that does not even need to be said in interpreting the need for introducing someone to another helping person.

Wayne Oates concludes his chapter on the pastor as minister of introduction with an interpretation of Anton Boisen's description of the kinds of persons with whom a pastor must deal. It continues to be a useful reminder. There are persons who can take care of themselves rather well and who will get along well regardless of the kind of care the pastor offers. There are others who for one reason or another are likely to get worse no matter what the pastor does. But there are some "who stand at the crossroads, and the outcome of their lives will be *largely determined* by the patient efforts of a pastor in his ministry to them."[28]

Pastoral Counseling's Moral Contexts

For more than fifteen years Don Browning has made pastoral practitioners aware that there is a moral context to pastoral care. In one of his early efforts to illustrate the moral context in which pastoral care and counseling take place, Browning told the story of Mary Jones, a twenty-seven-year-old public school nurse who came to see a Protestant chaplain in a metropolitan hospital.[29] Mary is Roman Catholic, but has come to the Protestant clergyperson to get advice about having an abortion. Mary has been married, but has been divorced for slightly over one year. When she got her divorce she returned to the city where she grew up and where her father and siblings reside. She has no plans to marry the man with whom she became pregnant. She was referred to the chaplain by her psychotherapist, who felt that he was unable to help her make the decision about abortion.

On one hand, Mary believes that divorce, extramarital sex, and abortion are all sins. On the other hand, she is somewhat attracted by the possibility of actually having the child and wonders whether her traditional Catholic values will serve her well at this time. Browning describes Mary's thoughts about the possible abortion as "a kind of cost-benefit analysis."

> On the cost side, if she had the abortion she would probably feel guilty; lose a child which, in fact, she had always wanted; and incur some health risks. On the benefit side, she would not jeopardize her relationship with her family; be free of the burden of raising a child; not lose her nursing job, and not incur other embarrassments.

The focus of the chaplain's counseling work was on Mary's developmental history. She was the oldest child of a lower-middle-class Irish Catholic family of three children. She remembers having strained relations with her mother, which appeared to be due to jealousy that existed between herself and her younger sister, for which her mother always held her responsible. When Mary was eleven years old, her mother died and Mary assumed the position of the head of the household. She did all the cooking, cleaning, and other work around the house and, consequently, received praise from her father for this. Although her father had a persistent problem with alcohol, Mary spoke of him as the "most wonderful man in the world."

After graduating from high school, Mary went to nursing school and married a medical student. She helped put her husband through medical school, but after her husband became established as a doctor and seemed not to need her anymore, they divorced. Having the baby, Mary said, would at least mean "having someone to take care of," and "someone who would appreciate her."

What Browning does with this case is quite interesting. First, he comments on the kind of ethical thinking that Mary is doing and notes that it is "anything but classically Catholic in character." It is teleological in its cost-benefit analysis—trying to determine which act will bring about the greatest amount of good. But it is not the good of the greatest number of people with which she is concerned, but rather her own good, and thus, as Browning puts it, she is employing "an ethical egoist perspective." In terms of Lawrence Kohlberg's stages of moral development, Mary appears to be somewhere between the instrumental-hedonistic stage and the conventional good-girl, bad-girl orientation.

Browning then asserts that pastoral care involves dealing with both the kind of ethical issues evident in Mary's presenting problem and the psychodynamic ones, such as her need to nurture and be nurtured, to be affirmed and appreciated. I would say that it involves dealing with moral and other contextual issues, with issues of the persons involved, and with the message of the classical Christian tradition.

Central to this book has been the conviction that God remembers and that God's people remember what God has done for them. Christian worship is centered around remembering that God has declared unconditional love for us through the cross and resurrection. Regardless of what we do, God will not desert us, and it is from this assurance of God's memory that pastoral care proceeds. Sometimes pastors will be able to communicate this faith explicitly, but what determines how explicitly it is communicated in pastoral care is a judgment about how well it can be related to the particular human situation at hand. In my experience, it is most often received when communicated indirectly by the way the pastor hears, remembers, and responds to the situation experienced by the counselee. The good news is not good news if it comes in words that satisfy only the pastor. Pastoral skill depends a great deal upon sensitivity to the right time that the news may be heard.

Responding to the moral context of pastoral care, therefore, involves accurately hearing the issue, reframing or placing it in a larger context, and communicating it back to the counselee in a different way. That different way needs to be one that the counselee understands to be relevant to her situation. The pastor does not usually make a direct challenge to a person's way of thinking, because such a procedure is more likely to confirm the person in his or her position. Instead, the pastoral counselor suggests another way of considering the issue and encourages the counselee to consider options other than the ones that have occurred to her or him. In this case, the pastor holds on to the possibility that Mary's perception of her situation might change under the impact of God's grace, because the real question for Mary is not "What must I do?" (the way of law), but "What am I free to do?" (the way of grace).

Responding to the moral context of pastoral care involves relationally supporting parishioners or counselees to risk action in spite of the fact that their choices are never without ambiguity.

An avoidance of choice is itself a choice and a lesser one than a decision that faces head-on the guilt or failure involved in any of our serious decisions. Assessing the situation as best we can, we are free to decide in the knowledge that the grace of God will not desert us regardless of the outcome. Pastoral counseling involves the kind of communication that makes the human risk of choosing possible.

I affirm much of what Browning has done in calling attention to the moral context of pastoral care and counseling. His attempts to address the hiddenness of norms in our culture and his attempts to make them more explicit is an important contribution to our understanding of our pastoral work. As pastors we cannot simply apply the principles and values of the psychologists. We cannot avoid ethical issues and the discussion of ethical principles under the guise of letting persons decide for themselves. If they have come under our pastoral care, they have a right to expect us to engage with them in consideration of moral issues. They also have a right to have us respect them and the ambiguity of human choice enough for us not to act as if the answer to the moral question is a simple one. It must take into account who they are as well as what we think they should do.

Stating it too simply, I think Browning has dealt too much with moral context as offering principles for right living. More important, I believe, is moral context understood as a reminder to persons of who they are. In contrast to Browning's concern with ways of avoiding future sins or clarification of the gravity of present sin, moral context may also be a reminder of my identity and an exhortation "to live, as Paul might put it, in accordance with our new nature in Christ."[30] Morality as action and rule for action is important, but more important is our action in relation to our being, who we are in the light of God's memory of and care for us.

I want now to explore the issue further by looking at the situation of another Mary Jones who was concerned about an abortion, one who came to see me for pastoral counseling. She was referred by a pastor who was leaving town on vacation and had told her that he was unable to meet with her. Mary had had an abortion six weeks prior to coming to see me, and she began her story by saying she could not get over what she had done. Prior to her abortion she had seen a counselor at one of the family counseling centers who had told her, as she remembers it, "There's no right or wrong here. It's what's right for you." She also remembered her physician saying to her that the heart of the fetus is not formed until eight weeks. Mary said that she had the abortion because her husband would not even talk with her about having the baby. She had thought it would be better after the first week, but now after six weeks she is still not better. She cries all the time and is afraid that her two sons, one twelve and one eighteen, who is leaving for college in the fall, will find out what happened. I remember Mary looking at me with what seemed to be a mixture of desperation and anger, "Have I sinned? Have I killed a child?"

I responded as matter-of-factly as possible, "Those are two different questions, and it's important that you answer them separately. But give me a chance to get to know you. That's really the only way that I can help you answer them." I then proceeded to get acquainted with Mary in my usual way, not ignoring the problem she presented to me, but trying to put what had happened into the larger story of her life. Generalizing, one might say that my clinical perspective insisted on an anthropology as well as an ethics, a history as well as an act or a circumstance to deal with.

She told me of her life with a hardworking husband. She was forty, her husband somewhat older. They had been married twenty years, and over the years of their marriage there had been a slow increase in the family's economic well-being. At the same time, there seemed to be an increased pressure on her husband to maintain their success.

In the course of our talking about children and parenting, she admitted that she really felt that having another child would be great—she would have one at home until she was sixty. But her husband's attitude was another thing. He told her that she already had no time for him, always seeming to choose to do something for the boys rather than for him. She heard her husband saying that she must choose between him and her pregnancy.

I asked Mary to tell me some more about the sexual dimension of her life with her husband. She said that her husband worked so hard that they seldom had intercourse. She had been happy when they had sexual relations, but it was from that infrequent sexual act that she had gotten pregnant. "I wonder," I said, "if in some way you wanted to get pregnant." Mary did not respond to this, so I moved around that issue by asking about contraception. Mary said that they had always used the rhythm method, but this time she had counted wrong. When she told her husband that she was pregnant, he became enraged, and she felt that she had to have the abortion even though she didn't want to.

I asked Mary about her religious faith. She said that she was a strong believer in God and God's power and that she was looking for an answer from God. She had always tried to do what was right. Still, she could find no peace, and felt that in some way she hadn't turned things over to God. After hearing Mary's story—and

I have touched on only a portion of it here—I said to her something like this: "Let me tell you what I've been hearing from you.
You're hurting a great deal and trying to find a way to get over
the hurt. Your faith has been important to you, but somehow it
doesn't seem to be helping as much as it seems it should. And you
experience yourself in a moral dilemma which seems to be the
reason for your pain. I think your problem has to do with where
you are in your life and what you are going to do with the second
half of it, but a lot of other things have gotten mixed up in this
question—the pregnancy, the abortion, your worry about your
husband's working too hard, his relationship to you, having your
first son go away to college.

"You asked me awhile ago whether you had sinned and killed a
child, and I told you that those questions really had to be separated. The answer to the first one is, yes, you are a sinner, but I
don't think you are really dealing with the worst of your sins."
"What do you mean?" Mary asked. "It's certainly not that you
and your husband are responsible for the death of a six-week-old
fetus. You may not want to look at it the way I do, but I agree
with your physician as far as his comments to you went. A fetus
in the early stage of a pregnancy is not the same as a child. I believe that the pain over the abortion will gradually go away, but
the pain of what you are to do with the second half of your life
will last longer and is even harder to deal with. Your worst sin is
avoiding that."

"Pray for me," said Mary.

"I'll be glad to pray for you, but right now I don't want what I
say in a prayer to get in the way of your thinking about your life
and not just your abortion. Your own prayers about that are able
to say more about your life than I can. I will pray for you, and I
will pray with you the next time we meet, but this time I want
you to think about how I responded to your story." In the two interviews that followed I pursued the same general course and did,
as I got to know her better, pray with her during our counseling
session.

In presenting this pastoral event, I am not attempting to pre-
scribe what the reader should do in a similar situation. You might
have felt, for example, that it was wrong for me not to have
prayed with Mary in that interview. I am less concerned with
whether or not I did the right thing than I am in challenging the
reader to consider what he or she would say or not say to Mary
Jones. How does one bring together ethics, theology, and pastoral
skill in ministering to the Mary Joneses? Look again at what happened in the event.

First and foremost, Mary had focused everything in her recent life on that decision to have an abortion. The question she framed so desperately was, "Have I sinned? Have I killed a child?" In not attempting to give a quick answer I was not playing the kind of Rogerian counseling games we learned years ago, where you do anything to avoid a direct answer to a question. I was intentionally trying to meet the intensity of her feelings with calmness and trying to reduce the demand in the situation—the demand that "something must be done now." I was trying to move away from what the philosopher Alfred North Whitehead called the "fallacy of misplaced concreteness," in this case Mary's insistence that she and I look only at the abortion and her inability to get free of her guilt about it. What I am talking about here—this attempt to calm things down without saying, "Now, Mary, just calm down"—is pastoral care. It is beginning to build a trustable relationship with a person in pain, believing that the relationship itself will contribute to addressing the problem.

I continue my pastoral caring as I try to hear her story as well as her problem. I am not trying to develop a situation ethic dependent entirely on Mary's story or to follow the course of the counselor who said there is no right and wrong. Mary's story provides only part of the data for dealing with the ethical questions, but it does provide an indispensable part. Now, moving to the ethical dimension of the situation, not apart from but in the context of Mary's life situation, my assumption is that there is more than one moral problem here. It is too simple—I think, wrong—to deal with Mary in terms of abortion's being right or wrong. We could have very different views on that question, and the ethical and pastoral way of dealing with Mary would still be open for discussion.

My initial way of dealing with the moral dilemma of Mary's situation was to hear her one question as two. My answer, when I did respond to her, was (1) "Yes, you are a sinner"; and (2) "No, you have not killed a child." Whether or not you agree with me on either answer is much less important than your agreeing that a simple answer to the question is neither good pastoral care nor good ethical reasoning and response. Not to identify a six-week-old fetus as a child does not mean that I am for abortion or against it. In fact, that is not the main concern here, whatever position you and I take on the general issue of abortion. The main concern, pastorally, is to develop a trusting relationship that will help Mary with her pain and reduce her anxiety and guilt so that she can look at more of her life, not just her abortion. The main concern, ethically, is to assist her in becoming aware of the moral choices she still has in life as well as the one that she has already made. The main concern theologically is to clarify her identity as a person related to, not estranged from, God. If she can broaden her perspective enough to consider that, she may be able to see the abortion within the context of her whole life situation, and her pain will gradually subside.

There are various psychodynamic issues in this event which are interesting, but not necessary to explore in any detail. Mary may indeed have had an unconscious wish to get pregnant. It seems unimportant, however, that she develop insight into her motivations. Her beautifully naive wish to have a child at home with her until she is sixty is fascinating, but does not need to be pushed. The issue can be dealt with more appropriately by focusing on what Mary is going to do with the second half of her life. She is much more likely to see that as a relevant issue. "How are you going to improve your life and relationship with your husband?" is more appropriate to pursue than "Why did you think you had to have a child to insulate you from your husband?"

The ethical and pastoral dimensions of the situation need to be enriched by the pastor's theological understanding. For pastoral reasons, he or she will convey that understanding only indirectly to Mary, but what is done pastorally and ethically is deepened by a theological view of the human being as a sinner who is responsible and redeemable. Theologically, the pastor cannot afford to attend only to the abortion to which Mary attributes her pain. He or she must understand the pain and the sin more deeply—as having to do with her lack of faith in being able to deal with life as a middle-aged and older woman who is not actively caring for or being cared for by a child. The pastor's task is to convey through relationship Mary's importance to God and to others, even when she is not doing what she knows how to do best—caring for a child. Part of that affirmation is conveying the belief that although you are in fact a sinner, God cares and will continue to care.

Some Final Reflections

Just as Paul Pruyser has argued that the minister should be a specialist in attending to the religious dimension of persons' lives when determining their particular need for care, I have argued that the pastor who has little specialized training in counseling is, in fact, a specialist in availability and introduction.

The pastor's availability to persons helps to convey the truth that asking for help is not only a legitimate and reasonable thing to do, it is also a means of their discovering the importance of giving and receiving care at all stages of life. Pastoral counseling is a type of pastoral care that is not offered without a person's asking for it. And therein lies some of its importance. Pastoral counseling helps persons discover that acknowledging their need for help is not a liability, but an asset.

Questions for Consideration

1. What is pastoral about pastoral counseling? How is what the minister does influenced by what she or he is?

2. What are some of the things that "[to] see how you listen" may mean in pastoral counseling? How does a pastor listen, and what does she listen for?

3. Discuss the relationship between accountability and confidentiality in parish pastoral counseling.

4. What is the power of a pastor in a pastoral counseling relationship? In what way does the gender of the pastor affect that power? How does transference or the bringing of past relationships into the present affect it?

5. What are the most important elements in introducing a parishioner or counselee to another person for help? What is the pastor's responsibility to the parishioner after a referral has taken place?

6. What does it mean to say that pastoral counseling "involves the kind of communication that makes the human risk of choosing possible"?

7. What is your understanding of moral context in pastoral counseling? What factors influence the pastor's use of that context in dialogue with a counselee? Again, in this context, how is what one *is* related to what one *does*?

10

Theological Reflection on Pastoral Caring

> Theological reflection always involves a mutually informative dia-
> logue between its normative sources and human experience in a
> particular political, economic, cultural, and historical environment.
> —Shirley C. Guthrie[1]

Although this is a book on pastoral care, not theology, one of the
assumptions of this chapter and of the entire book is that it is important to think about pastoral care as well as to do it. This chapter,
therefore, is a theological reflection on pastoral care and an example of pastoral theological method. I begin with some concepts that
are often used to think about the method of theology in general
and practical theology in particular. This is followed by two examples of methods of reflecting theologically on the practice of ministry. Finally there is a reflection on the method of this book. This is
not because of the importance of the method itself, but to give another example of theological reflection on pastoral care.

Pastoral Theological Methods

In thinking theologically about pastoral care it is useful to be
aware of the three languages of theology. First-order language is
the collection of phrases like "God loves me" or "God remembers
me," which in story, hymn, or ritual express the way an individual or a community affirms its relationship with God. It is also the
first language used to give voice to religious experience. It is expressive, but essentially uncritical or comparative.

The second-order language of theology is distinguished by critique and comparison. It examines the essential religious meanings

growing out of first-order language and experience and compares them with the beliefs of a particular community of faith. In that process, theology further explicates and reinterprets the doctrines of the faith community in relation to ongoing religious experience of the first order.

Third-order theological language deals with how theology is done. It involves the method of theology. It steps back from both first-order experiencing and second-order formulations and examines the process of doing theology. What are the materials or sources of theology? What is the relative authority of each source? In what way are the materials put together in a liturgical, doctrinal, or other form?[2]

Pastoral theology involves "a two-way movement between (theological) theory and (pastoral) practice," according to Theodore Jennings. This move between theory and practice takes place something like this: "Pastoral practice provides a norm as well as a source for theological reflection and formulation." Only if theological or doctrinal assertions prove to be actually illuminating in pastoral practice "do they retain the general interpretive power which is necessary for second order discourse. Thus with respect to a particular proposal or doctrine it is appropriate to inquire whether it has implications for understanding of or intervention in situations of pastoral care and counseling."[3]

Thinking from practice to theory takes place when a pastor asks whether what took place in a particular pastoral encounter is in keeping with the doctrines and values of his or her religious tradition. There may be a confirming relation between these practices and theology or a disconfirming one, so that a particular practice is abandoned because it is inconsistent with beliefs, for example, about human responsibility and freedom.

Another two-way dialogue that is discussed by Jennings and which has been a part of the method of this book is the dialogue between theology and the human sciences. This dialogue is most likely to be productive under two conditions: (1) when it is focused on theories about phenomena common to both disciplines, such as human nature and its transformation; (2) when each discipline takes seriously the other's claim to offer a theoretical, reflective, and useful way of interpreting human phenomena comparable to the other's scheme of explication and interpretation. This kind of dialogue is second-order to second-order or concept to concept, dialogue. It cannot reduce first-order descriptions of religious experience to second-order psychological categories or judge powerful experiences without obvious religious content to be unimportant because they do not fit in second-order or theological categories.

Such dialogue allows theoretical material from outside one's field to be used to enrich the understanding of the human within one's primary field.[4]

Methods of Theological Reflection Related to Practice

One of the most widely known methods of theological reflection related to the practice of ministry is found in James and Evelyn Whitehead's *Method in Ministry*. They work with "three sources of religiously relevant information—Christian Tradition, the experience of the community of faith, and the resources of the culture."[5] "Tradition," in contrast to the other two sources, is capitalized, suggesting, as some who have used the model have said, that the Whiteheads give it more weight than the other sources. Whether or not that is the case, the way the Whiteheads do it can be an encouragement to others thinking about pastoral care to make their own "third order" theological decision about the relative weight that they give to these sources. "The minister does not look to the Christian Tradition," say the Whiteheads,

> to provide a simple, proof-text answer to a contemporary pastoral question, but to provide parameters for a solution—examples of how Christians, in faith, have addressed similar problems. Different responses within Scripture, the Church Fathers, medieval theology, and in twentieth-century Christianity guide the minister to a genuinely Christian resolution of the question.[6]

Interestingly, the Whiteheads speak of the alienation that many Christians feel in relation to the Tradition. Their gentle argument is not that the average minister needs to be an expert on the Tradition but that he or she needs to "befriend" it. This, they say, includes "both critical awareness of and comfort with the diverse testimony of the Tradition on a specific pastoral concern."[7]

With respect to the "experience of the community of faith," the Whiteheads appeal to the Vatican II document *Lumen Gentium* as recognizing the "sense of the faithful as a powerful, unerring expression of Christian faith," but attempt to go around the emphasis on uniformity in the document to affirm instead the "diverse expressions in many communities which comprise the Christian Church."

Cultural information includes historical and contemporary analyses of culture, philosophy, political interpretations of human community, social sciences of the person and society, and information from other religious traditions. Cultural information, say the Whiteheads, "represents not a realm of unredeemed nature, but a mixed environment, partly antithetical to and partly complementary to Christian life."[8]

Using these three sources for theological reflection, the Whiteheads' three-stage method involves (1) *attending*—seeking out information on a particular pastoral concern; (2) *assertion*—engaging the information from the three sources in a process of mutual clarification and challenge in order to deepen religious insight; and (3) *decision*—moving from insight through decision to concrete pastoral action.[9]

James Whitehead, in a later writing, brings in the imagination as a major element in theological reflection and in the interplay of the three authorities. "Our deepest convictions and biases abide not in clear and available intellectual concepts, but in the images and fantasies often hidden somewhere within us." Moreover, effective and enjoyable interplay

> happens only if these authorities really engage one another. If tradition overwhelms a person's experience with its interpretation, no interplay occurs; likewise, if one's experience is so absorbing that it ignores or rejects any information from the religious tradition, no exchange happens.[10]

Another method of theological reflection on ministry has been developed by James N. Poling. In a book coauthored with Donald E. Miller, Poling developed a method of theological reflection which he related both to the phenomenological philosophical tradition and to the Chicago School of empirical theology, particularly the theology of Bernard E. Meland. The elements in that method are:

1. Description of lived experience;

2. Critical awareness of one's own or the reflecting community's own biases and interests;

3. Correlation of perspectives from culture and the Christian tradition;

4. Interpretation of meaning and value, a "confessional moment" or moment of theological affirmation;

5. Community critique of the interpretation or affirmation; and

6. Guidelines for practical application.[11]

This listing of the elements in Poling and Miller's method is too brief to capture the richness of the method, but it serves as an excellent example of what theological reflection on practice may involve. More recently, Poling has revised his method in the light of a particular issue in practical theology in which he has been deeply involved—physical, emotional, and sexual abuse. His definition of practical theology as "theological interpretation of unheard voices of personal and community life for the purpose of continual transformation of faith in the true God of love and power toward renewed ministry practice" changes his starting place for theological reflection from the general rubric of "lived experience" to a more specific one. The revised steps of the method are as follows:

1. Experience of difference and otherness. Perception of difference and otherness enables one to experience step 2:

2. Awareness of tensions within the self. This kind of reflection requires a reformulation of one's personal identity, and eventually of one's theological anthropology. This, in turn, leads to:

3. Awareness of the tension between oppression and liberation in the institutions and ideologies of the communities that shape human lives and of which one is a part. From this awareness one is led to:

4. Consideration of one's ultimate horizon, one's understanding of truth or God, and questions about whether the metaphors and images used to describe God are abusive or redemptive.

This fourth reflection, Poling believes, leads to a reformulation of the doctrine of God. The results of his reformulation, it seems to me, are less important than is his bold affirmation that the theology growing out of pastoral practice can go beyond anthropology to speak about the doctrine of God.[12]

Reflection on the Argument and Method of This Book

Each of the three methods I have discussed involves moving dialogically between two or more of the sources for theology. Sometimes the reflection moves out of an individual pastoral event. Sometimes it involves a composite of experiences in caring or other types of ministry. The reader who has moved all the way through this book with me may find it useful to look at the method and argument of the book as another example of the way theological reflection on practice works. The method I have used in this book involves moving toward theological reflection from some specific pastoral experiences, but mostly grows out of a composite of experience over a thirty-year period, with reflections on that experience modifying previous reflections. One could also describe my function in relation to this experience as that of both participant and observer. I have been both a pastor doing pastoral care and working with my own experience and an observer and interpreter of what others are doing in the field and how they are reflecting upon it.

With respect to the argument and method of this book, it began with an observation that, increasingly, it was not just the ordained pastor who was doing pastoral care—it was a caring community itself that was involved, with a pastor as a consultant and teacher for that community. Although I had done various types of training of laity in churches for many years, what seemed to be happening required more than this. It involved a reinterpretation of who the pastoral carer was and a reinterpretation of the function of the ordained clergyperson.

Growing out of that observation as well as conversations and more formal interviews with laity who were doing good pastoral care, I made a theological judgment that the modifier "pastoral," although still strongly associated with the ordained clergy, must have a more inclusive meaning. Pastoral means "representative of" and "accountable to" a community of faith, not necessarily being ordained. The theological assumption about the involvement of the community and the theological judgment about the meaning of "pastoral," in effect, changed or enlarged the meaning of pastoral care and called for further theological decisions or judgments.

I began with observations of care being done by caring communities, not just clergy. I then began to broaden the meaning of pastoral to fit my observations. Although my observations and theological judgments were not done apart from "second order" theology, the changes in my thinking seemed now to require more specific engagement with what I had previously learned about pastoral care. I also looked at ways that changes had been interpreted in related areas of thought and noted the use of "paradigm change" as an interpretive device. Following the pattern of the three paradigms for Christian theology, I identified three paradigms for pastoral care: the *classical*, the *clinical pastoral*, and the *communal contextual*. Each of these paradigms, understood as patterns, examples, or models, emphasized a different element in pastoral care. The classical emphasized the Christian message that is conveyed in pastoral care. The clinical pastoral focused on an understanding of the person giving and the persons receiving the message as essential to the care. The communal contextual emphasized the community's influence on the message and the messenger and the fact that there are important differences in the persons who give and receive the message.

Both observation and theological judgment suggested to me that the three paradigms do not succeed each other, although the influence of one or the other may be greater at a particular period of time. The book's argument has been that pastoral care today requires attention to all three. Pastoral carers, lay or ordained, need to be aware of, in touch with, and able to share the Christian message. They also must be in touch with themselves, have some understanding of their own person and sensitivity to other persons. They must be aware that it is the community's message of care that they bring, oftentimes to persons quite different from themselves. Their knowledge of persons is knowledge that takes seriously the context in which persons live and the differences between persons.

Although the paradigm scheme was a type of thesis to guide the development of the book, it was more related to the sources of knowledge about pastoral care, about method, than a statement about what pastoral care was or what it involved. I looked, therefore, at the two concepts I had begun with, care and community, to find my thesis. How are care and community related to each other? Or how do communities care, and how does care contribute to community? The answer, after a period of reflection, seemed clearly to be memory, or more accurately, remembering, anamnesis, something that is also in the very center of the Christian community's worship. And with respect to pastoral care, as I reflected on my experience, what came back to me was the request that came time after time when I was a chaplain in a hospital: "Remember me, Reverend. Remember me." Remembering seemed to be at the heart of community and of care.

The theological thesis that emerged was based on reflection upon my experience as a pastor, the discovery of an important, but insufficiently explored theme in the biblical message, a longtime commitment to the inseparability of the message and the pastoral relationship, and an emerging awareness of the importance of community and context in conveying care. It was stated in the following way: *God created human beings for relationship with God and with one another. God continues in relationship with creation by hearing us, remembering us, and bringing us into relationship with one another. Human care and community are possible because of our being held in God's memory; therefore, as members of caring communities, we express our caring analogically with the caring of God by also hearing and remembering.*

Although a good portion of the first chapter was an argument for the importance of remembering for care and community, the thesis was not something that the book attempted to prove. It was, as I suggested, intended to be a guide that emerged periodically, in the midst of the discussion of particular human problems, to give direction to the discussion and a reminder of what pastoral care is. It is not problem solving. It is the community's care expressed as hearing and remembering.

It is obvious that care as hearing and remembering is not the only thesis or the only way to think about pastoral care. It is, however, a theological judgment that claims to be near the center of Christian convictions about God. There may indeed be other convictions about God that are a part of the Christian tradition and which may also serve as guides for rethinking pastoral care, but I believe this is an important one that deserves further reflection.

The assertion about God as rememberer and God's people as those who remember is a part of the Christian tradition and of the experience of those who do pastoral care today. "Will God remember me?" and "How will God remember me?" are questions implicit in virtually every situation of care. I have heard these questions explicitly stated and implied in many ways and for many years. It is important for me to be in touch with a message that responds to those questions. It is important that I have enough knowledge of persons to know how and when to convey the message. It is important to be sufficiently aware of the context to know when and how the message might be heard and understood.

There are a number of other elements in the structure of the book that might be reflected upon theologically, such as, the way the relation of context to care was dealt with, the interpretation of the "characteristics of the carers," and the image of the pastor as teacher/consultant. Probably more influential on both the structure and the content of whole discussion, however, was the decision to treat the major problems that carers are called to address as the context rather than the focus of care. That decision involved a theological judgment about what a pastor is and an observation based on experience of what a pastor can offer most effectively to a person in need.

There were two other essentially theological decisions made concerning the question of how to deal with pastoral problems. The first judgment was that there are certain problems persons face that are important not only because they profoundly affect the lives of persons experiencing them, but also because those problems reveal something important about what human beings are and what they should be. The second judgment was simply deciding what those problems are. My decision to deal with loss, patienthood, abuse, and relationship involved the judgment that these four problems had the greatest potential for challenging and changing persons and for revealing the nature and possibility of human being. The dialogue between human problems and knowledge about the human condition is a major element in pastoral theological reflection which needs far more exploration than I have been able to do in this book.

This reflection on my own thinking about pastoral care that has taken place in this book is shared to illustrate some of the things that I believe pastoral carers need to do when they think seriously about their care in the light of their faith. Some of this thinking will grow out of their own particular way of hearing and remembering God's message for them. Reflecting upon or sharing something of what they have heard in that primary relationship involves "first-order" theological language. Other theological thinking about care will take place in a community of other carers when they try to improve on the kind of care they have offered and at the same time work with others on what it all means for life and faith.

With the experiences of care or failure to care that are most meaningful or most painful, theological reflection will involve what I described earlier as a theological journey or a search for God when God seems absent. Fortunately, such a journey can be affirmed and supported by other members of a caring community and be inspired by other searching theologians like Edward Schillebeeckx and the night elevator man at the hospital.

Appendix

As I suggested early in the book, the most effective learning of pastoral care involves reflection upon one's own experience of caring and being cared for. The assignments below are intended to facilitate this process when they are discussed with a dialogue partner or a small group of other carers. They are related to the various chapters of the book.

Chapter 1

Write a brief story (no more than two pages double-spaced in length) to be shared and reflected upon in a small group of your peers. This story should give a picture of what it feels like to be cared for.

Write a brief story of an experience of community in which you participated.

Reflect upon and recall an event in which you discovered the importance of being remembered.

Chapter 2

Write a brief story about an experience in which you became aware of something about your own context and another context different from your own.

Chapter 3

Write a brief paper entitled: "A Personal Response to 1 Timothy 3:5."

Chapter 4

Write a story about an experience you have had in being supervised or in supervising another.

Chapter 5

Write a story describing an experience of limit and loss that you have had to face.

How has your faith affected or failed to affect that experience of limit and loss? Write a brief reflection paper separate from the story.

Chapter 6

What has been your experience with pain? Write a brief story of your experience "from the inside."

Chapter 7

Write a brief story of your encounter with someone's abuse of self and/or others.

Chapter 8

How does the story of a special relationship affect the way in which ethical principles are applied? Illustrate what you say by describing a particular relationship.

Notes

Introduction

1. James C. Fenhagen, *Ministry and Solitude* (New York: Seabury Press, 1981), p. 2.

2. Peter Hodgson, *Revisioning the Church: Ecclesial Freedom in the New Paradigm* (Philadelphia: Fortress Press, 1988), p. 12.

3. See Thomas C. Oden, *Pastoral Theology* (New York: Harper & Row, 1982); *Care of Souls in the Classic Tradition* (Philadelphia: Fortress Press, 1984); *Becoming a Minister* (New York: Crossroad, 1987); and *Pastoral Counsel* (New York: Crossroad, 1989).

4. Edward E. Thornton in an editorial tribute to Frederick C. Keuether, *The Journal of Pastoral Care* 25, no. 2 (June 1971): 75.

5. Hodgson, *Revisioning the Church*, p. 17.

6. See William B. Oglesby's *Biblical Themes for Pastoral Care* (Nashville: Abingdon Press, 1980).

7. Walker Percy, *The Last Gentleman* (New York: Farrar, Straus & Giroux, 1966), p. 4.

8. The term "minister of introduction" was used by Wayne E. Oates in his book *The Christian Pastor* (Philadelphia: Westminster Press, 1964), ch. 8.

Chapter 1 The Communal: Care as Remembering

1. Annie Dillard, as quoted by Parker Palmer in an address to the Association for Clinical Pastoral Education (A.C.P.E.), November 3–5, 1987.

2. Claus Westermann, *Genesis 1–11* (Minneapolis: Augsburg Publishing House), 1974, pp. 159–60; Jürgen Moltmann, *God in Creation* (New York: Harper & Row, 1985), pp. 29–31.

3. Joseph Sittler, *Gravity and Grace: Reflections and Provocations* (Minneapolis: Augsburg Publishing House, 1986), p. 18.

4. Joseph Sittler, "Ecological Commitment as Theological Responsibility," *Zygon: Journal of Religion and Science* 5 (1970): 174.

5. Douglas John Hall has made use of Sittler's work in several of his theological writings where he has emphasized the ecological dimension of care. In one of them he focuses on the concept "steward" as "a biblical symbol come of age." God's covenant with human beings left them with the task of stewardship. See Hall, *The Steward: A Biblical Symbol Come of Age* (New York: Friendship Press, rev. ed., 1990).

6. In John Macquarrie, "Will and Existence," in *The Concept of Willing*, ed. James N. Lapsley (Nashville: Abingdon Press, 1967), p. 78.

7. Martin Heidegger, *Being and Time*, trans. John Macquarrie and Edward Robinson (New York: Harper & Row, 1962), pp. 370–71, 375.

8. Nel Noddings, *Caring: A Feminist Approach to Ethics and Moral Education* (Berkeley, Calif.: University of California Press, 1984), pp. 40–42.

9. Ibid., pp. 24–26.

10. Ibid., pp. 79–81.

11. Ibid., p. 99.

12. Barbara Houston, "Prolegomena to Future Caring," in *Who Cares?* ed. Mary B. Brabeck (New York: Praeger Publishers, 1989), p. 96. For a more critical evaluation of care as a central ethical concept, see Jeffrey Blustein, *Care and Commitment* (New York: Oxford University Press, 1991).

13. Daniel Day Williams, unpublished lecture dated April 25, 1950, transcribed and distributed by students of the Federated Theological Faculty of the University of Chicago.

14. William H. Willimon, "The Priestly Task in Creating Community," in *The Pastor as Priest*, ed. Earl E. Shelp and Ronald Sunderland (New York: Pilgrim Press, 1987), p. 105.

15. Parker Palmer, *The Company of Strangers* (New York: Crossroad, 1981), pp. 119–20.

16. Ibid.

17. Ibid., p. 125.

18. Douglas John Hall, *Imaging God: Dominion as Stewardship* (Grand Rapids: Wm. B. Eerdmans Publishing Co., 1986), p. 120.

19. Frank G. Kirkpatrick, *Community: A Trinity of Models* (Washington, D.C.: Georgetown University Press, 1986).

20. Ibid., p. 140.

21. Martin Buber, *I and Thou*, trans. Ronald Gregor Smith (New York: Charles Scribner's Sons, 1958), p. 4.

22. Buber, as quoted in Kirkpatrick, *Community*, p. 142.

23. John Macmurray, *The Self as Agent* (New York: Harper & Brothers, 1957), and *Persons in Relation* (New York: Harper & Row, 1961).

24. John Patton, *From Ministry to Theology: Pastoral Action and Reflection* (Nashville: Abingdon Press, 1990), ch. 2.

25. Peter Hodgson, *Revisioning the Church: Ecclesial Freedom in the New Paradigm* (Philadelphia: Fortress, 1988), p. 52.

26. Ibid., pp. 22–23 and 35–36. Hans Küng in *The Church* (Garden City, N.Y.: Doubleday & Co., 1976) developed a similar *basileia-ecclesia* dialectic prior to Hodgson.

27. Hodgson, *Revisioning the Church*, pp. 58–63.

28. Edward S. Casey, *Remembering: A Phenomenological Study* (Bloomington, Ind.: Indiana University Press, 1987), pp. 273–74.

29. Palmer, A.C.P.E. conference address (see n. 1).

30. I have been influenced in my reading and thinking about this section by two series of lectures given to members and supervisors of the Association for Clinical Pastoral Education. The first was a lecture series by Henri J. M. Nouwen and was published by Seabury Press in 1981 under the title *The Living Reminder*. The second series was given by Fred Craddock, and I was influenced more by the spirit of the third lecture, a reflection on Philippians 1:3, than by any of its specific content.

31. Don E. Saliers, *Worship and Spirituality* (Philadelphia: Westminster Press, 1984), pp. 24–25.

32. Brevard S. Childs, *Memory and Tradition in Israel* (Naperville, Ill.: Alec R. Allenson, 1962), p. 34.

33. Ibid., p. 72.

34. Ralph W. Klein, as quoted by John S. Kselman, "The Book of Genesis: A Decade of Scholarly Research," *Interpretation* 45, no. 4 (October 1991): 384.

35. Gerhard von Rad, *Genesis: A Commentary* (Philadelphia: Westminster Press, 1961), p. 128.

36. Walter Brueggemann, *Genesis: A Bible Commentary for Teaching and Preaching* (Atlanta: John Knox Press, 1982), pp. 85–87.

37. Ibid., pp. 85–87.

38. See also the theme of remembering relationships in 1 Thessalonians.

39. Casey, *Remembering*, p. 8.

40. Sigmund Freud, "Further Recommendations in the Technique of Psychoanalysis. Recollection, Repetition and Working Through" (1914) in *Collected Papers*, vol. II (London: Hogarth Press, 1953), pp. 366–76.

41. Joachim Scharfenberg, *Sigmund Freud and His Critique of Religion*, trans. O. C. Dean, Jr. (Philadelphia: Fortress Press, 1988).

42. Milan Kundera, *The Unbearable Lightness of Being*, trans. Michael Heim (New York: Harper & Row, Perennial Library, 1987), p. 5. See also Kundera's *The Book of Laughter and Forgetting* (New York: Penguin Books, 1986).

43. Martin Heidegger, *What Is Called Thinking?* trans. J. Glenn Gray (New York: Harper & Row, Torchbooks, 1968), p. 11.

44. Ibid., p. 140.

45. John A. Mourant, *Saint Augustine on Memory* (Villanova, Pa.: Villanova University Press, 1980), p. 23.

46. Edward S. Casey, "Imagining and Remembering," an unpublished

paper quoted in Barbara DeConcini, *Narrative Remembering* (Lanham, Md.: University Press of America, 1989), p. 46.

47. Saliers, *Worship and Spirituality*, pp. 16–17.

48. See *The Confessions of St. Augustine*, Book X. See also J. G. Kristo, *Looking for God in Time and Memory: Psychology, Theology, and Spirituality in Augustine's Confessions* (Lanham, Md.: University Press of America, 1991).

49. Perhaps the most influential of the psychological skills training books are Charles B. Truax and Robert R. Carkhuff's *Toward Effective Counseling and Psychotherapy* (Chicago: Aldine Publishing Co., 1967) and Gerard Egan's *The Skilled Helper* (Monterey, Calif.: Brooks/Cole Publishing Co., 1982). A more recent skills training book describes Truax and Carkhuff as "essential reading for those who wish to become as empathic, warm and genuine as possible and to learn to gauge their progress in these dimensions." See Alfred Benjamin, *The Helping Interview* (Boston: Houghton Mifflin Co., 1987), p. 278.

50. Eugene Gendlin, "Client Centered Therapy: A Current View," in David A. Wexler and Laura North Rice, *Innovations in Client-Centered Therapy* (New York: John Wiley & Sons, 1974), p. 214.

51. Ibid., p. 215.

52. Casey, *Remembering*, p. 183.

53. Ibid., p. 189.

54. Susan Allen Toth, "The Importance of Being Remembered," *New York Times Book Review* 92 (June 18, 1987): 1.

55. Ibid., p. 37.

56. Henri J. M. Nouwen, *The Living Reminder* (New York: Seabury Press, 1977), pp. 24–25.

Chapter 2 The Contextual: Care as Re-membering

1. Douglas John Hall, *Thinking the Faith: Christianity in the North American Context* (Minneapolis: Augsburg Press, 1989), p. 78.

2. Seward Hiltner and Lowell G. Colston, *The Context of Pastoral Counseling* (Nashville: Abingdon Press, 1961).

3. See Douglas John Hall, *Thinking the Faith*, and Peter Hodgson, *Revisioning the Church: A Theology of the Church in the New Paradigm* (Philadelphia: Fortress Press, 1988).

4. Letty Russell, as quoted in David W. Augsburger, *Pastoral Counseling Across Cultures* (Philadelphia: Westminster Press, 1986), p. 239.

5. Elaine Pinderhughes, *Understanding Race, Ethnicity, and Power* (New York: Free Press, 1989), p. 24.

6. Ibid., p. 44.

7. Ibid., pp. 65–66, 69.

8. Clyde Kluckhohn and Henry Murray, *Personality in Nature, Society, and Culture* (New York: Alfred A. Knopf, 1948).

9. Augsburger, *Pastoral Counseling Across Cultures*, p. 18.

10. Ibid., pp. 20–21.

11. Ibid., p. 42.

12. Arthur Kleinman, *The Illness Narratives* (New York: Basic Books, 1988), pp. 232–33.

13. Clifford Geertz, *The Interpretation of Cultures* (New York: Basic Books, 1973), p. 14.

14. Ibid., p. 23.

15. Ibid., p. 33.

16. Ibid., pp. 35–36.

17. Ibid., p. 49.

18. Ibid., pp. 52–53.

19. Eugene Robinson and Miriam A. Needham, "Racial and Gender Myths as Key Factors in Pastoral Supervison," *The Journal of Pastoral Care* 45, no. 4 (Winter 1991): 333–42.

20. Madonna Kolbenschlag, *Kiss Sleeping Beauty Goodbye* (San Francisco: Harper & Row, 1988), p. 12.

21. Robinson and Needham, "Racial and Gender Myths," pp. 340–41.

22. Lynne Iglitzin and Ruth Ross, eds., *Women in the World: A Comparative Study* (Santa Barbara, Calif.: ABC-CLIO, 1976), p. 15.

23. William J. Doherty, "Can Male Therapists Empower Women in Therapy?" *Women and Power: Perspectives for Family Therapy*, ed. Thelma Jean Goodrich (New York: W. W. Norton & Co., 1991), p. 152.

24. Deborah Anna Luepnitz, *The Family Interpreted: Feminist Theory in Clinical Practice* (New York: Basic Books, 1988), pp. 19–20.

25. Ibid., p. 20.

26. Ibid., pp. 21–22.

27. Ibid., p. 275.

28. Ibid., p. 148.

29. Ibid., p. 195.

30. Pinderhughes, *Understanding Race, Ethnicity, and Power*, p. 109.

31. Linda Webb Watson, "The Sociology of Power," in *Women and Power*, p. 53.

32. Carolyn Heilbrun, *Writing a Woman's Life* (New York: Ballantine Books, 1989), p. 18.

33. Michael Basch, "Toward a Theory That Encompasses Depression: A Revision of Existing Causal Hypotheses in Psychoanalysis," in James Anthony and Theresa Benedek, eds., *Depression and Human Existence* (Boston: Little, Brown & Co., 1975), p. 513.

34. Michael Lerner, *Surplus Powerlessness* (Oakland, Calif.: Institute for Labor and Mental Health, 1986), pp. 2–5.

35. Judith Lynn Orr, "Ministry with Working-Class Women," *The Journal of Pastoral Care* 45, no. 4 (Winter 1991): 343. See also Judith Lynn Orr, *A Dialectical Understanding of the Psychological and Moral Development of*

Working-Class Women with Implications for Pastoral Counseling (Ann Arbor, Mich.: University Microfilms, 1990).

36. See also Pamela D. Couture, *Blessed Are the Poor?* (Nashville: Abingdon Press, 1991).

37. Christine Y. Wiley, "A Ministry of Empowerment: A Holistic Model for Pastoral Counseling in the African American Community," *The Journal of Pastoral Care* 45, no. 4 (Winter 1991): 355–64.

38. Pinderhughes, *Understanding Race, Ethnicity, and Power*, pp. 111 and 138.

39. Monica McGoldrick, "For Love or Money," in *Women and Power*, p. 243.

40. See John Patton, "Problem Solving," *Dictionary of Pastoral Care and Counseling*, ed. Rodney J. Hunter (Nashville: Abingdon Press, 1990), p. 955.

41. Shirley C. Guthrie, *Christian Doctrine* (Atlanta: John Knox Press, 1968), p. 11.

42. John Patton, "The 'Secret' of Pastoral Counseling," *The Journal of Pastoral Care* 36, no. 2 (June 1982): 73–75.

43. Shirley C. Guthrie, "Human Condition/Predicament (Theological Perspective)," pp. 542–43, and Rodney J. Hunter, "Human Condition/ Predicament (Clinical Pastoral Perspective)," p. 541, in *Dictionary of Pastoral Care and Counseling*.

44. Don S. Browning, *The Moral Context of Pastoral Care* (Philadelphia: Westminster Press, 1976).

45. Pinderhughes, *Understanding Race, Ethnicity, and Power*, pp. 24–25.

46. Geertz, *The Interpretation of Cultures*, pp. 52–53.

Chapter 3 Characteristics of the Carers

1. John Patton and Brian H. Childs, *Christian Marriage and Family: Caring for Your Generation* (Nashville: Abingdon Press, 1988), pp. 213–14.

2. Wayne E. Oates, *The Christian Pastor* (Philadelphia: Westminster Press, 1964), p. 72.

3. *COCU Consensus*, ed. Gerald F. Moede, approved and commended to the churches by the Sixteenth Plenary of the Consultation on Church Union, November 30, 1984 (Princeton, N.J.: Consultation on Church Union, 1985), p. 42; World Council of Churches, *Baptism, Eucharist, and Ministry*, Faith and Order Paper No. 111, 1982 (Geneva: World Council of Churches, 1982), p. 25. See also *The Documents of Vatican II*, ed. Walter M. Abbott, S.J. (New York: American Press, 1966), pp. 56–60 and 491–95.

4. David Duncombe, *The Shape of the Christian Life* (Nashville: Abingdon Press, 1969).

5. David Duncombe, "Christian Life," *Dictionary of Pastoral Care and Counseling*, ed. Rodney J. Hunter (Nashville: Abingdon Press, 1990), p. 148.

6. Ibid., pp. 148–49.

7. Karl Barth, *Church Dogmatics: The Doctrine of Creation,* vol III, part 2 (Edinburgh: T. & T. Clark, 1960), pp. 220–43.

8. Ibid., pp. 250, 252, 260, 267, 273.

9. McKenzie Brown, *Ultimate Concern: Tillich in Dialogue* (New York: Harper & Row, 1965), p. 145.

10. Ibid., p. 161.

11. Paul Tillich, *Systematic Theology,* III (Chicago: University of Chicago Press, 1963), p. 237.

12. Brown, *Ultimate Concern,* p. 185.

13. Tillich, *Systematic Theology,* III, p. 231.

14. Ibid., pp. 232–33.

15. Ibid., pp. 235–36.

16. Oates, *The Christian Pastor,* ch. 3.

17. Søren Kierkegaard, *Fear and Trembling—Repetition,* ed. and trans. Howard V. Hong and Edna H. Hong (Princeton, N.J.: Princeton University Press, 1983), pp. 38–41.

18. Duncombe, *Shape of the Christian Life,* p. 149.

19. Edward E. Thornton, "Awaking Consciousness: The Psychological Reality in Christ-Consciousness," *Review and Expositor* 76, no. 2 (Spring 1979): 187.

20. Ibid.

21. Edward E. Thornton, *Being Transformed: An Inner Way of Spiritual Growth* (Philadelphia: Westminster Press, 1984).

22. Seward Hiltner, *Preface to Pastoral Theology* (Nashville: Abingdon Press, 1958), pp. 18–19.

23. Paul Tillich, "The Theology of Pastoral Care," *Pastoral Psychology* 10, no. 97 (October 1959): 21–26.

24. See the interpretation of Kierkegaard's concept of repetition in John D. Caputo's *Radical Hermeneutics* (Bloomington, Ind.: Indiana University Press, 1987) and Romney C. Mozley's *Becoming a Self Before God* (Nashville: Abingdon Press, 1990), pp. 62–63.

25. In this section I am following the outline and argument of my article on "Authority Issues in Pastoral Care," *Dictionary of Pastoral Care and Counseling,* pp. 62–63.

26. Richard Sennett, *Authority* (New York: Vintage Books, 1980).

27. Ibid., p. 63.

28. Patton and Childs, *Christian Marriage,* pp. 227–28.

29. Bernard Cooke, *Ministry to Word and Sacraments: History and Theology* (Philadelphia: Fortress Press, 1976), p. 197.

30. John Hunter, "Dear Master, in Whose Life I See," *The Methodist Hymnal* (Nashville: Board of Publication of the Methodist Church, 1964).

31. Paul Tillich, *Systematic Theology,* II (Chicago: University of Chicago Press, 1957), p. 121.

32. Ibid., p. 124.

Chapter 4 Care Through Consultation on Caring

1. Heije Faber, *Pastoral Care and Clinical Training in America* (Arnhem: VanLoghum Slaterus, 1961), pp. 30–32, 59–60.

2. James C. Fenhagen, *Ministry and Solitude* (New York: Seabury Press, 1981), p. 7.

3. World Council of Churches, *Baptism, Eucharist, and Ministry*, Faith and Order Paper No. 111, 1982 (Geneva: World Council of Churches, 1982), pp. 25–26.

4. James C. Fenhagen, *Mutual Ministry* (New York: Seabury Press, 1977), p. 105.

5. Ronald H. Sunderland, "Training Clergy to Be Supervisors: A Mandate for Theological Education," *Journal of Supervision and Training in Ministry* 10 (1988): 229.

6. Paul Tillich, "The Theology of Pastoral Care," *Pastoral Psychology* 10, no. 97 (October 1959): 21–26.

7. Fenhagen, *Mutual Ministry*, pp. 27–28.

8. John T. McNeil, *A History of the Cure of Souls* (New York: Harper & Brothers, 1951).

9. William A. Clebsch and Charles R. Jaekle, *Pastoral Care in Historical Perspective: An Essay with Exhibits* (Englewood Cliffs, N.J.: Prentice-Hall, 1964).

10. See Thomas C. Oden, *Pastoral Theology: Essentials of Ministry* (New York: Harper & Row, 1983); *Care of Souls in the Classic Tradition* (Philadelphia: Fortress Press, 1984); *Pastoral Counsel* (New York: Crossroad, 1989). See also Philip L. Culbertson and Arthur Bradford Shippee, eds., *The Pastor: Readings from the Patristic Period* (Minneapolis: Fortress Press, 1990).

11. Oden, *Care of Souls*, pp. 12–13.

12. See the discussion of this method in David Tracy's *Blessed Rage for Order* (New York: Seabury Press, 1979), pp. 45–46.

13. David A. Steele, *Images of Leadership and Authority in the Church* (Lanham, Md.: University Press of America, 1986), pp. 18–19.

14. John Patton, "Supervision, Pastoral," in *Dictionary of Pastoral Care and Counseling*, ed. Rodney J. Hunter (Nashville: Abingdon Press, 1990), pp. 1242–43.

15. Steele, *Images of Leadership*, p. 78.

16. Bernard Cooke, *Ministry to Word and Sacraments: History and Theology* (Philadelphia: Fortress Press, 1976), p. 197.

17. Patton, "Supervision, Pastoral," p. 1242.

18. Ibid.

19. See Richard Robert Osmer, *A Teachable Spirit: Recovering the Teaching Office of the Church* (Louisville, Ky.: Westminster/John Knox Press, 1990).

20. I am not claiming that this is the dominant theory and practice of supervision in the C.P.E. movement. I believe, however, that it is quite relevant to this point in history. See John Patton, "Self-evaluation Through Relational Experience: A C.P.E. Perspective," in *Clergy and Career*

Development, ed. Richard A. Hunt, John E. Hinkle, Jr., and H. Newton Maloney (Nashville: Abingdon Press, 1990), pp. 123–28.

21. *COCU Consensus,* ed. Gerald F. Moede, approved and commended to the churches by the Sixteenth Plenary of the Consultation on Church Union, November 30, 1984 (Princeton, N.J.: Consultation on Church Union, 1985), pp. 42–43.

22. World Council of Churches, *Baptism, Eucharist, and Ministry,* Faith and Order Paper No. 111, 1982 (Geneva: World Council of Churches, 1982), pp. 24–25.

23. See also Isidore Gorski, "Commentary on the Decrees on the Apostolate of the Laity," in *The Church Renewed: The Documents of Vatican II Reconsidered,* ed. George P. Schner (Lanham, Md.: University Press of America, 1986), pp. 73–80.

24. Lynn Rhodes, "Supervision of Women in Parish Contexts," *Journal of Supervision and Training in Ministry* 10 (1988): 200, 202.

25. Ibid., p. 204.

26. Eldon L. Olson, "Lay Care Ministries: A Pastoral Theological Assessment," *Journal of Supervision and Training in Ministry* 10 (1988): 170–73.

27. Tillich, "The Theology of Pastoral Care," pp. 21–22.

28. William Lloyd Roberts, "The Pastoral Supervisor as Participant-Observer in the Small Affection-Centered Church," *Journal of Supervision and Training in Ministry* 10 (1988): 142.

29. Ibid., pp. 146–48.

30. See John Patton, "Self-evaluation Through Relational Experience."

31. O. L. Delozier, "Consultation," *Dictionary of Pastoral Care and Counseling,* p. 223.

32. *The Journal of John Wesley,* as abridged by Nehemiah Curnock (New York: Capricorn Books, 1963), p. 41.

Chapter 5 Limit and Loss—The Risks of Care

1. Thomas C. Oden has contributed significantly to the development of classical pastoral care through his research on the pastoral contributions of major figures in Christian theology and history. His work has reawakened many of us to the value of these resources and provided bibliographical aid in finding them. See Thomas C. Oden, *Pastoral Theology* (New York: Harper & Row, 1982); *Care of Souls in the Classic Tradition* (Philadelphia: Fortress Press, 1984); *Becoming a Minister* (New York: Crossroad, 1987); and *Pastoral Counsel* (New York: Crossroad, 1989).

2. Daniel L. Migliore, "Death, Meaning of (Christian)," *Dictionary of Pastoral Care and Counseling,* ed. Rodney J. Hunter (Nashville: Abingdon Press, 1990), pp. 261–62.

3. Peter C. Hodgson and Robert H. King, *Christian Theology: An Introduction to Its Traditions and Tasks* and *Readings in Christian Theology,* rev. eds. (Philadelphia: Fortress Press, 1985).

4. Jaroslav Pelikan, *The Shape of Death* (Nashville: Abingdon Press, 1961), p. 5.

5. Clement as quoted in Pelikan, p. 52.

6. Pelikan, *The Shape of Death,* p. 123.

7. Karl Barth, *Church Dogmatics,* vol. III, part 2 (Edinburgh: T. &. T. Clark, 1960), pp. 514–73.

8. Eberhard Jungel, *Death: The Riddle and the Mystery* (Philadelphia: Westminster Press, 1974), pp. 115, 120.

9. Migliore, "Death, Meaning of," p. 262.

10. Jürgen Moltmann, "Eschatology and Pastoral Care," *Dictionary of Pastoral Care and Counseling,* ed. Rodney J. Hunter (Nashville: Abingdon Press, 1990), pp. 361–62.

11. Frederick Buechner, *Open Heart* (New York: Harper & Row, 1984, orig. ed., 1972), pp. 129–30.

12. Frederick Buechner, "All's Lost—All's Found," in *A Room Called Remember* (New York: Harper & Row, 1984), pp. 186–87.

13. Judith Viorst, *Necessary Losses* (New York: Ballantine Books, Fawcett Book Group, 1986), pp. 2–3.

14. Jonathan Bloom-Feshbach and Sally Bloom-Feshbach, *The Psychology of Separation and Loss* (San Francisco: Jossey-Bass, 1987), p. 3.

15. Robert J. Lifton, Preface, *The Inability to Mourn,* by A. Mitscherlich and M. Mitscherlich (New York: Grove Press, 1975), p. vii.

16. Anna Freud, *War and Children* (New York: International Universities Press, 1944), p. 37.

17. John Bowlby, *Attachment and Loss* (New York: Basic Books, 1969), p. 208.

18. Ibid., pp. 27–29.

19. John Bowlby, *Separation* (New York: Basic Books, 1973), p. 377.

20. John Bowlby, *Loss* (New York: Basic Books, 1980), p. 167.

21. Bloom-Feshbach and Bloom-Feshbach, *The Psychology of Separation and Loss,* p. 9.

22. Daniel N. Stern, *The Interpersonal World of the Infant: A View from Psychoanalysis and Developmental Psychology* (New York: Basic Books, 1985).

23. Kerry P. Duncan, "Loss and Suffering and Its Impact Upon the Separation-Individuation Process of Mourning," unpublished Th.M. thesis, Columbia Theological Seminary, 1990.

24. Erich Lindemann, "Symptomatology and Management of Acute Grief," *The American Journal of Psychiatry* 101 (September 1944): 141–48.

25. Granger Westberg, *Good Grief* (Philadelphia: Fortress Press, 1962).

26. Elisabeth Kübler-Ross, *On Death and Dying* (New York: Macmillan Co., 1969).

27. C. Knight Aldrich, "The Dying Patient's Grief," *Journal of the American Medical Association* 184, no. 5 (May 4, 1963): 329–31.

28. Vanderlyn R. Pine et al., eds., *Unrecognized and Unsanctioned Grief* (Springfield, Ill.: Charles C. Thomas, 1990); and Kenneth J. Doka, ed., *Disenfranchised Grief: Recognizing Hidden Sorrow* (Lexington, Mass.: Lexington Books, 1989).

29. "Your Present and Silence," editorial in *The Journal of Pastoral Care* 26, no. 2 (June 1972): 73.

30. Larry R. Churchill, "The Human Experience of Dying: The Moral Primacy of Stories Over Stages," *Soundings* 62 (Spring 1979): 26.

31. Ibid., pp. 29–30.

32. Ibid., pp. 31–32.

33. Ibid., pp. 35–36.

34. Louis Richard Lothman, "Pastoral Family Therapy: Systemic Mourning and the Evocation of Human Vulnerability," unpublished S.T.D. dissertation, Columbia Theological Seminary, 1989.

35. Ibid., p. 181.

36. Ruth H. Collins, "WHO Cares About Widows," *Response,* January 1973: 43–44.

37. Tore-Kristian Lang, "A Pastoral Anthropology of Loss and Grief," unpublished S.T.D. dissertation, Columbia Theological Seminary, 1990, pp. 181–85.

38. Ibid.

Chapter 6 Patience and Patienthood—The Need for Care

1. John Florio, *Firste Fruites,* fo. 44 (1578), from *The Home Book of Proverbs, Maxims and Familiar Phrases,* ed. Burton Stevenson (New York: Macmillan Co., 1948).

2. Eric Partridge, *Origins: A Short Etymological Dictionary of Modern English* (New York: Macmillan Co., 1959), p. 475.

3. Warren Thomas Reich, "Speaking of Suffering: A Moral Account of Compassion," *Soundings* 72.1 (Spring 1989): 83–85.

4. Andrew Purves, *The Search for Compassion* (Louisville, Ky.: Westminster/John Knox Press, 1989), p. 15.

5. Martin Luther, *Letters of Spiritual Counsel,* ed. Theodore G. Tappert, vol. 18 of Library of Christian Classics (Philadelphia: Westminster Press, 1955), p. 39.

6. William A. Clebsch and Charles R. Jaekle, *Pastoral Care in Historical Perspective: An Essay with Exhibits* (Englewood Cliffs, N.J.: Prentice-Hall, 1964), p. 263.

7. Ibid., p. 265.

8. Reich, "Speaking of Suffering," p. 93.

9. Susan Sontag, *Illness as Metaphor and AIDS and Its Metaphors* (New York: Doubleday, Anchor Books, 1990), p. 3.

10. Arthur Frank, *At the Will of the Body: Reflections on Illness* (Boston: Houghton Mifflin Co., 1991), pp. 40–41.

11. Ibid., p. 128.

12. Ibid., p. 85.

13. Virginia Woolf, "On Being Ill," *The Moment and Other Essays* (New York: Harcourt, Brace & Co., 1948), p. 11.

14. Elaine Scarry, *The Body in Pain* (New York: Oxford University Press, 1985).

15. Ibid., p. 4.

16. Wilbert George Patterson, "The Pastoral Care of Persons in Pain," *Journal of Religion and Aging* 1, no. 1 (Fall 1984).

17. Quoted in ibid., pp. 21–22.

18. Wayne E. Oates and Charles E. Oates, *People in Pain* (Philadelphia: Westminster Press, 1985), p. 22.

19. Robert J. Lifton, *The Broken Connection* (New York: Basic Books, 1979), pp. 172–73.

20. Ibid., pp. 173.

21. Oates and Oates, *People in Pain,* pp. 14–19.

22. David Bakan, *Disease, Pain, and Sacrifice: Toward a Psychology of Suffering* (Chicago: University of Chicago Press, 1968), p. 40.

23. Ibid., pp. 50–59.

24. Ibid., pp. 64–66.

25. Ibid., p. 84.

26. James G. Emerson, *Suffering: Its Meaning and Ministry* (Nashville: Abingdon Press, 1986), pp. 21–23.

27. Eric J. Cassell, "Recognizing Suffering," *Hastings Center Report* 21, no. 3 (May–June 1991): 24.

28. Ibid., p. 25.

29. Eric J. Cassell, "Life as a Work of Art," *Hastings Center Report* 14, no. 5 (October 1984): 35–37.

30. Reich, "Speaking of Suffering," p. 86.

31. Ibid., p. 87.

32. Dorothee Soelle, *Suffering* (Philadelphia: Fortress Press, 1975), p. 127.

33. Reich, "Speaking of Suffering," p. 89.

34. Leston Havens, *Participant Observation* (New York: Jason Aronson, 1976), p. 125.

35. Reich, "Speaking of Suffering," pp. 88–90.

36. Anton Boisen, *The Exploration of the Inner World* (New York: Harper & Brothers, 1936), p. 11.

37. Ibid., p. 56.

38. Ibid., pp. 15–16.

39. Ibid., p. 192.

40. Ibid., p. 202.

41. Ibid., p. 240.

42. Arthur Kleinman, *The Illness Narratives* (New York: Basic Books, 1988), p. 26.

43. A. L. Kroeber, *Anthropology* (New York: Harcourt, Brace and Co., 1948).

44. H. K. Beecher, *Measurement of Subjective Differences* (New York: Oxford University Press, 1959).

45. Paul Tillich, *The Courage to Be* (New Haven, Conn.: Yale University Press, 1952), p. 74.

46. Nel Noddings, *Women and Evil* (Berkeley, Calif.: University of California Press, 1989), pp. 93–95. See also Noddings, "Educating Moral People," in *Who Cares,* ed. Mary M. Brabeck (New York: Praeger Publishers, 1989), pp. 216–32.

47. Thomas C. Oden's "A Theodicy for Pastoral Practice," ch. 15 in his *Pastoral Theology* (New York: Harper & Row, 1982), pp. 223–48, is an excellent example of what I am speaking of.

48. Paul S. Fiddes, *The Creative Suffering of God* (Clarendon, N.J.: Clarendon Publishing Group, 1988), pp. 214, 221.

49. Karl Barth, *Church Dogmatics* (Edinburgh: T. & T. Clark, 1960), vol. III, part 3, p. 366.

50. Ibid., vol. IV, part I, pp. 175–76.

51. Ibid., vol. III, part 3, pp. 351, 361–65.

52. Alfred North Whitehead, *Religion in the Making* (New York: Meridian Books, 1960), p. 60.

53. Fiddes, *The Creative Suffering of God,* p. 262.

54. Ibid., p. 266.

55. Belden C. Lane, "Grace and the Grotesque," *The Christian Century* 107, no. 33 (November 14, 1990): 1068.

Chapter 7 Abuse of Self and Others—The Failure to Care

1. Virginia Goldner, "Making Room for Both/And," *The Family Therapy Networker* 16, no. 2 (March–April 1992): 60.

2. Douglas John Hall, *The Steward: A Biblical Symbol Come of Age* (New York: Friendship Press, rev. ed., 1990), pp. 31–32, 71. See also James M. Gustafson's discussion of stewardship in *Ethics from a Theological Perspective* (Chicago: University of Chicago Press, 1984), vol. 2.

3. Hall, *The Steward,* pp. 33–34.

4. S. J. DeVries, "Shame," *Interpreter's Dictionary of the Bible,* vol. 4, ed. George Arthur Buttrick et al. (Nashville: Abingdon Press, 1962), pp. 305–6.

5. Johannes Pedersen, *Israel: Its Life and Culture* 1 (New York: Oxford University Press, 1926), pp. 241, 243.

6. Gerhard von Rad, *Genesis: A Commentary* (Philadelphia: Westminster Press, 1961), pp. 91–92.

7. Claus Westermann, *Genesis 1–11* (Minneapolis: Augsburg Press, 1984), pp. 250–51.

8. Heinz Kohut, *The Nature of Psychoanalytic Cure* (Chicago: University of Chicago Press, 1984), pp. 52–53, 63.

9. Heinz Kohut, *The Analysis of the Self* (New York: International Universities Press, 1971), pp. 300–7.

10. Heinz Kohut, *The Restoration of the Self* (New York: International Universities Press, 1977), p. 197.

11. Jerome D. Levin, *Treatment of Alcoholism and Other Addictions* (Northvale, N.J.: Jason Aronson, 1987), pp. 229–31. Levin quotes from Kohut's *The Restoration of Self* (New York: International Universities Press, 1977), 197n.

12. Rebecca Patton Falco, "Sex Crimes Against Female Children by Trusted Adults: A View from Nineteenth Century American Appellate Court Opinions," unpublished M.A. thesis, Duke University, 1991, pp. 4–5 and 68–69.

13. Roland C. Summit, "The Child Sexual Abuse Accommodation Syndrome," *Child Abuse and Neglect* 7:177–93.

14. Mary Field Belenky, Blythe McVicker Clinchy, Nancy Rule Goldberger, and Jill Mattuck Tarule, *Women's Ways of Knowing* (New York: Basic Books, 1986), pp. 58–59.

15. Nancy Ramsey, "Sexual Abuse and Shame: The Travail of Recovery," *Women in Travail and Transition: A New Pastoral Care,* ed. Maxine Glaz and Jeanne Stevenson Moessner (Minneapolis: Fortress Press, 1991), pp. 114–15.

16. Ibid., pp. 118–19.

17. Ibid., pp. 115–16.

18. Ellen Goodman, "If She Says No, then It's Rape," in *Sexual Assault and Abuse,* by Mary D. Pellauer, Barbara Chester, and Jane A. Boyajian (New York: Harper & Row, 1987), pp. 17–19.

19. Merle A. Fossum and Marilyn J. Mason, *Facing Shame: Families in Recovery* (New York: W. W. Norton & Co., 1986), p. 6.

20. Ibid., p. 8.

21. Ibid., pp. 8–9.

22. Bruce K. Alexander, "The Disease and Adaptive Models of Addiction: A Framework Evaluation," in *Visions of Addiction,* ed. Stanton Peale (Lexington, Mass.: Lexington Books, 1988), pp. 46–47.

23. George E. Valliant, "We Should Retain the Disease Concept of Alcohol," in *The Harvard Medical School Mental Health Review,* monograph on *Alcohol, Abuse and Dependence,* 1990, pp. 13–15.

24. Pia Mellody, *Facing Codependence* (New York: Harper & Row, 1989), pp. 207–8.

25. Charlotte Davis Kasl, *Women, Sex, and Addiction: A Search for Love and Power* (New York: Ticknor & Fields, 1989), p. 31.

26. Ibid., p. 33.

27. Wendy Kaminer, "Chances Are You're Codependent Too," *New York Times Book Review,* February 11, 1990: 1, 26ff., see also Kaminer, *A Fearful Freedom: Women's Flight from Equality* (Reading, Mass.: Addison-Wesley Publishing Co., 1990).

28. Harriet Goldhor Lerner, "12 Stepping It: Women's Roads to Recovery, A Psychologist Tells Why," *Lillith* (Spring 1991): 15–16.

29. Gail Unterberger, "12 Stepping It: Women's Roads to Recovery, A Psychologist Tells How," *Lillith* (Spring 1991): 16–17.

30. Fossum and Mason, *Facing Shame*, p. 72.

31. James Newton Poling, *The Abuse of Power: A Theological Problem* (Nashville: Abingdon Press, 1991), p. 69.

32. Fossum and Mason, *Facing Shame*, p. 79.

33. Marie M. Fortune, *Sexual Violence: The Unmentionable Sin: An Ethical and Pastoral Perspective* (New York: Pilgrim Press, 1983), pp. 87–89, 135–37. See also her *Violence in the Family: A Workshop Curriculum for Clergy and Other Helpers* (Cleveland: Pilgrim Press, 1991).

34. On the issue of confidentiality, see Sissela Bok, "The Limits of Confidentiality," *A Hastings Center Report* (February 1983): 24–25.

35. Marie M. Fortune, "Confidentiality and Mandatory Reporting: A Clergy Dilemma," cited in Lee W. Carlson, *Child Sexual Abuse* (Valley Forge: Judson Press, 1988), p. 33.

36. Peggy Halsey, "What Can the Church Do?" in Pellauer et al., *Sexual Assault and Abuse*, p. 219.

37. Poling, *The Abuse of Power*, p. 148.

38. Pellauer et al., *Sexual Assault and Abuse*, p. xi.

39. John Patton, *Is Human Forgiveness Possible? A Pastoral Care Perspective* (Nashville: Abingdon Press, 1985).

40. Richard P. Lord, "Personal Perspective," in *The Christian Century,* October 9, 1991: 902–3.

41. Sidney B. Simon and Suzanne Simon, *Forgiveness: How to Make Peace with Your Past and Get On with Your Life* (New York: Warner Books, 1990), pp. 15–20.

42. Carl D. Schneider, "Shame," *Dictionary of Pastoral Care and Counseling,* ed. Rodney J. Hunter (Nashville: Abingdon Press, 1990), pp. 1162–63.

43. See Karen Lebacqz, *Professional Ethics: Power and Paradox* (Nashville: Abingdon Press, 1985), and Karen Lebacqz and Ronald G. Barton, *Sex in the Parish* (Louisville: Westminster/ John Knox Press, 1991).

Chapter 8 Special Relationships—The Balances of Care

1. Anne Tyler, *Dinner at the Homesick Restaurant* (New York: Berkley Publishing Group, 1983, published by arrangement with Alfred Knopf), p. 189.

2. Richard Bondi, *Fidelity and the Good Life: Special Relationships in Christian Ethics* (Ann Arbor, Mich.: University Microfilms, 1981), p. 38.

3. Ibid., pp. 38–39, 43–44.

4. John Patton, *Is Human Forgiveness Possible? A Pastoral Care Perspective* (Nashville: Abingdon Press, 1985), p. 28.

5. Lillian B. Rubin, *Just Friends: The Role of Friendship in Our Lives* (New York: Harper & Row, 1986), p. 34.

6. Ibid., p. 26.

7. I believe that one can make the case that all but the most casual relationships involve story as well as principle, but in special relationships as
I am using the term here, the story or history of the relationship is involved to a very significant degree.

8. John Patton and Brian M. Childs, *Christian Marriage and Family:
Caring for Our Generation* (Nashville: Abingdon Press, 1988).

9. Martin Luther, in vol. XVIII of The Library of Christian Classics, ed.
and trans. Theodore G. Tappert (Philadelphia: Westminster Press, 1955),
pp. 263–64.

10. Ibid., pp. 272–74.

11. William Johnson Everett, *Blessed Be the Bond* (Philadelphia: Fortress
Press, 1985), pp. 10, 20, and ch. 3.

12. Roland H. Bainton, *What Christianity Says About Sex, Love, and Marriage* (New York: Association Press, 1957), pp. 17–18.

13. Ibid., p. 63.

14. Ibid., p. 100.

15. Everett, *Blessed Be the Bond*, ch. 6.

16. Peter L. Berger, *Facing Up to Modernity: Excursions in Society, Politics,
and Religion* (New York: Basic Books, 1977), p. 7.

17. Ibid., p. 10.

18. Lyman Wynne and Adele Wynne, "The Quest for Intimacy," *Journal
of Marital and Family Therapy* 12 (1986), no. 4, 383–94.

19. See also Lyman Wynne, "An Epigenetic Model of Family Processes,"
in *Family Transitions,* ed. Celia Jaes Falicov (New York: Guilford Press,
1988), pp. 81–106.

20. Wynne and Wynne, "Quest for Intimacy," pp. 383–94.

21. Thomas Patrick Malone and Patrick Thomas Malone, *The Art of Intimacy* (Englewood Cliffs, N.J.: Prentice Hall, 1987).

22. Ibid., pp. 22, 24.

23. Ibid., pp. 26–27.

24. Ibid., pp. 27–29.

25. Ibid., p. 49.

26. Ibid., p. 64.

27. Ibid., p. 90.

28. Ibid., p. 152.

29. Deborah Anna Luepnitz, *The Family Interpreted: Feminist Theory in
Clinical Practice* (New York: Basic Books, 1988), pp. 21–22.

30. Ibid., p. 110–11.

31. Ibid., p. 145.

32. Ibid., p. 180.

33. Ibid., p. 183.

34. Ibid., p. 20.

35. Nancy Boyd-Franklin, *Black Families in Therapy* (New York: Guilford
Press, 1989), pp. 5ff.

36. Ibid., p. 247.

37. Patton and Childs, *Christian Marriage,* p. 78.

38. Ibid.

39. Kenneth R. Mitchell and Herbert Anderson, "You Must Leave Before You Can Cleave," *Pastoral Psychology* 30, no. 2 (Winter 1981): 71–88.

40. Patton and Childs, *Christian Marriage,* p. 81.

41. Ibid., p. 96.

42. Ibid., pp. 93–95.

Chapter 9 Pastoral Counseling: A Ministry of Availability and Introduction

1. Seward Hiltner, *Pastoral Counseling* (Nashville: Abingdon Press, 1949), p. 121.

2. John Patton, "Pastoral Counseling," *Dictionary of Pastoral Care and Counseling,* ed. Rodney J. Hunter (Nashville: Abingdon Press, 1990), p. 849.

3. John Patton, *Pastoral Counseling: A Ministry of the Church* (Nashville: Abingdon Press, 1983).

4. Patton, "Pastoral Counseling," p. 850.

5. Thomas C. Oden, *Pastoral Counsel* (New York: Crossroads, 1989), p. 5.

6. See Kittel's *Theological Dictionary of the New Testament,* ed. Gerhard Kittel, trans. and ed. Geoffrey W. Bromiley, vol. 5 (Grand Rapids: Wm. B. Eerdmans Publishing Co., 1967), pp. 343–50.

7. Patton, *Pastoral Counseling,* pp. 20–22.

8. See John Patton, "A Not So Private Practice," ch. 3 in *Pastoral Counseling,* pp. 58–82.

9. Elaine Pinderhughes, *Understanding, Race, Ethnicity and Power* (New York: Free Press, 1989), p. 139.

10. Ibid, p. 138.

11. Karen Lebacqz, *Professional Ethics: Power and Paradox* (Nashville: Abingdon Press, 1985) and Karen Lebacqz and Ronald G. Barton, *Sex in the Parish* (Louisville, Ky.: Westminster/John Knox Press, 1991).

12. The American Association of Marriage and Family Therapists, of which I am a member and an approved supervisor, has as its official "party line" that marriage and family therapy is a profession. This is an understandable political strategy for a group seeking recognition through licensing, but I believe that a more accurate view is that psychotherapy in its many forms, including marriage and family therapy, is a therapeutic practice that may be performed by a variety of professions, including ministry.

13. See Brian H. Childs, *Short-Term Pastoral Counseling* (Nashville: Abingdon Press, 1990).

14. Translator's note in Gabriel Marcel's *Creative Fidelity,* trans. Robert Rosthal (New York: Farrar, Straus & Co., 1964), p. 57.

15. Joe McCown, *Availability: Gabriel Marcel and the Phenomenology of Human Openness* (Missoula, Mont.: Scholars Press, 1978), pp. 17–21.

16. Gabriel Marcel, *The Philosophy of Existence* (New York: Philosophical Library, 1949), pp. 25–26.

17. Marcel, as quoted in McCown, *Availability,* p. 74.

18. See Henri J. M. Nouwen, *Reaching Out* (Garden City, N.Y.: Doubleday & Co., 1975), pp. 45–78; and Thomas W. Ogletree, *Hospitality to the Stranger* (Philadelphia: Fortress Press, 1985), pp. 1–9.

19. See John Patton, "The Dialectical Relationship Between Mystery and Ministry," *Quarterly Review* 1, no. 4 (Fall 1981).

20. Patton, *Pastoral Counseling,* pp. 90–93, 139–42, 182.

21. Paul Pruyser, *The Minister as Diagnostician* (Philadelphia: Westminster Press, 1976).

22. Charles V. Gerkin, *The Living Human Document* (Nashville: Abingdon Press, 1984).

23. Wayne E. Oates, *The Christian Pastor* (Philadelphia: Westminster Press, 1964), pp. 220–21.

24. Ibid., p. 224.

25. Patton, *Pastoral Counseling,* pp. 164–166. See also William B. Oglesby, Jr., *Referral in Pastoral Counseling* (Englewood Cliffs, N.J.: Prentice-Hall, 1968), pp. 36–57.

26. Oates, *The Christian Pastor,* p. 232.

27. John Patton, "Harry Stack Sullivan's 'Expert in Interpersonal Relations,'" *Journal of Religion and Health* 9, no. 2 (April 1970).

28. Oates, *The Christian Pastor,* p. 236.

29. Don S. Browning, "Pastoral Theology in a Pluralistic Age," in *Practical Theology,* ed. Don S. Browning (New York: Harper & Row, 1983), pp. 188, 190.

30. My discussion here is informed by an unpublished paper by Brad Binau, a Lutheran pastor in California.

Chapter 10 Theological Reflection on Pastoral Caring

1. Shirley C. Guthrie, "Theology, Christian," *Dictionary of Pastoral Care and Counseling,* ed. Rodney J. Hunter (Nashville: Abingdon Press, 1990), p. 1266.

2. Theodore Jennings, "Pastoral Theological Methodology," *Dictionary of Pastoral Care and Counseling,* pp. 862–63.

3. Ibid., p. 863.

4. Ibid., p. 864.

5. James D. Whitehead and Evelyn Eaton Whitehead, *Method in Ministry* (New York: Seabury Press, 1981), p. 13. My own structure for theological reflection may be found in John Patton, *From Ministry to Theology: Pastoral Action and Reflection* (Nashville: Abingdon Press, 1990).

6. Ibid., p. 15.

7. Ibid., p. 17.

8. Ibid., p. 21.

9. A method of theological reflection on experience, somewhat similar to the Whiteheads', was developed by Robert L. Kinast, formerly of Catholic University in Washington, D.C., and now director of a center for theological reflection in Florida. See Robert L. Kinast, "How Pastoral Theology Functions," *Theology Today* 37 (1981): 425–38; "A Process Model of Theological Reflection," *The Journal of Pastoral Care* 37 (1983): 144–55; and *Handbook for Theological Reflection: Let the Ministry Teach,* The Center for Theological Reflection, P.O. Box 86035, Madeira Beach, FL 33738-6035.

10. James D. Whitehead, "The Practical Play of Theology," in *Formation and Reflection,* ed. Lewis S. Mudge and James N. Poling (Philadelphia: Fortress Press, 1987), p. 40.

11. James N. Poling and Donald E. Miller, *Foundations for a Practical Theology of Ministry* (Nashville: Abingdon Press, 1985), pp. 62–99.

12. James Newton Poling, *The Abuse of Power: A Theological Problem* (Nashville: Abingdon Press, 1991), pp. 186–91.

Index